MODERNIST LIFE HISTORIES

Edinburgh Critical Studies in Modernist Culture
Series Editors: Tim Armstrong and Rebecca Beasley

Available

Modernism and Magic: Experiments with Spiritualism, Theosophy and the Occult
Leigh Wilson
Sonic Modernity: Representing Sound in Literature, Culture and the Arts
Sam Halliday
Modernism and the Frankfurt School
Tyrus Miller
Lesbian Modernism: Censorship, Sexuality and Genre Fiction
Elizabeth English
Modern Print Artefacts: Textual Materiality and Literary Value in British Print Culture, 1890–1930s
Patrick Collier
Cheap Modernism: Expanding Markets, Publishers' Series and the Avant-Garde
Lise Jaillant
Portable Modernisms: The Art of Travelling Light
Emily Ridge
Hieroglyphic Modernisms: Writing and New Media in the Twentieth Century
Jesse Schotter
Modernism, Fiction and Mathematics
Nina Engelhardt
Modernist Life Histories: Biological Theory and the Experimental Bildungsroman
Daniel Aureliano Newman

Forthcoming

Modernism, Space and the City
Andrew Thacker
Slow Modernism
Laura Salisbury
Primordial Modernism: Animals, Ideas, Transition (1927–1938)
Cathryn Setz
Modernism and the Idea of Everyday Life
Leena Kore-Schröder
Modernism Edited: Marianne Moore and The Dial *Magazine*
Victoria Bazin
Modernism and Time Machines
Charles Tung

www.edinburghuniversitypress.com/series/ecsmc

MODERNIST LIFE HISTORIES

Biological Theory and the Experimental *Bildungsroman*

Daniel Aureliano Newman

EDINBURGH
University Press

Edinburgh University Press is one of the leading university presses in the UK. We publish academic books and journals in our selected subject areas across the humanities and social sciences, combining cutting-edge scholarship with high editorial and production values to produce academic works of lasting importance. For more information visit our website: edinburghuniversitypress.com

Edinburgh University Press Ltd
The Tun – Holyrood Road
12(2f) Jackson's Entry
Edinburgh EH8 8PJ

First published in hardback by Edinburgh University Press 2019

Typeset in 10/12.5 Adobe Sabon by
IDSUK (DataConnection) Ltd

A CIP record for this book is available from the British Library

ISBN 978 1 4744 3961 9 (hardback)
ISBN 978 1 4744 3962 6 (paperback)
ISBN 978 1 4744 3963 3 (webready PDF)
ISBN 978 1 4744 3964 0 (epub)

CONTENTS

FIGURES

PREFACE

This book reflects a belief acquired during my scientific training and fostered by my readings of modernist literature: that experiment is the best way of resisting the force of habit which reduces complex realities to simple myths, experience into slogans, cultural constructs into immutable truths and curiosity into complacency. Many literary innovators have said as much. And while T. H. Huxley and Alfred Whitehead defined science as disciplined common sense, I agree with literary critic Gillian Beer, who counters that 'most major scientific theories rebuff common sense' (2000: 1), and with developmental biologist Lewis Wolpert, who insists that science is 'counterintuitive' and therefore 'requires a conscious awareness of the pitfalls of "natural" thinking' (1992: 1). Few statements better capture the vision of biology and literature in *Modernist Life Histories: Biological Theory and the Experimental Bildungsroman.*

Focusing on biology, this book leaves the main current of Modernism and Science Studies, which tends to favour the New Physics of relativity and quantum mechanics. Physics was certainly important to the modernists, but 'biology', writes Aldous Huxley in *Literature and Science*, 'is more immediately relevant to human experience than are the exacter sciences . . . Hence, for all writers, its special importance' (1963: 67). Taking Huxley's lead, I explore how early twentieth-century biology informs modernist experiments with the *Bildungsroman*. My focus is motivated by the genre's exemplary status among what Fredric Jameson calls '"natural" forms' (1982: 132), plot structures so deeply embedded in our culture that we can no longer detect their constructed nature, or their 'vitality' (Jameson 1982: 132). *Modernist Life Histories* seeks this 'vitality' in biological allusions and narrative structures, often finding them in seemingly trivial details: James Joyce's 'law of heredity' (*PA* 230), E. M. Forster's 'throw back' (*HE* 320), Aldous Huxley's 'axolotl' (*EG* 612) and Samuel Beckett's 'Darwin's caterpillar' (*MU* 122; *W* 194). Such allusions are just the visible part of a veritable intertextual iceberg, a substantial and systemic literary dialogue with biological models of development and evolution.

Not knowing where such allusions would lead was one of the greatest thrills of researching what would become *Modernist Life Histories*. As Gérard Genette quips, 'the inconvenience of "research" is that by dint of searching you can find . . . what you weren't looking for' (1982: 8). This view on literary criticism seems to me fundamentally congenial with the spirit of scientific enquiry, though its objects and objectives are and should remain different from those of the humanities. In any case, seeing modernist literature in such a light helped me envision my project beyond the alternatives outlined by Eve Sedgwick: on the one hand, a 'hermeneutics of suspicion', on the other a 'hermeneutics of recovery of meaning' (2003: 125). I will call it a hermeneutics of discovery, as does Susan Stanford Friedman when she advocates for 'the humanities' capacity for discovery, for building knowledge in ever new forms' (2017: 347). Discovery may overlap with recovery, but by avoiding the implication of exegetical unveiling, it comes closer to scientific exploration and experimentation than to religious revelation. Discovery implies not the restoration of lost wholeness but an act which combines finding with creating new knowledge.

Espousing this ideal, *Modernist Life Histories* aligns itself with appeals by several recent advocates of 'post-critique' (Friedman 2017: 344). The book is especially sympathetic with Elaine Freedgood and Cannon Schmitt's plea that 'we need to know something other than what we already know' (2014: 12). Knowing more, they continue, comes from 'reading more' (2014: 12) – not more books but more *in* books. The germ of new knowledge is in the details, in 'what we have ruled out, what we have ignored, what we have found too boring or opaque to deal with, what we have passed by', and only by looking there 'will texts come alive in ways that are not simply re-visions of our present ideas of the past or our preformed ideas of the present' (Freedgood and Schmitt 2014: 12). Closer attention to the meaning of textual details, as Freedgood and Schmitt imply, necessarily demands more respect for their context. The impulse behind post-critique is not in any way opposed to historicism, though it may question the methodological biases of certain Historicisms. These biases can result in historical blind-spots as serious as those of vulgar formalism.

The aspirations linking various strands of post-critique reflect a growing recognition of critique's limited ability to recognise specificity, novelty and opposing perspectives. Critique sees texts as case studies, illustrations of ideology in action; it is thus, as Sedgwick portrays it, 'averse above all to surprise' (2003: 146). Critique is indispensable and often bracing, but it is on its own an insufficient approach to art. Working on this book has repeatedly given me the thrill of unexpectedness I first encountered in the sciences.

Focusing closely on scientific ideas and models in the context of their historical emergence, the book uses concepts and terms which may be alien to many readers. I have striven to write plainly, avoiding superfluous terminology and detail. The lexicon of early twentieth-century biology is byzantine and protean, and for the sake of concision and parsimony I have preferred to commit anachronism rather than negotiate a semantic quagmire whose details are, frankly, irrelevant to the novels at hand. Unless specificity serves my argument, I choose general terms. That said, I have tried hard not to sacrifice scientific accuracy. Throughout the book, I maintain a crucial distinction between 'development' and 'evolution', reserving 'development' for individual (ontogenetic) change and 'evolution' for historical, population or species (phylogenetic) change. Also confusing is the language of narrative theory. I use 'story' and 'discourse' exclusively as equivalents of *fabula* and *syuzhet*, and 'plot' in roughly the same way as Peter Brooks does in *Reading for the Plot*. Translations from French are mine, unless otherwise indicated in the Bibliography.

ACKNOWLEDGEMENTS

Over the course of this book's long gestation, I have been blessed with support and assistance in many forms, from many sources. For research funding, I thank the Social Sciences and Humanities Research Council of Canada, the Avie Bennett Foundation, Massey College and the English Departments at the University of Toronto and McGill University. I am grateful to Duke University Press for permission to reprint an earlier version of Chapter 5 originally published in *Twentieth-Century Literature* 62: 4 (2016). I also acknowledge Faber & Faber, as well as Houghton Mifflin Harcourt, for permission to reprint a passage from T. S. Eliot's *Four Quartets*. Finally, I thank Cambridge University Press for permission to reprint a diagram from D'Arcy Thompson's *On Growth and Form*.

Scholarship is collaboration, and this book owes its existence to many critics, colleagues, mentors and friends. My greatest debts are to the invaluable insights, invigorating criticisms and unflagging support of Cannon Schmitt and Melba Cuddy-Keane at the University of Toronto and Allan Hepburn at McGill. I am grateful to many readers and reviewers, most notably Gregory Castle, for suggestions, questions and scepticism which spurred me to dig deeper. Countless others have contributed, in innumerable ways more or less direct, to the book's coming-to-form. Especially helpful were Claire Battershill, Alyson Brickey, Fiona Coll, Greig Henderson, Judith Herz, Cari Hovanec, Heather Jessup, Christine Lehleiter, Inder Marwah, Spencer Morrison, Elise Newman and Cynthia Quarrie. Unparalleled support came from my family: Elise, David-Marc, Jack and especially my mother Adèle. In Loïc Édouard and Tevia Émile, born while the book took shape, I keep finding new reasons to see literature and the natural world with eyes attuned to detail and wonder. My greatest thanks go to Kellie Davis. She made this book possible by, among untold other ways, teaching me to love literature. To her I literally owe my vocation.

SERIES EDITORS' PREFACE

This series of monographs on selected topics in modernism is designed to reflect and extend the range of new work in modernist studies. The studies in the series aim for a breadth of scope and for an expanded sense of the canon of modernism, rather than focusing on individual authors. Literary texts will be considered in terms of contexts including recent cultural histories (modernism and magic; sonic modernity; media studies) and topics of theoretical interest (the everyday; postmodernism; the Frankfurt School); but the series will also re-consider more familiar routes into modernism (modernism and gender; sexuality; politics). The works published will be attentive to the various cultural, intellectual and historical contexts of British, American and European modernisms, and to inter-disciplinary possibilities within modernism, including performance and the visual and plastic arts.

Tim Armstrong and Rebecca Beasley

ABBREVIATIONS

James Joyce

FW	*Finnegans Wake* (1939)
PA	*A Portrait of the Artist as a Young Man* [1916] (1968b)
SH	*Stephen Hero* (1969)
U	*Ulysses: The 1992 Text* [1922] (1993)

E. M. Forster

AN	*Aspects of the Novel* [1927] (1974)
HE	*Howards End* [1910] (1973)
TC	*Two Cheers for Democracy* (1972b)

Virginia Woolf

EVW	*The Essays of Virginia Woolf* (1986–2011), 6 vols
O	*Orlando: A Biography* [1928] (1993)
ROO	*A Room of One's Own* [1929] (1998)

Aldous Huxley

AS	*After Many a Summer Dies the Swan* (1939)
EG	*Eyeless in Gaza* (1936a)

EM	*Ends and Means* (1937)
PCP	*Point Counter Point* (1928)

George Eliot

SM	*Silas Marner* [1861] (1996)

Samuel Beckett

HII	*How It Is* [1961] (2007)
MD	*Malone Dies* [1956] (1997b)
MO	*Molloy* [1955] (1997a)
MU	*Murphy* [1938] (1973)
UN	*The Unnamable* [1958] (1997c)
W	*Watt* [1953] (1959)

Other Authors

EE	Gavin de Beer (1930), *Embryology and Evolution*
OP	Stephen Jay Gould (1977), *Ontogeny and Phylogeny*
OS	Charles Darwin [1859] (1964), *On the Origin of Species*

INTRODUCTION

> It is . . . very odd to find all the little follies and virtues, and developments and retrogressions, written out in the big world's book that you find in your little internal self.
>
> – Olive Schreiner, *Story of an African Farm* (1999: 165)

Modernist fiction radically reimagines human development. It offers, in most critical accounts, a bleak picture of wasted potential, stunted growth, perpetual adolescence, or premature senescence.[1] This book offers a different perspective: rather than failed development, new kinds of development. If they look like failures, it may be because our understanding of growth and self-formation is, even today, shaped by a particular model of organic change which arose in the nineteenth century. Linear, accretive and above all progressive, this model seems so natural that other ways to chart a life are almost unimaginable.

This model is memorably captured in Aldous Huxley's *Point Counter Point* (1928), when the pregnant Marjorie Carling considers 'the astounding process of creation' unfolding within her:

> Something that had been a single cell, a cluster of cells, a little sac of tissue, a kind of worm, a potential fish with gills, stirred in her womb and would one day become a man – a grown man, suffering and enjoying, loving and hating, thinking, remembering, imagining. And what had been a blob of jelly within her body would invent a god and worship; what had been a kind of fish would create and, having created, would become the battle-ground of disputing good and evil; what had blindly

> lived as a parasitic worm would look at the stars, would listen to music, would read poetry. A thing would grow into a person . . . (*PCP* 2)

The life of Marjorie's unborn son, progressing from a 'single cell' to 'a human body, a human mind' (*PCP* 3), from bodily formation to aesthetic and spiritual maturity, is plotted as both a primer in nineteenth-century embryology and a Victorian *Bildungsroman*. Its path and end are as optimistic as they are confident in the future course of the unborn child. Yet Marjorie feels 'only of sickness and lassitude' (*PCP* 3), and the following 500 pages strongly suggest that the narrator's optimism is rank with sarcasm. No evidence of successful development is to be found in this novel teeming with 'pre-human monsters' (*PCP* 180) and cases of 'atavismus', 'atrophy' and 'infantility' (*PCP* 143, 417, 439): Lord Edward is 'a kind of child, a fossil boy preserved in the frame of a very large middle-aged man' (*PCP* 27–8); Maurice Spandrell is a 'Peter Pan . . . stuck at a sillier age' (*PCP* 184); John Bidlake is a 'dotard in his second childhood' (*PCP* 192); and Denis Burlap ends up on 'a romp' with his secretary Beatrice, 'pretend[ing] to be two little children and ha[ving] their bath together' (*PCP* 601). In short, the initial rosy picture of human development, which is also a condensed version of human evolution, is treated with an irony typical of modernist attitudes towards vulgar progressivism.

The point is clinched later in the novel when the painter Mark Rampion presents a diptych showing 'two Outlines of History', contrasting pictures of human evolution. The first half of the diptych shows history 'according to H. G. Wells', as 'a simple crescendo', an 'uninterrupted' growth in physical (and by extension moral) stature beginning with 'a very small monkey', passing through 'a slightly larger Neanderthal man' to the 'quite respectable dimensions' of 'Galileo and Newton' (*PCP* 290). Progress then leads to the giants 'Faraday and Darwin' and the even bigger contemporary 'figures of Mr. H. G. Wells himself and Sir Alfred Mond', until 'through the radiant mist of prophecy the forms of Wells and Mond, growing larger and larger at every repetition, wound away in a triumphant spiral clean off the paper, towards Utopian infinity' (*PCP* 290–1). An obvious parallelism links this evolutionary scenario to the life envisioned for Marjorie's son – and both are undercut by the second half of the diptych, which charts history according to Rampion himself. Mirroring the contrapuntal method of *Point Counter Point*, this half of the painting shows a series of 'peaks and declines' (*PCP* 291):

> The small monkey very soon blossomed into a good-sized bronze-age man, who gave place to a very large Greek and a scarcely smaller Etruscan. The Romans grew smaller again. The monks of the Thebaid were hardly distinguishable from the primeval little monkeys. There followed a number of good-sized Florentines, English, French. (*PCP* 291)

From this point on, as far as the painting reveals, the history of humankind is a steady decline: early modern and eighteenth-century figures including Calvin and Wesley are 'revolting monsters', 'the Victorians' are 'dwarfish and misshapen', 'their twentieth-century successors were abortions', and the future promises 'little gargoyles and foetuses with heads too large for their squelchy bodies, the tails of apes and the faces of our most eminent contemporaries' (*PCP* 291). Shocking next to the Wellsian view, this 'Outline of History' is actually not wholly pessimistic. Though currently in decline, the stature of its 'representative men' (*PCP* 291) has grown as well as shrunk, leaving hope for future reversals. What Rampion attacks is not progress itself but a version of progress intimately tied to the arrow of time.

Eccentric as he seems, Rampion illustrates a broader modernist reaction to the classical *Bildung* plot which impinges with such force on the protagonist of Robert Musil's *Verwirrungen des Zöglings Törleß* (1906): 'a rigid, iron constraint was imprisoning him, forcing his whole life into this forward movement, step by step along this single straight line' (2013: 14). Nor is Rampion's painting merely reactive: in deforming the 'crescendo' into 'peaks and declines', his art is an experiment in alternative life histories. His diptych targets not History, Evolution, Human Endeavour, or even Progress but, rather, a specific model of organic change, which is all but identified by name in the account of Marjorie's pregnancy. During foetal growth, her baby has been reliving its own evolutionary past: it has 'been' an amoeboid 'single cell', a 'worm', and a 'fish' on its triumphant way to being first a 'man' and then, with the acquisition of culture, 'a person' (*PCP* 2). At issue, then, are two overlapping plots. The first is a stereotyped version of the *Bildungsroman*, a genre Huxley mocked as early as *Crome Yellow* for its predictable course – from a hero's tormented childhood to his 'disappear[ance], at the end of the book, into the luminous Future' (2004: 14). The second plot transposes the hero's *Bildung* into historical and evolutionary time. In the optimistic scenarios associated with Marjorie and H. G. Wells, the two plots are parallel: each step in development (ontogeny) represents a concomitant advance in evolution (phylogeny). Placing tiny 'foetuses' at a late stage where one would expect big adults, Rampion decouples these plots. The result is a miniature modernist *Bildungsroman* which uses biology to deform, and re-form, the developmental plot.

Decoupling individual development from rectilinear time is one of two key features of the modernist novels investigated in this book. These texts, I argue, deploy various formal strategies to extricate the ideal of *Bildung* from the historical developmentalism with which it had long been associated. The second feature, inextricably linked to the first, is the role biology plays in confirming or enabling the modernist resistance to chronological plotting. That biology could inspire alternatives to chronological plotting may seem counterintuitive. The chronological structure of life narratives is 'predictable', writes Terry Eagleton, because such is the temporality of the body: 'the structure of biography is biology' (qtd in DiBattista 2009: 9). Chronology, agrees Peter Brooks, matches plot to the 'biological pattern' (1985: 88). In *Aspects of the Novel*, E. M. Forster similarly distinguishes 'life in time' – our bodily existence, subject to physical laws – and 'life by values' (*AN* 19). Conceding time's arrow, Forster admits that 'of course we grow old. But a great book', he adds, 'must rest on something more than an "of course"' (*AN* 26), suggesting that the art must transcend the biological scaffolding of biographical narratives. This conclusion, however, is premised on the equivalence of chronology and ontogeny (biological development and growth). This equivalence may hold in the theories of organic change which dominated the study of ontogeny and phylogeny from the late eighteenth through the late nineteenth centuries, but theories too can change. In the early twentieth century, the emerging fields of experimental embryology and genetics were demanding radically new explanatory models, some of them so strange I call them *modernist biology*. These models helped the novelists featured in this book, Forster included, find ways to narrate development more or less unbound to the 'of course' of 'life in time'.

I am suggesting that modernism's apparently unnatural ways of narrating development might be to some extent mimetic – not in a naïve or literal sense, but in the sense that they resemble or even borrow from the natural world revealed by modernist biology. That nature might permit development to occur variously, along multiple lines and to multiple ends, is suggested in André Gide's *Les Faux-monnayeurs*: 'It seems nature has tested one by one every way of being alive, of moving, and has exploited everything permitted by matter and its laws' (1975: 147). That such natural exuberance might inspire fiction is suggested by Gide's writer-protagonist, Édouard, who seeks a form which does not 'always cut in the same direction, with the grain of time' (1975: 184).

Modernist experiments might seem inhospitable to biological models for another reason. By and large, studies of modernism have ignored biology. We have thankfully mostly outgrown the once common belief that modernism was anti-science, and since 2002 much has been done to heed Mark Morrisson's appeal for closer ties between Modernist Studies and Science Studies. And yet attention to the sciences is partial and largely asymmetrical. It is telling that even recent anthologies or reference works on modernism tend either not to mention biology or to mention it in passing.[2] This relative neglect stems in part from a suspicion of biology's associations with scientific racism and eugenics; in part from the increasing specialisation and difficulty of the life sciences of the period; and in part from the overwhelming critical interest in Darwin himself. For these reasons, studies on modernism and biology tend to read twentieth-century literature with nineteenth-century science.[3] After Conrad, claims George Levine, Darwinism in fiction became 'so diffused and various, so much part of the Freudian mythology, of the deconstructive turn, of the largest movements of mind in the twentieth century[,] that efforts to trace it further become futile' (1988a: 272). Once Darwin was domesticated, Levine implies, evolution's power to shock and inspire dwindled. Another factor in biology's relative obscurity in Modernist Studies is the undeniable appeal of contemporary physics, whose dazzling novelty fed the sense that it would be for the twentieth century what biology had been for the nineteenth: 'So it was with Darwin, so it is with Einstein', quips Wyndham Lewis (1927: 104). In Aldous Huxley's *Those Barren Leaves*, the ageing Tom Cardan, 'almost a twin to *The Origin of Species*', pits familiar materialist biology against 'that disquieting scientific modernism which is now turning the staunchest mathematical physicists into mystics' (1925: 35).

'Scientific modernism' was more than physics, however. Nor did biology end with Darwin. Many major discoveries and controversies occurred between his death in 1882 and the description of the double helix in 1953. This period saw the rise of classical genetics, beginning with the rediscovery of Mendel's theories in 1900, and the Evolutionary Synthesis of Mendelism and Darwinism from roughly 1920 to 1940. The new biology was challenging and potentially inspiring. Relativity and quantum mechanics profoundly alter our view of reality, but although biology is less hard-hitting, it hits closer to home. It speaks directly to our bodily formation and functions, to the mundane but pleasurable activities of nutrition and sex, and to our place in a network of other living things. Biology was increasingly posthuman, ever less amenable to humanist notions of selfhood and individuality. As Haldane asserts in his 1923 lecture 'Daedalus', biological discoveries do more than surprise and frighten: they shock and insult us with their 'indecent and unnatural' implications (1995: 36).

Haldane's claim finds its clearest literary test case in the novel it directly inspired, *Brave New World*. But it also resonates in modernist treatments of the body, from the modernism of content in frank discussions of sex in D. H. Lawrence and Djuna Barnes or decrepitude in Beckett, to the modernism of form in Wyndham Lewis and Virginia Woolf, who insists in *A Room of One's Own* that 'the novel has somehow to be adapted to the body' (*ROO* 101). Modernism's attentiveness to the body has inevitable consequences for its rendering of *Bildung*. 'A mind is not fully grown', writes Aldous Huxley in 'The Idea of Equality', 'until the body with which it is connected through the brain has passed the age of puberty. The mind of a young child . . . [d]oes not become completely itself until the body is more or less fully grown' (1927: 16). What characters want, fear and perceive alters as their bodies grow, change in appearance and ability and face the onset of sexual desire and frustration which comes with puberty. Stephen's struggles with lust in *A Portrait of the Artist* amply demonstrate how a changing body participates in personal and social formation; Orlando's sex change is an extreme version of the same correlation. In *Howards End*, there is a clear connection between 'los[ing] the life of the body and fail[ing] to reach the life of the spirit': frustrating Leonard Bast's attempt 'to acquire culture' is not a lack of will but the physical conditions of his dark, stuffy flat (*HE* 113, 37).[4]

More specifically, many modernists were aware of contemporary biological issues, as allusions in their essays, poems and fiction attest. Unfortunately, there is a tendency in modernist scholarship to treat even obvious allusions to biology as incitements to symbolic, allegorical, or psychoanalytic analysis, rather than opportunities for more literal investigations. A case in point, one relating to a key aspect of this book, is the critical response to modernism's most notorious engagement with biology. In the 'Oxen of the Sun' episode of *Ulysses*, Joyce travesties the expected parallelism between ontogeny and phylogeny, much as Huxley does with Rampion's painting in *Point Counter Point*. A potted history of English prose styles, the episode also mimics, as Joyce wrote to Frank Budgen, 'the natural stages of development in the embryo and the periods of faunal evolution in general' (*U* 907). But Joyce plays fast and loose with chronology, mimicking Pater before Carlyle, for example. More significant is the 'tailpiece' of the episode (*U* 906). Rather than building progressively to a glorious end, the episode descends into gibberish and slang, concluding not with the latest addition to the noble genealogy of English prose but, rather, with the stylistic equivalent of the mind of Stephen Dedalus as a very drunk young man.

Mark Gaipa rightly insists that the biological structure of 'Oxen of the Sun' has 'everything to do with its meaning' (1995: 197) and expresses frustration with critics who ignore or downplay Joyce's reference to 'faunal evolution'. It has been called unserious or misleading by scholars including Richard Brown (1985: 68–70), Don Gifford (1989: 408), Robert Janusko (1983: 4), Weldon Thornton (1987: 269n38) and even John Gordon, who is otherwise acutely attentive to scientific issues (2003: 7, 143–55). Leo Bersani goes as far as rejecting the bulk of 'Oxen' scholarship since Stuart Gilbert's *James Joyce's Ulysses* (1930), wondering, 'in what way is the historical transformation (which is of course *not* a "development" or the maturation of an organism) of English prose styles "parallel" or "analogous" to . . . the biological development of an embryo in a womb?' The question is rhetorical: the very idea 'is so absurd that it is difficult even to find the term in which to object to it' (Bersani 2004: 221–2). Bersani fails to see that, for Joyce's contemporaries, the parallel between 'development of an embryo' and 'historical transformation' (cultural or biological) would have been anything but 'absurd'. Called the theory of recapitulation, the parallel is best known by Ernst Haeckel's 'biogenetic law' that individual development replays species evolution: 'Ontogeny is a recapitulation of Phylogeny' (1883: 6). One of the nineteenth century's grandest grand narratives, it was, in Gillian Beer's words, 'the most productive, dangerous, and compelling of creative thoughts for our culture' (1996: 6).[5]

Derived from the analogical tradition, revived in the historicist framework of late eighteenth-century philosophy, anthropology and biology, and easily adapted to post-Darwinian evolutionism, recapitulation theory posits the isometry of embryonic growth and evolutionary change. As Arthur Milnes Marshall writes in *Vertebrate Embryology*, 'evolution tells us that each animal has had a pedigree in the past. Embryology reveals to us this ancestry, because every animal in its own development repeats its history, climbs up its own genealogical tree' (1893: 26). This charming image is no mere analogy or metaphor: development literally repeats evolution, in miniature. Marjorie Carling's foetus was not merely like a fish but 'had been' a fish (*PCP* 2). Marshall continues:

> the fact that a frog commences its free existence as a tadpole, i.e. to all intents and purposes as a fish, is a very extraordinary one, but it becomes at once intelligible if we interpret it as meaning that frogs are descended from fish, and that every frog is constrained to repeat or recapitulate its pedigree in the course of its own individual development. (Marshall 1893: 26)

The model is necessarily progressivist, conserving but modernising the Great Chain of Being by translating its static hierarchies into temporal phases (Bowler 1984: 100).[6] The frog must pass through a fish stage because fish are lower on the purported evolutionary scale; by this logic, human embryos must rise through both fish and frog stages, and many more besides, before reaching their place, fully mature, at the top of the evolutionary ladder.

Most biologists in the later nineteenth century were recapitulationists, though with varying zeal. The reasons for this dominance were as much empirical as metaphysical, and the stakes were high. Writing in 1928, a sceptical Edwin Conklin describes recapitulation theory's promise 'to reveal not only the animal ancestry of man and the line of his descent but also the method of origin of his mental, social, and ethical faculties' (1928: 70). Such sweeping claims were encouraged by Haeckel, who promoted his biogenetic law as the foundation of a 'universal Theory of Development, which embraces in its wide range the whole domain of human knowledge' (1876: 1–2). Certainly, recapitulation exerted considerable and lasting influence outside biology. So elegantly simple and mythic in scope, recapitulation suited an ideological need to unite diverse historical phenomena within a single law of Progress. These various phenomena found a perfect model in embryogenesis because embryonic changes are relatively easy to observe, because their succession seems clearly progressive and end-directed, and because the history of organicism is inextricable from the study of embryogenesis in the late eighteenth century (Bowler 1984: 119). It is in 'the growing embryo' that Herbert Spencer finds a model for 'the law of all progress':

> whether it be in the development of the Earth, in the development of Life upon its surface, in the development of Society, of Government, of Manufactures, of Commerce, of Language, Literature, Science, Art, this same evolution of the simple into the complex, through a process of continuous differentiation, holds throughout. (H. Spencer 1878: 3)

By the late nineteenth century, indeed, the biogenetic law was lending scientific heft to fields ranging from anthropology and developmental psychology to art history and literary criticism (*OP* 115–66).

Given my focus on the *Bildungsroman*, the most pertinent extensions of the biogenetic law were in pedagogy and kindred subfields of psychology. In these fields recapitulation had practical implications, for instance in curriculum development and evaluation, and its normative assumptions about how children learn as they mature reveals a lot about the shape of narratives about early life, growth and self-formation. The modern notion of childhood as an especially formative period is captured in Wordsworth's dictum, 'the Child is father to the Man' (1958: 85); recapitulation theory adds simply that the child is also the man's ancestor. Theories of education founded on recapitulatory thinking thus assigned special importance to the natural chronology of knowledge acquisition. In *Education*, then, Herbert Spencer stresses the need to match the curriculum to the history of ideas:

> if there be an order in which the human race has mastered its various kinds of knowledge, there will arise in every child an aptitude to acquire these kinds of knowledge in the same order. So that even were the order intrinsically indifferent, it would facilitate education to lead the individual mind through the steps traversed by the general mind. But the order is *not* intrinsically indifferent; and hence the fundamental reason why education should be a repetition of civilization in little. (H. Spencer 1861: 76)

In Spencer's synthetic world view, as in Haeckel's monistic philosophy, it is but a short step between intellectual history and evolutionary history – a short step often taken, as Jessica Straley and Ruth Murphy demonstrate, by late nineteenth- and early twentieth-century pedagogues as well as didactic novelists. Nicholas Butler observes in 1900 that 'the course of evolution in the race and in the individual furnishes us . . . with the clue of the natural order and the real relationships of studies' (qtd in *OP* 149), a point repeated more sensationally by John Tyler in *Growth and Education*:

> the child is naturally successively animal, anthropoid, half-barbarian, and then civilized . . . If we regard the lower stage as useless or pernicious, if we try to repress or obliterate it, we are knocking out the rounds of the ladder up which, with Nature's assistance, the child is climbing to manhood. (Tyler 1907: 53)

Crazy as they may now seem, such views were dominant in the late nineteenth century. I return in Chapter 1 to the role of proper order in recapitulation theory, but it should be clear that chronology would play a more than incidental role in a *Bildungsroman*'s developmental logic.

Proper order mattered because it is a constitutive aspect of progressive change, which, as Dana Seitler argues, depends on the 'notion of time as a one-way street and history as motivated by unidirectional causation' (2008: 13). The past is necessary, but only as an origin or period of apprenticeship. It must remain safely where it belongs, to be visited through the safe lens of ironic retrospective or paternalistic condescension: it must be past and must have been *passed* – passed through and passed by. To grow up, in recapitulation theory's progressivist framework, is therefore not merely to develop one's own potentialities but also to traverse and transcend what Darwin called the 'stamp of our lowly origin' (1981: ii.405). This biological ascent is analogous to the 'lawlike development' in Dilthey's seminal discussion of the *Bildungsroman*:

> A lawlike development is discerned in the individual's life; each of its levels has intrinsic value and is at the same time the basis for a higher level. Life's dissonances and conflicts appear as necessary transitions to be withstood by the individual on his way towards maturity and harmony. (Dilthey 1985: 336)

If recapitulation depicts development as a climb up the species' family tree, the final step in this ascent is to affix a new branch at the top, making way for further evolutionary progress in the future. Again, for thinkers like Haeckel, this biological progress would have been inextricable from the cultural and imperial project of civilisation, 'the master narrative of modernity, which encompasses the plot of individual development within the broader storyline of the civilizing process' (Bixby 2009: 38).

This developmentalist vision is a consistent target of modernist *Bildungsromane*. This is not to imply it was blindly accepted by classical *Bildungsromane*, whose visions of acculturation are as complex and critical as they are various. What distinguishes modernist *Bildungsromane* is the blatancy with which they attacked the recapitulatory model, as well as the specific forms they used in their attack. One of the features which make *Story of an African Farm* so recognisably modernist, despite its publication in 1883, is its attempt to imagine individual (and female) development beyond 'the analogy there always is between the progress and development of one individual and of a whole nation; or again, between a single nation and the entire human race' (Schreiner 1999: 165). Similar attempts animate the novels featured in this book: James Joyce's *A Portrait of the Artist as a Young Man* (1916), E. M. Forster's *Howards End* (1910), Virginia Woolf's *Orlando* (1928), Aldous Huxley's *Eyeless in Gaza* (1936) and Samuel Beckett's so-called Trilogy (1955–8) and *How It Is* (1961). During this period, as we have seen, a similar reaction was shaking up biology: slowly, then abruptly, recapitulation lost its supremacy. By the 1920s, the biogenetic law was effectively repealed, displaced by the non-linear models of experimental embryology and the statistical laws of Mendelian inheritance (*OP* 167–206). I make no general claim about the demise of recapitulation and the concurrent rise of literary modernism. But in the several cases of modernist *Bildungsromane* evidently engaging genetics and embryology, the question arises: did biology participate in modernist attempts to reimagine human life histories?

Modernist Life Histories: Biological Theory and the Experimental Bildungsroman explores relations between modernist biology and formal innovations in modernist novels of formation. My title plays on the various nuances of 'life history'. As 'the history or narrative of a person's life' (*OED n*[1]), it denotes the *Bildungsroman*, arguably the most influential of biographic forms. The compound of 'life' and 'history', moreover, brings to mind the *Bildungsroman*'s particular vision of biographical narrative, most eloquently expressed in Bakhtin's formula of the genre as the 'image of man growing in national-historical time' (1984: 25). Reflecting epochal changes in national development, the individual's social, aesthetic and spiritual maturation coincides with, and indeed participates in, the 'border between two epochs' and 'reflects the historical emergence of the world itself' (Bakhtin 1984: 23). The protagonist is 'forced to become a new, unprecedented type of human being . . . It is as though the very foundations of the world are changing, and man must change along with them' (Bakhtin 1984: 23–4). In his essay on the *Bildungsroman*, in fact, Bakhtin does gesture towards a recapitulatory model of individual development: 'to understand the image of emerging man in Goethe', he writes, 'it is immensely important to consider the idea of education as it took shape during the Enlightenment and particularly that specific category that we find on German soil as the idea of the "education of the human race"' (Bakhtin 1984: 24). Though Bakhtin refers to social change, it is impossible to ignore the implication of a third meaning of 'life history': 'the life cycle of an individual organism or of a species' (*OED n*[2]). This definition, derived from ecology and evolutionary theory, is rather congenial with the other two; it is biology's counterpart to literary life narratives. Like the *Bildungsroman*, it narrates the life of individuals and the larger community, substituting the evolution of the species for the history of the nation. This connection, which is central to my argument, is treated at length in Chapter 1.

For now, the point is this: as long as the biogenetic law dictated understandings of growth and education, normal development was hard to imagine in other terms; deviations from its expectations made sense only as developmental failures or pathologies, as what Tennyson calls, in 'Locksley Hall', 'the sickly forms that err from honest Nature's rule' (1958: 106). As Tennyson returns to his theme in 'Locksley Hall Sixty Years After', development was either with 'Evolution ever climbing after some ideal good', or against it, with 'Reversion ever dragging Evolution in the mud' (1958: 509). This binary and normative logic, combined with pre-existing hierarchies, made recapitulation a powerful tool and scientific justification for prejudice. When individuals climb their family tree, some get stuck part-way up on a primitive, even sub-human branch. The political implications of such thinking are obvious, but an explicit statement by G. Stanley Hall is worth quoting: 'If we could . . . correlate animals, infancy, and savagery, we should then have a standard to measure and also to compare progress in different civilizations' (1904: ii.359). The practical consequence of such thinking is 'the legitimation of marginalization' because 'the diverse possible modes of cultural development that these societies represent are displaced by a single model of historical development within which other cultures can only be envisaged as underdeveloped, imperfect, childlike, or . . . inauthentic, perverse, or criminal' (JanMohamed and Lloyd 1990: 4–5). Because recapitulation assumes perfectibility, groups deemed imperfect were thus primitive, immature or degenerate,[7] and the standard of perfection was unsurprisingly white, male, heterosexual and upper class. By this standard James Frazer would assert that 'a savage is to a civilized man as a child is to an adult' (2007: 162); Edward Drinker Cope would note more 'embryonic characters' in 'the Negro' and 'the Mongolian' than in 'the Indo-European', and more 'quadrumanous [simian] indications . . . in the lower classes of the most developed races' than in the upper classes (1887: 287, 293); and James McGrigor Allan would observe that 'physically, mentally and morally, woman is a kind of adult child' who also 'preserves . . . the earlier stage from which the race or tribe has been developed' (1869: 104, 110).

As recapitulation theory lost its hold over the developmental imagination, however, its power to determine the narrative grammar of *Bildung* became weaker, more contingent, even arbitrary. Released from the structural and ideological constraints of recapitulation theory, *Bildung* was free, so to speak, to explore new forms of developmental narrative. A developmental 'advance in a zigzag fashion' which had once seemed to corrupt the true course of evolution (Ewart 1894: 350) might now be seen as the normal effect of the complex genetic, cellular, physiological and environmental factors involved in ontogeny. By thus becoming 'modernist', biology made itself a congenial source of concepts and narrative structures for modernist *Bildungsromane*.

The Modernist *Bildungsroman*

Once considered an oxymoron, notably by Franco Moretti and Weldon Thornton, the modernist *Bildungsroman* now enjoys the exclusive or significant focus of several monographs and articles. Whereas Moretti finds the historical conditions after 1914 inimical to the *Bildungsroman*'s survival (2000: 229), recent studies tend to follow Rita Felski in characterising the genre not as a set form but as a set of dynamic relations between individual and historical change. These relations may shift, thus deforming the classical *Bildung* plot, but the ideals of *Bildung* still inform the narrative. Most of the best recent scholarship on the genre therefore assumes continuity between nineteenth- and twentieth-century versions of the genre. Not only do modernist novels retain many elements of the classical *Bildungsroman*, but the classical *Bildungsroman* is also far less formally straightforward or ideologically complacent than many accounts suggest.[8] It is therefore worth stressing, then, that the critical energies of the modernist *Bildungsroman* are directed less against its Victorian predecessors, which are often engaged in similar critiques (albeit less extravagantly), than against a culture steeped in the ideology of Progress and what T. S. Eliot calls 'superficial notions of evolution' (2001: 26). Doctrinal declarations of progressivism, such as those in Spencer's *Illustrations of Universal Progress* (1864) and Haeckel's *Evolution of Man* (1874), are not endorsed unchecked in contemporaneous *Bildungsromane*. Few if any of these novels match their common caricature as uncritical narratives of simple forward and upward growth, ending in the resolution of personal and social contradictions. The genre is 'intrinsically contradictory' (Moretti 2000: 6), and *Bildung* itself was conceived by the Weimar classicists as both linear and recursive (A. Berman 1992: 47; Minden 1997: 28–9). Friedrich Schlegel emphasised both movements, writing of 'the steady improvement and natural cycle of education [*Bildung*]' in the growth of 'each individual, as well as of the whole species' (1997: 433). Similarly, Goethe, a key player in the history of the *Bildungsroman* and developmental biology, tempered his progressivism with a non-linear model of growth. From the genre's emergence, indeed, *Bildungsromane* have staged insoluble conflicts between the forward-looking ideal of personal freedom and the individual's historical reality. This tension complicates the naïve 'sequential and additive understanding of history' often attributed to classical *Bildungsromane*, and 'the resulting asynchronicities undermine simplistic narratives about national consciousness and its putative quest for closure' (Boes 2012: 33–4). As scholars of modernism, we should refrain from caricaturising the nineteenth century in order to highlight the peculiarities of the twentieth.

The putative linear *Bildungsroman* is indeed, as Marc Redfield argues, a 'phantom *Bildungsroman*' (1996: 39), a critical construct. Yet the notion of linearity has its uses, if only as a relative measure, and to dismiss it entirely would be to obscure the fact that, in structure at least, nineteenth-century *Bildungsromane* do tend to limn closer than their modernist successors to the ideals embodied in recapitulation theory: chronological plotting, gradual change and the wise authority of maturity. These ideals are embodied in one of the great heroines of the genre, Jane Eyre, who states with unwitting metafictional acuity that her 'circumstances knit themselves, fitted themselves, shot into order; the chain that had been lying hitherto a formless lump of links, was drawn out straight – every ring was perfect, the connection complete' (Brontë 2008: 390–1). Though Jane under-reads the intricacies of her own narrative, she ably describes a vision of plot and character development which had become, and still is, thoroughly naturalised. For Victorian fiction, then, alternative forms of change tend to manifest as Gothic horror or pathology, as with the abrupt transformations of Dr Jekyll and Trilby O'Ferrall and the developmental arrests of Silas Marner and Dorian Gray.

Modernist novels, by contrast, flaunt their disregard for the expected ends and endings of the *Bildung* plot. As if gradual and progressive plotting no longer reflected natural laws of change, modernist *Bildungsromane* chart development which stalls, as with Imogen in *Told by an Idiot*, or which happens too fast or too dramatically, as with Gregor Samsa. Sometimes it moves backwards, as in Gertrude Atherton's *Black Oxen* (1923). Growth is uneven: in *Jacob's Room* Florinda's father 'died from the growth of his bones which nothing could stop' (Woolf 1992a: 65), while the drones of *Brave New World* are specialised for their jobs but stunted in every other faculty. Elsewhere cumulative growth gives way to cycles of repetition, as in *Good Morning, Midnight*, or, as Birkin puts it in *Women in Love*, to 'a series of accidents – like a picaresque novel?' (D. H. Lawrence 1981: 340). In T. E. Hulme's view, development itself is a lie: 'Man is an extraordinarily fixed and limited animal whose nature is absolutely constant' (1994: 61). In at least two modernist *Bildungsromane*, what is abnormal is *linear* development. In Rosamond Lehmann's *Dusty Answer*, Mariella is a case of 'arrested development' (2013: 65) not because she stops growing but because she has 'grown most alarmingly' in her immature form: 'Her body had merely been stretched out without much alteration of the long vague curves of childhood' (Lehmann 2013: 29). Young Frankie in Carson McCullers's *The Member of the Wedding* worries her recent growth spurt will continue at a constant rate:

> If she reached her height on her eighteenth birthday, she had five and one-sixth growing years ahead of her. Therefore, according to mathematics and unless she could somehow stop herself, she would grow to be over nine feet tall . . . She would be a Freak. (McCullers 2004: 22, 19).

Such strange representations of development elicit three primary classes of explanation: some critics point to the effects of new historical pressures (the symptomatic model), others to the critical energies of irony (the immanent-critical model), and a few to explorations of new kinds of developmental narrative (the performative or experimental model).[9]

The symptomatic model links genres to a historical moment, specific literary forms serving particular ideological functions which new historical conditions can render unnecessary, obsolete, or incoherent. Certainly, the Great War made the picture of an optimistic youth at the cusp of real life difficult to sustain. Much of the critical power of *Jacob's Room* derives from the irony, painfully obvious to readers of 1922, that many young men like Jacob Flanders would never experience maturity, marriage, vocation, or even the regrets of older age. In *Unseasonable Youth*, the best exemplar of the symptomatic model, Jed Esty chronicles the collapse of *Bildung*'s 'soul-nation allegory' (2012: 13) in novels set in imperial peripheries, where maturity and nationhood – 'mutually reinforcing versions of stable identity' (2012: 39) – are delayed and desynchronised, producing new and inharmonious correspondences between individual and historical becoming. The material conditions of 'colonial contact zones' intensify the forces which 'thwart the realist proportions of biographical time that had, from its inception, defined the bildungsroman' (Esty 2012: 2); yet such disruptions also typify metropolitan *Bildungsromane* whose protagonists do not match the humanist ideals of personhood or citizenship.[10]

While the symptomatic view stresses how historical pressures affect the integrity of the classical *Bildung* plot, the immanent-critical model foregrounds the more active role of critique or experimentation. For Gregory Castle, the apparent failures of *Bildung* in modernist novels are in fact attempts to rehabilitate the 'aesthetico-spiritual' ideal of inner culture conceived by Goethe, Schiller and Humboldt, while recognising the impossibility of ever achieving it (2006: 63). Echoing Susan Fraiman's feminist readings, Castle reads modernist deformations of the *Bildung* plot as manoeuvres designed to critique ideology from within the text of 'a self-deconstructing *Bildungsroman*' (2013: 629). It is typical of modernism to approximate generic forms in order to undercut their ideological complicity. This is true of many narrative forms – witness modernist marriage plots (*Women in Love*, *The Last September*) and quests (*Heart of Darkness*, *Ulysses*) – but the *Bildungsroman*'s central concern with identity, agency and social life makes it a privileged site of modernist critique.

Though closely aligned with this immanent-critical model, my own approach draws also on the symptomatic. It recognises the need to contextualise the modernist impulse towards experimentalism and, more specifically, stresses that the availability of experimental forms is largely contingent on historical circumstances. That said, *Modernist Life Histories* highlights the agency of authors as producers of new literary formulations. Though I share with Castle an investment in the critical, even adversarial stance of modernism relative to grand narratives, my focus on the traffic of narratives from science to literature shifts the emphasis towards modernism's productive exploration of alternative plots.[11] As Michael Levenson puts it, 'one cannot alter the movement of history. But it is possible to change the form and style of one's response' (1991: 80). Like others working on science and literary form,[12] I approach innovative fictions as thought experiments, following Lionel Trilling's suggestion that

> plot is to the novelist what experiment is to the scientist . . . Experiment, with its artificiality, is our best way of making things act so that we can learn about their nature. And plot in the novel does the same for human nature. (Trilling 1962: 57–8)

Dirk Van Hulle has similarly identified 'the function of special forms of narration' as a means of investigation akin to the 'sciences of the mind' (2014b: 26). I would add that even conventional narrational modes and generic structures have correlatives in our models of the world, including scientific models.

Science can spur new narrative forms because its findings can force us to see beyond the plots which structure our experience. In this, it resembles modernism. Though science is often linked to the instrumental reason so hated by modernists, 'it is also possible to see science as an open-minded inquiry into the physical world, as a discipline that maintained the ideals of Enlightenment, and that resisted their assimilation into instrumentalism' (Whitworth 2010: 445). But science is often unequipped for, or unconcerned with, clarifying the meaning of its defamiliarising discoveries. Fiction, however, is ideally suited to testing out the implications of difficult ideas without reducing them to propositions. This thesis is implicit in Tobias Boes's argument against treating the *Bildungsroman* as a normative form which 'privilege[s] finality, and focus[es] on the perfected form revealed at the end of the protagonist's development' (2012: 59); Boes cites Morgenstern's definition of the genre 'as an infinitely varied instrument by which the equally multiform achievements of future generations might be measured' (Boes 2012: 59). Thus, Boes continues, 'theories of *Bildung* . . . are concerned with process rather than finality or . . . "performance" rather than "form"' (2012: 59). By this logic *Bildungsroman* is a kind of thought experiment, designed to test any number of narrative grammars for representing self-formation.

Particularly apt is Michel Butor's metaphor of the novel as a 'laboratory'. Unlike nonfiction, which relies on external verification, 'the novel must create what it seeks to show us. This is why it is the phenomenological domain *par excellence*, the site *par excellence* for studying how reality appears to us or how it might appear' (Butor 1992: 9). Butor emphasises formal questions because 'new forms will find new things in reality', and thus 'formal innovation in the novel, far from being opposed to realism . . . is the *sine qua non* of a greater realism'

(1992: 10, 11). Unlike the realism Elizabeth Deeds Ermarth equates with normative standards of time and perception, Butor's 'greater realism' requires unsettling formal manoeuvres – 'not arts of consensus but, rather, instruments for exploring and transforming the real' (Butor 1992: 182). Writing on verbal models in science, Richard Dawkins makes the same point: 'thought experiments are not supposed to be realistic. They are supposed to clarify our thinking about reality' (2008: 4).

Through their narrative contortions modernist *Bildungsromane* enact not only a deconstruction of the classical *Bildung* plot but also an 'experimentalism that seeks constantly to find new ways to convey self-formation' (Castle 2013: 629). This re-formation therefore participates in the critical approach to genre studies advocated by Fredric Jameson in order to prevent genres from becoming 'thought of as 'natural' forms' (1982: 145). Because they play with the conventions of the *Bildungsroman* without rejecting its fundamental concern with acculturation, modernists can be grouped with the practitioners of a 'genre criticism [which] recovers its freedom and opens up a new space for the creative construction of experimental entities' (Jameson 1982: 145). The *Bildungsromane* featured in this book are thus viewed as explorations of the narrative space beyond those conventions. The need for such exploration is surely one of the implications of Woolf's famous claim: 'on or about December 1910 human character changed' (*EVW* iii.421).

The old conventions are resilient, however, so naturalised it takes a shock to recognise their conventionality. In the *Bildungsromane* featured in this book, the shock comes at least in part from modernist biology. These novels exploit the correlation, explored in Chapter 1, between models of bodily formation (ontogenesis) and the narrative shape of a life, in order to generate previously unimaginable plots. If, as Punday argues, the history of the novel is bonded to developmental biology (2003: 17), new theories of sexual generation and gestation redefine not only how we view the body and identity but also how we tell, read and theorise narratives. If new biological theories 'produce a new way of thinking about character identity as the basis for narrative' (Punday 2003: 41), then the modernist *Bildungsroman* emerges as a particularly powerful and revealing privileged discursive site for revisionary experiment.

Recapitulation and the Modernists

In advancing my argument I am not suggesting that biology holds the key to the modernist *Bildungsroman* – to speak of *the* modernist *Bildungsroman* is itself to create a fictional character. Nor do I seek to refute other recent explanations of unusual development in modernist fiction. Every text is overdetermined and thus admits of multiple, even opposing explanations. There is no necessary contradiction, for example, between my thesis and Esty's account of stunted growth as a symptom of global capitalism. One reason for my focus on biology is simply its underappreciated yet recurrent presence in modernist life writing. Consider the musings on Darwin bookending Dorothy Richardson's *Pointed Roofs*; the metaphor linking biography to the reconstruction of a fossil in Somerset Maugham's *The Moon and Sixpence*; Nancy's paleontological ambitions in Bryher's *Development*; and Marya's interest in the monogenic origin of *Homo sapiens* in Jean Rhys's *Quartet*. Consider the biological conceit of H. G. Wells's *Experiments in Autobiography* and the chapters on 'Heredity' and 'Environment' in Evelyn Waugh's *A Little Learning*. The 'bio' in biographical writing, as Alexis Harley points out, has overlapped with the 'bio' in biology since the nineteenth century (2015: 6), though the overlap would grow increasingly vexed as scientific findings challenged literary conventions. I focus on biology for another, more specific reason: because one of its most important contributions to modern thought, recapitulation theory, undergirds so much of what is rejected in modernist *Bildungsromane*. When they borrowed from recent embryology or genetics in their developmental fictions, modernists could, wittingly or not, use biology to release *Bildung* from the 'mental strait-jacket of recapitulation' (*EE* 97).

Perhaps the most pointed modernist reaction to recapitulation is in the opening of Joyce's essay on 'The Universal Literary Influence of the Renaissance' (1912):

> The theory of evolution, in the light of which our society basks, teaches us that when we were little were we not yet grown up. Hence, if we consider the European Renaissance as a dividing line, we must come to the conclusion that humanity up to that epoch possessed only the soul and body of a youth, and only after that epoch did it develop physically and morally to the point of meriting the name of adult. It is quite a drastic conclusion, and not very convincing. In fact . . . I should like to attack it with drawn sword. (J. Joyce 1977: 19)

Joyce's sarcasm is clear from the whimsical tautology, 'when we were little we were not yet grown up'. But his target is not, as Weldon Thornton assumes, 'the theory of evolution' in general (1987: 269n38). Joyce's 'we', conflating individual and species, suggests the more specific theory of recapitulation. And 'attack it' he does – in the travesties of 'Oxen of the Sun', in the recirculations of the *Wake*, and also, as I argue in Chapter 2, in the *Bildungsroman* he was writing at the time of his 'Renaissance' essay. Plotting *A Portrait of the Artist* as 'the gestation of a soul' (R. Ellmann 1965: 307), Joyce relies on the ontogenetic substrate of the classical *Bildung* plot. One of the manifestations of the novel's modernism, however, is the wilful decoupling of its ontogenetic plot from plots of historical (national, racial, evolutionary) emergence. The history refracted through Stephen Dedalus's development is 'reticulated', to borrow

Kevin Ohi's term for Walter Pater's vision of history. Against the dominant framework of recapitulation, Ohi argues, Pater favours 'the innumerable forms of development . . . that merely intersect (or indeed are entirely skew to) the line of history'; Joyce's Stephen may not accept it, but his 'ontogeny', like the model promoted by Pater, 'shelters within it multiple uncoordinated and not necessarily hierarchically organized developments' (Ohi 2015: 84–5). In a felicitous formulation, Ohi enlists Pater's 'historical recovery and aesthetic *Bildung*' (2015: 82) against historical developmentalism – another way in which Pater anticipates Joyce in particular and modernism more generally. Decades later, T. S. Eliot's 'The Dry Savages' would recognise a vision of historical reticulation likewise pitted against the neat parallelism of recapitulation:

> It seems, as one becomes older,
> That the past has another pattern, and ceases to be a mere sequence –
> Or even development: the latter a partial fallacy
> Encouraged by superficial notions of evolution,
> Which becomes, in the popular mind, a means of disowning the past.
>
> (Eliot 2001: 26)

These lines reject the recapitulation implied in the analogy of 'development' and 'evolution'. Its headlong progressivism, 'a means of disowning the past', fails to account for the range of human temporalities and for 'the meaning' which re-experiencing the past gives to the present. Stressing 'sudden illumination', Eliot uses epiphany to dissociate ontogeny ('one grows older') from phylogeny ('evolution'), translating the process of *Bildung* from 'mere sequence' into a new configuration, 'restor[ing] the experience' of life 'in a different form' (Eliot 2001: 26).

Eliot, Pater and Joyce express a discontent with recapitulation remarkably consistent among modernists, especially in their *Bildungsromane*. In addition to challenging the narrative structure and political implications of recapitulation, the novels examined in *Modernist Life Histories* respond positively to models of development which helped overthrow the biogenetic law and resemble in many ways modernist narrative techniques. Where recapitulation posits a linear ascendance towards evolutionary perfection, the new models normalise recursive and relativistic dynamics; where recapitulation represents ontogeny as the miniature repetition of a singular, true evolutionary history, the new models partition the organism into many independent organs, each forming at its own speed in a 'mosaic sort of differentiation' (Oppenheimer 1967: 161); where recapitulation equated the past with ancestral forms, the new models recognised the coevalness of what biologists call basal (primitive) and derived (advanced) forms; and where recapitulation implicitly viewed heredity as an additive process, each generation building progressively on the inherited experience of its predecessors, modern genetics radically separated the processes of development from those of genealogy.

Unlike the advent of Darwinism, the overthrow of the biogenetic law cannot be described as a cultural revolution. It took place, for the most part, in specialised journals and monographs. When modernists engage with the new biology, they do so pell-mell, opportunistically, unsystematically, often eccentrically – the way T. E. Hulme interprets Hugo de Vries's genetics as the death-knell of 'Romanticism' (1994: 61). The authors featured in *Modernist Life Histories* engage with biology variously. Joyce's uses are general, while Huxley's are specific, thoroughgoing and up-to-date; between the extremes fall Forster, Woolf and Beckett. The biological models and phenomena are likewise diverse. Joyce explores the atavistic corporeality of language, Forster the mechanisms of Mendelian genetics, Huxley neoteny (the retention of juvenile traits), Woolf alterations in anatomical sex and Beckett interrupted metamorphosis. Despite their differences, however, each of these phenomena involves a retrogressive deviation from the norms set by the biogenetic law; the umbrella term I use to group them together is *reversion*. Whatever their specific form, reversions disrupt the neat parallelism of recapitulation, blocking the forward-moving stream of life history, or troubling it with eddies and diversions. Time reversals do not merely obscure a developmental plot; they erode the philosophical underpinnings of nineteenth-century developmentalism, including recapitulation theory. 'Deviations from chronology', writes Gregory Castle, 'challenge the idealist conception of self-identity conveyed in the classical ideal of achieved Bildung by unveiling the contrast between that ideal and its manifestation in material existence' (2013: 269). As a category of reactions and strategies, reversion is the governing trope of my study of modernist *Bildungsromane*.

Reversion and the Narratology of Modernist *Bildung*

The term reversion has some currency in biology. Darwin used it, for example, to describe cases in which an organism 'is arrested in its development, but still continues growing until it closely resembles a corresponding structure in some lower and adult member of the same group' (1981: i.113). My own use of *reversion*, intentionally loose, describes any developmental and narrative deviation from the expected sequence. Franco Moretti alludes to a kindred phenomenon when he denies the possibility of the modernist *Bildungsroman* because 'when the process of socialization becomes more violent', as it does following the Great War, 'regression inevitably acquires its symbolic prominence' (2000: 234). My vision of reversion, however, is not as negative or inimical to development as Moretti's 'regression' appears to be. A character who fails to develop, as has been said of Leonard Bast, Rachel Vinrace, or Anna Morgan, does not merely embody a critique of developmentalism. The inability (or refusal) to develop along the lines of the ideal or archetypal plot is also to embrace a kind of atavism, to regress towards or become entrapped in juvenile or ancestral stages. In the more familiar lexicon of Freudian psychology, modernist reversions embrace disruptive effects akin to perversion and neurosis. If the end-point of Freud's model of psychosexual development maps onto the achievement of reproductive heterosexuality and the release of sexual climax, then, as Judith Roof argues, 'perversions, chronologically and analogically linked to infancy and foreplay, threaten to substitute themselves for this normal end pleasure' (1996: xx). Because recapitulation provides the structural bedrock of Freudianism, it follows that modernist *Bildungsromane* make good on this threat by means of reversion.

Reversions are evident in Mark Rampion's painting in *Point Counter Point*, in Frank Norris's *Vandover and the Brute* and in Somerset Maugham's *The Moon and Sixpence*, but the logic of recapitulation assigns similarly atavistic interpretations to Orlando's change from male to female, to Maurice Hall's idyllic ending with Alec and even to Stephen Dedalus's choice of artistic over spiritual vocation. Each case exposes the refractory presence of the biological past throughout the trajectory of developmental change, and in so doing demands that we either recognise atavism everywhere, or admit that the pejorative notion of atavism is an artefact of a particular way of conceptualising time, development and modernity. The modern notion of Progress requires a past, but as a system of roots, as something to transcend. Jung's method, founded on recapitulation, is illustrative. Though Jung brings to light 'the residues of . . . man's animal ancestry', he also warns against allowing these residues outside their rightful place deep in 'the collective unconscious'; otherwise they 'are extremely liable, when activated, not only to retard the pace of development, but actually force it into regression until the store of energy that activated the unconscious has been used up' (1990: 98). The recapitulatory structure of Freudianism underpins Peter Brooks's statement that 'the progressive, educative plots, the plots of repression and social advancement, are threatened by a repetitive process obscurely going on underneath and beyond them' (1985: 123). But as Faulkner reminds us, 'the past is never dead. It's not even past' (2011: 73).

Reversionary processes characterise modernism in its various forms, linking thinkers from Nietzsche, Pater, Bergson and Ortega y Gasset to artists from Henri Rousseau, Stravinsky, D. H. Lawrence and Djuna Barnes. One of modernism's most eloquent descriptions of the 'reversionary process' occurs in Henri Bergson's *L'Évolution créatrice*, in a seamless blend of art, culture, psychology and biology. Tempering his usual human exceptionalism, Bergson admits that

> the evolutionary line culminating in man is not the only one. Other forms of consciousness have developed on other, divergent lines, and

> though these have not succeeded in escaping external constraints or regaining control over themselves as human intelligence has done, they express nonetheless something immanent and essential about evolutionary movement. Were the various lines brought together and fused with intelligence, might we not obtain a consciousness coextensive with life and capable, by turning back abruptly against the life force pushing it forwards, of encompassing, if only fleetingly, the whole of life? (Bergson 2007: viii)

Longing for life's potential fullness, but aware that the *élan vital* pushes life forwards in time, Bergson is forced to imagine an anti-chronological movement, a 'turning back abruptly' against the clock. Such temporal dynamics riddle modernist *Bildungsromane*, whether they engage or not with biology; in those that do, however, reversion cuts to the very heart of *Bildung* as an organic process as well as a spiritual goal, allowing life to be, 'if only fleetingly', human and animal, present and past, differentiated and whole.

If chronology supplies much of the *Bildungsroman*'s rhetorical and ideological power, it is also a vulnerability: any deviation is a potential subversion of that power. If the *Bildungsroman* becomes politically inert and ideologically suspect because it is taken for a natural form, as Jameson suggests, then its potential for renewal may lie in disrupting its most common-sense, natural-seeming feature; as Lewis Wolpert points out, it is intuitive and thus 'natural' to 'see change in terms of a simple linear causal sequence or chain of events. This may be the root of the difficulty . . . with concepts involving reversibility' (1992: 15). To dechronify the *Bildungsroman* is not necessarily to abandon *Bildung*: experiments with the genre can rescue that ideal from the oblivion of natural thinking by making it unnatural and strange.

Reversions are not limited to the formal devices which decouple discourse order from story order. In a *Bildungsroman*, the story of development is inextricable from its telling, so any plot event which is somehow untimely amounts to a formal disruption of chronology. As Marc Redfield observes, 'the "content" of the bildungsroman instantly becomes a question of form, precisely because the content is the forming-of-content, "Bildung"' (1996: 42). Redfield's formulation has important implications for my argument, because it stresses how thematic departures from the expected developmental trajectory are also structural deformations (and vice versa). The new-born senility of Benjamin Button and Mary Zattiany's glandular rejuvenation in *Black Oxen* are deviations of content, but they have structural and generic effects. When Orlando becomes a woman, the change occurs at the story level, but also at the level of form. Contemporary developmental hierarchies ranked femaleness lower than maleness; Orlando's change from male to female therefore upsets a 'natural' order of progressive growth. More generally, and radically, the simple fact of featuring a female (or non-white, working-class, homosexual) protagonist is a structural deformation of the *Bildung* plot because such protagonists are always belated.

Writing on time in Forster's *Maurice*, Jesse Matz suggests that the novel's temporal anomalies occur not in the discourse as typically understood but, rather, 'at the level of *story*' (2000: 191). Though this formulation neglects the fact that anachrony occurs not in discourse or in story *per se* but in their interaction, Matz adds another possibility which clarifies how the *Bildungsroman*, as a particularly seamless union of form and content, relates to the genre's recapitulatory structure. The 'anachrony' in *Maurice*, proposes Matz, occurs instead 'at some level prior to that of *story* and *discourse* alike' (2000: 191). If this solution seems vague, it is only because narratology offers no clear concept for the 'level prior' to story and discourse. Perhaps the missing level in this case is *genre*, for generic expectations impose their own temporality, which can be resisted by either or both story and discourse. Thus the reversionary dynamics of modernist *Bildung* can occur in any number of ways, as long as they disrupt the expected order and nature of the developmental sequence. In *Orlando* the resistance is enacted largely at the level of story, in *Eyeless in Gaza* at the level of discourse; in both, however, the specific and individual moves out of step with the generic. By incorporating reversionary temporalities from biological models, the modernist *Bildungsromane* featured in this book reclaim the 'regressive metamorphosis' Goethe recognised as a normal part of development yet could not help but devalue compared with the 'progressive metamorphosis' which 'ascends – as on a spiritual ladder – to the pinnacle of nature' (1988: 76).

Modernist experiments with the *Bildung* plot, then, are not always (or not merely) iconoclastic. Many, including the novels featured in the upcoming chapters, more productively suggest that if 'growing up . . . is not necessarily growing better' (O 282), then growing better might mean growing *down* – reverting. An exemplary figure in this respect is Edward Carpenter, the Whitmanesque philosopher and art critic now best known for his influence on Lawrence and Forster. Relying on 'a large analogy of all growth', Carpenter argues that if 'modern life has come to an *impasse* and a point of arrest', the remedy must be 'a return to an earlier and more primitive stage in social development, as to a point from which to branch out afresh'. This 'reversionary process', Carpenter argues, is as manifest 'in the growth of the Individual as in the progress of Society' (1898: 246–7). Unlike Huysmans going against nature, Carpenter reimagines natural development to include multiple trajectories, not only the inexorable forward movement of 'the existing line of progress' (1898: 244). What Carpenter means by reversion can be distilled to his folksy definition of returning to Nature:

> When, in walking over a mountain country, you miss the path or find it running out into mere sheep-trails, you generally *go back* till you reach the main track from which you strayed, and then go forward again . . .

> [T]here is a good deal to show that there is a similar tendency or law in human progress . . . May it not indeed be said that *all* growth takes place on some such principle as that indicated? (Carpenter 1898: 243–4)

This 'reversionary process' is not anti-progressive: its 'movements . . . point pretty distinctly to fresh developments from the earlier ideals they imply' (Carpenter 1898: 246). Carpenter's model is progressive in its optimism about better prospects for individuals and society. But it is not progressivist, because it challenges the equation of improvement and time.

Carpenter expands the definition of progressive development by reimagining Newton's absolute time as just one among a plurality of other temporalities. In this he joins other modernists from Mach and Einstein to Bergson, Proust and Woolf. For Bergson, evolution is the increasing dissipation of *élan vital* as it is channelled into divergent lineages, only some of which, notably humans, are progressive. Despite Bergson's faith in human progress, however, he objects to Herbert Spencer's crude vision of forward-moving development and sees harmony not ahead 'but behind'; only lineages capable of 'a return backwards' can reverse the entropic genealogical stream and recapture primitive energies (2007: 105). Like Bergson, Carpenter does not advise a literal movement back in history, which would be impossible; nor does he suggest a naïve return to earlier technologies *à la* Erewhon. He recognises time as having social, psychological and physical dimensions which do not necessarily move in unison. While clock time ticks onwards, others temporalities might progress in different directions. In *Orlando*, Woolf's narrator describes individuals as amalgams of such various, desynchronised temporalities, identifying '(at a venture) seventy-six different times all ticking in the mind at once' (*O* 308).

Contemporary biology was identifying and even celebrating similar reversions and self-divisions, as I discuss in detail in Chapter 1. In embryology, recapitulation's unidirectional and well-coordinated process gave way to models which partition development into a mosaic of simultaneous processes, each unfolding at its own rate. Processes which unfold more slowly, or stop earlier than others, thus move back in time – not literally, of course, but relative to the faster or longer-lasting processes.[13] Mosaic models were also transforming the study of heredity, with similarly radical implications for theories of development. These reconceptions had profound metaphysical implications: progress was no longer written in the very structure of a universe in which everything follows the law of gradual unfolding from primitive simplicity to advanced complexity. Nor would linear development suffice as a framework for ranking individuals along a simple scale or hierarchy. Progress did not vanish from politics or from biology, but given the findings of experimental embryology and Mendelian genetics any notion of progressive evolution would henceforth have to accommodate reversion.

Having examined, in Chapter 1, the biological substrate of the *Bildung* plot, the narrative structure of recapitulation theory and the reversionary mechanisms of modernist biology, I turn to my analyses of recapitulation and reversion in the novels. Chapter 2 explores reversion in *A Portrait of the Artist*. Foregrounding Stephen's unusual receptiveness to words with carnal and sexual connotations, I link his epiphanies to his unwilled ability to remember or imagine distant pasts, personal and ancestral, human and 'infrahuman' (*PA* 167). The history of words, tied to the evolutionary antiquity of the human body, repeatedly draws Stephen into the past, even as the conventions of the *Künstlerroman* demand a forward movement towards artistic achievement. Thus the very medium of Stephen's purportedly spiritual art leads him predictably back to the realm of the sexual body. Arguably the definitive modernist *Bildungsroman*, *A Portrait* illustrates how reversion allows for a non-linear *Bildung* plot by defensively, critically and productively extricating 'the slow and dark birth' of the individual soul from the history of 'country' and 'race' (*PA* 203, 253).

In Chapter 3 I read *Howards End* as a *Bildungsroman* whose plot of acculturation, fractured by procreation and reconstituted by genetic reversion, straddles two generations rather than following the formation of a single character. This approach enables conciliation between the queer, affiliative poetics which characterise most recent readings of Forster and the evident but often occluded centrality of biological reproduction in his plots. The reversionary process in this case is provided by Mendelian genetics, whose peculiar operations normalise evolutionary throwbacks and therefore provide Forster with a compelling alternative to the homogenisation he saw as an inevitable consequence of blind, unidirectional progress.

Chapter 4 reads *Orlando* alongside contemporary findings on the genetics of sex determination and biology's recognition that sex can be as fluid as gender and sexuality. Examining the protagonist's seemingly unnatural life history through the lens of biology helps foreground Orlando's extreme longevity, delayed ageing, and sex change as transformations in the body – a fact which has been overlooked and which has profound implications for the novel's feminism. By staging a bodily metamorphosis, Woolf frees her novel from the spectre of recapitulation which lingers in the sexological framework of other contemporary novels about homosexuality and gender dysphoria such as *Maurice* and *The Well of Loneliness*. Central to my reading of *Orlando* is the biological concept of *heterochrony*, basically an ontogenetic version of what Marxian economists call 'uneven development' (Esty 2012: 36–7). Dividing the body into multiple independent developmental trajectories, the heterochronic model of ontogeny provides a biological explanation for sex change in insects and an intriguing parallel to *Orlando*'s stated and structural challenges to classical temporality.

The possibilities of heterochrony are explored further in Chapter 5, focusing on *Eyeless in Gaza*, Aldous Huxley's only *Bildungsroman*. Where *Howards End* links progress to entropy, this novel links progress to the related ill of overspecialisation – the antithesis of *Bildung*. Readers have long struggled to comprehend *Eyeless in Gaza*'s disorienting and seemingly unmotivated use of anachrony, which I relate to the biological studies of Huxley's brother Julian (among others) on the embryology, endocrinology and evolution of amphibians. The novel's anachrony, I argue, is the narrative correlative of two related developmental phenomena, both of them seen by contemporary biologists as keys to progress in human evolution and culture: *heterochrony* (the relativity of developmental schedules and tempos) and *neoteny* (the retention of juvenile features). For Aldous, one of modernism's foremost advocates of the *Bildung* ideal, and surely the best versed in current science, these biological models suggest ways to narrate harmonious development in a modern world beset by overspecialised education and political tyranny.

The final chapter traces how an anecdote about interrupted metamorphosis in *The Origin of Species* spurred increasingly innovative reassessments of *Bildung* as a series of repeated beginnings. Starting with George Eliot's *Silas Marner* (1861), I explore adaptations of Darwin's 'much embarrassed' caterpillar (*OS* 208) through the eccentric fictions of Samuel Butler, Lewis Carroll and finally, as the chapter's primary focus, Samuel Beckett. Even as they push the novel of development far beyond its breaking point, Beckett's fictions engage in complex ways with the biographical plot, exemplifying through exaggeration the reversionary dynamics which modernists use to challenge and, at the same time, preserve the genre of the *Bildungsroman*.

In a brief conclusion, I outline how writers after Beckett continue to experiment with narrative with the help of contemporary biology. By broadening my scope to include fiction from the later twentieth and twenty-first centuries, I propose that literature continues to play a crucial role as an interpreter of biological knowledge, even as the biological sciences continue to challenge, surprise, endanger, but also inspire us today. Far from being the antithesis of literary aesthetics, ethics and conceptions of self and time, 'the sciences of life', as Aldous Huxley writes in *Literature and Science*, 'can confirm the intuitions of the artist, can deepen his insights and extend the range of his vision' (1963: 67). Probably unconsciously, Huxley echoes his brother Julian who, along with H. G. Wells and G. P. Wells, suggest in *The Science of Life* that as our knowledge of biology 'change[s], deepen[s], and intensifie[s]', we require new ways of seeing and representing 'life as it goes on about us and within us' (1937: 2). Biology thus 'reflects upon the conduct of our lives throughout; it throws new light upon our moral judgments; it suggests fresh methods of human co-operation, imposes novel conceptions of service, and opens new possibilities and new freedoms to us' (Wells et al. 1937: 2). Investigating how some modernist writers refracted biology's 'new light' and tested its 'new possibilities' is my goal in *Modernist Life Histories*.

Notes

1. Recent approaches to the modernist *Bildungsroman* are summarised in a review by Boes (2006) and, as part of a larger discussion of life writing, by John Paul Riquelme (2013). Adam Parkes's (2013) review of Esty's *Unseasonable Youth* and Max Saunders's *Self Impression* is an excellent synopsis of recent critical trends, as is the introduction to Patrick Bixby's *Samuel Beckett and the Postcolonial Novel* (2009: 19–33). Gregory Castle's *Reading the Modernist Bildungsroman* (2006), along with his newer essays on the topic (2013, 2015), remains a keystone study.
2. Biology goes unmentioned in Linda Henderson's 'Modernism and Science' in Eysteinsson and Liska's *Modernism* (2007), as in Hugh Crawford's 'Modernism' in *The Routledge Companion to Literature and Science* (2011). Michael Whitworth scatters a few references to Mendelism in his physics-heavy 'Science in the Age of Modernism' (2010). Notable studies of modernism and contemporaneous biology are Christina Alt's *Virginia Woolf and the Study of Nature* (2010); Tim Armstrong's essay on biology and the 1930s poets (2012); Bradley Clissold's essay on heredity in Joyce and Sinclair (2007); Caroline Hovanec's dissertation on 'zoological modernism' (2013); Paul Peppis's chapter on sexology and homosexuality in *Sciences of Modernism* (2014); and, most pertinent to this book, Susan Squier's brief but evocative 'Embryologies of Modernism' (1996).
3. On modernism and Victorian biology, see Gillian Beer (1996) and Sam See (2010) on Woolf; Margot Norris (1985) on Lawrence; Roger Ebbatson (1982) on Lawrence and Forster; Donald Childs (2001) on Eliot, Woolf and Yeats; and Scarlett Baron (2013), Paul Bowers (1999, 2009), Vike Martina Plock (2009) and Sandra Tropp (2008) on Joyce.
4. For the importance of the external environment on modern narratives of development, see Mao (2008).
5. Haeckel was widely read, influencing modernists including Fitzgerald, London, McKay, Wharton (Bender 2011: 59, 64) and Yeats (MacDonald 2014: 23). He influences the atheism of Alfred Milne in Ford Madox Ford's *Mr Apollo* (1908: 80–1) and the pantheism of Mary Olivier in May Sinclair's *Mary Olivier* (2002: 331). Joyce places Haeckel's epithet for God, 'the gaseous vertebrate', in Buck Mulligan's mouth (*U* 389).
6. What progress means in a biological context is not straightforward, as Michael Ruse demonstrates in *Monad to Man: The Concept of Progress in Evolutionary Biology* (2009).
7. On recapitulation and arguments for degeneration among various groups including women, homosexuals, non-whites and artists, see David Greenslade (1994), Valerie Rohy (2009) and Cynthia Eagle Russett (1991). On links between recapitulation theory or Haeckel himself and the rise of Nazism, see Gould (*OP* 77–8); for a rebuttal, Richards (2008: 448 ff.).
8. Part I of Tobias Boes's *Formative Fictions* includes an unparalleled rebuttal of simplistic and doctrinal definitions of the *Bildungsroman*, including those sharply distinguishing between classical and modern forms.
9. This tripartite division corresponds roughly with the three critical orientations recently discussed by Rita Felski: first, 'suspicious reading', which treats texts as

coded documents in need of ideological unmasking; second, a variant of suspicious reading which views critique as an imminent feature of the text; and, third, 'reflective reading', which 'assumes that literature's relation to worldly knowledge is not only suspicious, subversive, or adversarial, that it can also amplify and replenish our sense of how things are' (2009: 34). In methodology *Modernist Life Histories* is more closely aligned with the second and third orientations; in sympathy it is closest to the third. But the tripartite division is pragmatic, not doctrinal; the best work on the genre combines all three approaches.

10. Recent revaluations of the *Bildungsroman* owe much to feminist, queer and postcolonial studies. Female *Bildungsromane*, argues Susan Fraiman (1994), depict *Bildung* as a trajectory and goal but also as an ill-fitting imposition to be treated ironically and deconstructed. See also Elizabeth Abel (1983), Penny Brown (1992), Lorna Ellis (1999), Patricia Moran (2015), Ruth Parkin-Gounelas (1991) and Susan Stanford Friedman (2015). On queer *Bildung*, see Paul Morrison (2015), Kevin Ohi (2015) and Bonnie Zimmerman (1983); while not specifically about the *Bildungsroman*, Kathryn B. Stockton's *The Queer Child* and essays in McCallum and Tuhkanen's *Queer Times, Queer Becomings* characterise queer development as 'sideways' (Stockton 2009: 4 ff.) and queer time as 'contrapuntal, syncopated, and at worst, erratic, arrested' (McCallum and Tuhkanen 2011: 1). On colonial and postcolonial *Bildung*, see Jessica Berman (2011), Jonathan Bolton (2010), Pheng Cheah (2003), Janice Ho (2015), Maria Lima (1993), Richard Murphy (2013), Joseph Slaughter (2009) and Paula White (1998).
11. In recent essays, Castle is more receptive to the role of creative as well as critical interventions. Modernist *Bildungsromane*, he argues, do not stage developmental failure, which is after all a kind of closure; instead, they stress the process of 'failing', an indeterminate activity which 'opens up avenues of experience that would otherwise have been missed' (2015: 487).
12. On fiction as thought experiment, see Alexis Harley (2015), Simon Mawer (2005), Janine Rogers (2015) and Peter Swirski (2007). Jeremy Adler argues that the scientific interests of late eighteenth-century Germans like Haller and Goethe led them to a mode of literary production which 'not only adopts scientific insights, but actually performs a scientific role' (2005: 46). Alexander Welsh surveys the emergence of thought experiments, or 'models', in science and literature between 1870 and 1920; 'these decades', he notes, 'were critical for the attitude toward scientific fiction—as they would appear to have been for literary fictions' (1973: 139).
13. Modernist biology had precedents: in the 1760s, John Hunter tested the effects of cold on the organic functions of various animals and considered the possibility of multiple temporalities, thereby challenging the 'understanding of human time as having only one real directionality' (R. Mitchell 2014: 52).

I

BILDUNG, BIOLOGY AND THE NARRATIVE STRUCTURE OF DEVELOPMENT

> We are born, small and helpless, yet visibly stamped with humanity; day by day we change, but move with certainty in one direction . . . The changes affect size and structure, character and disposition, but are so orderly and familiar that we accept them without surprise.
>
> – P. Chalmers Mitchell, *The Childhood of Animals* (1912: 1)

I have claimed that biological theories of development participate in the narrative grammar of *Bildung* and thus in the structure of the *Bildungsroman*. Elaborating this claim is one purpose in this chapter, which surveys late eighteenth-century models of embryogenesis and their links with contemporary theories of self-cultivation. My point is that the ideal *Bildung* plot has, like the ontogenetic plot of embryology, a recapitulatory structure. This is not to reduce actual *Bildungsromane* to a formula, but it should contextualise the formal strategies of nineteenth-century *Bildungsromane*, as well as their modernist successors, by situating them within a dominant understanding of progressive development and linear time.

The chapter also presents the various forms of biological reversion which supply alternative developmental structures in the modernist *Bildungsromane* featured in subsequent chapters: atavism, Mendelian throwbacks, sex change, neoteny and interrupted metamorphosis. It will be useful to think of reversions as developmental dynamics which defer maturity or restore immaturity. Atavisms and Mendelian throwbacks are reversions to ancestral conditions which are, in the context of recapitulation, equivalent to immaturity; so is sex change, at least as it occurs in *Orlando*. Neoteny and interrupted metamorphosis delay or prevent the onset of adulthood. Treating the five forms of reversion together should help compare various biological phenomena which might otherwise seem unrelated.

Epigenesis and the Recapitulatory Shape of Life

With apologies to Mr Emerson in *A Room with a View*, *Bildung* is not the body, but it is (partly) *of* the body. Derived from Pietism and associated primarily with the spiritual, idealist and cultural, the modern concept of *Bildung* also reflects 'close affinities between the life-sciences and aesthetics models of autopoeiesis around 1800' (Pfau 2010: 28). Schelling, a central figure of Weimar classicism, theorised that biological processes 'were isomorphic with those acts delineated subjectively in the self' (Richards 2002: 116). Coevolving with new theories of embryogenesis and sexual generation, *Bildung* was by the turn of the nineteenth century partly 'a physiological concept' (Reill 1986: 143); it was 'education, acculturation, and ontogenesis bound up together' (Gigante 2009: 46).[1]

Overlaps between biological and cultural development have profound implications for literary history and literary practices, as Daniel Punday and Susan Squier have argued. The narrative forms we use are determined by the available theories of bodily form and formation, and 'developments in the scientific field of embryology – concerned as it is with the principle of individual development against a backdrop of species change over time – have a relationship to . . . the literary approach to character construction' (Squier 1996: 145). The cultural history of *Bildung* is, as several scholars have noted, inextricable from a paradigm shift in biological conceptions of generation and embryogenesis. Well into the 1700s, scientists were debating whether organisms are full formed from the start (preformationism) or gradually acquire form from original formlessness (epigenesis). Preformationism, which dominated embryological theories in the seventeenth and early eighteenth centuries, posits that development is effectively limited to growth in size; genealogy is thus like a set of nesting dolls, each offspring already contained in the egg (or sperm, depending on the version) of the parent, going all the way back to Creation. Epigenesis involves successive differentiations of an originally homogeneous cell, a progressive movement from simplicity to complexity. A decisive blow for preformationism came in 1781, when Johann Blumenbach theorised the existence of a formative drive (*Bildungstrieb*), a form-giving impulse guiding development in living things. The concept reverberated throughout German culture, influencing Kant's philosophy, Herder's notion of universal *Bildung*, Schelling's concept of organism and Goethe's theories of metamorphosis (Richards 2002: 216 ff.).

The triumph of epigenesis signalled a broader shift towards developmentalism and historicism. In the sciences, it meant 'natural history would have to redefine itself as a discipline devoted to the *histories* of living things' (Mensch 2013: 4). In the human realms of pedagogy, history and culture, it meant identity (individual or national) is not given but realised. Epigenesis is evident in Antoine Berman's definition of *Bildung* as 'a movement toward a form, *one's own form* – which is to say that, in the beginning, every being is deprived of *its* form' (1992: 44). No wonder the *Bildungsroman*, with 'origins in a longer history of aesthetics that converged with Romantic life science' (Gigante 2009: 46), has been called 'the epitome of epigenetic literature' (Müller-Sievers 1997: 20). Central to this history is Goethe, who played a key role in the history of the *Bildungsroman* as well as developmental biology. Widely if problematically credited with originating the genre with *Wilhelm Meisters Lehrjahre*, he also gave biology the concept of 'morphology in our modern and dynamic sense' (Oppenheimer 1967: 136). Like the cultural and spiritual concept of *Bildung*, Goethean morphology suggests more than finished form; it also implies active formation. In an 1807 entry in his journal *On Morphology*, Goethe deplores the stasis implied by the German word typically used to describe 'the complex of existence presented by a physical organism: *Gestalt*'. To see a living organism as a form is to neglect its constant 'flux'; 'this is why', Goethe argues, 'German frequently and fittingly makes use of the word *Bildung* to describe the end product and what is in process of production as well' (1988: 63).

Linking the two Goethean aspects of *Bildung* is its embodied context – the fact that social and spiritual formation unfolds in a corporeal substrate which changes over time. Well documented by historians, this biological context has received little attention from scholars of the *Bildungsroman*.[2] Yet it is intuitive that the body and its temporal changes would influence the content and form of the genre. Development 'is an aspect of life's temporal dimension' and therefore 'an inevitable condition and experience of living bodies' (Hartung 2016: 1). If, as Peter Brooks claims, 'modern narratives produce a semioticization of the body which is matched by somatization of story' (1993: xii), 'somatization' is most evident and literal in biographical narratives, whose plot of individual development unfolds in and around the protagonist's body. 'The body', Brooks adds, 'must be a source and locus of meanings, . . . a prime vehicle of narrative significance' (1993: xii).

A corollary of *Bildung* as an epigenetic process is that it is not only of the body, but of the body in time. In his essay on the *Bildungsroman*, Bakhtin identifies '"biological time" (the hero's age, his progress from youth to maturity)' as the physical substrate for the cultural life unfolding in '"biographical time" (birth, childhood, school years, marriage)' (1984: 11, 17). The insight was already clear to Karl Morgenstern who, in 1819, insisted that *Bildung* demands novelistic exposition: 'the novel has more time and space to develop and present its dispositions than in the drama and, furthermore, . . . the characters stand fully formed in the latter, whereas in the novel they are supposed to develop before our eyes' (2009: 651). Morgenstern's formulation links the drama to a preformationist view of character, whereas the gradually unfolding novel is epigenetic. This understanding of novelistic time explains why Bakhtin considers the *Bildungsroman* exemplary of the modern novel, in which 'changes in the hero himself acquire *plot* significance' (1984: 21). Character is incident, as Henry James said of fiction in general, but in the *Bildungsroman* the unity of character and plot is especially seamless: a *Bildung* plot is *about* the making of the character. The *Bildungsroman*'s focus on one character ensures that it is in the changing body, as well as in the changing mind and social ties, that 'time, as it were, thickens, takes on flesh, becomes artistically visible; likewise, space becomes charged and responsive to the movements of time, plot and history' (Bakhtin 1981: 84). Fusing time and space, content and form, the *Bildungsroman* is the modern novel *par excellence*.

A Narratology of *Bildung*: Linearity and Progress

Since the Introduction, I have identified the *Bildung* plot with linearity. The issue is in fact more complicated than it may sound, for *Bildung* is not reducible to a unidirectional movement. Echoing Michael Minden's model of the *Bildung* plot as both progressive and circular, Tobias Boes warns that to 'focus exclusively on the linear and forward-moving dimensions of the protagonist's development' is to ignore the fact that 'historical time in the *Bildungsroman* . . . acquires an iterative as well as a sequential character' (2012: 34). These dynamics are evident in early readings of *Wilhelm Meister*, and they are even clearer in Goethe's studies on *The Metamorphosis of Plants* (1790). According to Goethe, plant organs follow one of three modes of development. Only one, 'accidental metamorphosis', is in any sense abnormal (it results from damage by insects or herbivores). The other two, 'regular' and 'irregular metamorphosis', involve successive complexification and simplification, respectively. Both are normal, necessary for generating the various parts of a mature plant (Goethe 1988: 76). Each plant has many organs whose development is progressive or regressive in relation to others.[3] Thus 'a stamen is a contracted petal or, with equal justification, . . . a petal is a stamen in a state of expansion' and it is in concert that 'these manifestations both forward and backward' produce an organism (1988: 97). A plant's growth therefore involves the same multiple temporalities which scholars like Boes attribute to the *Bildungsroman* in both classical and modern forms. Nevertheless, linearity and progressivism remain an undeniable aspect of the *Bildung* plot.

Goethe is again exemplary. Though he explicitly recognises many developmental trajectories, he cannot help but moralise them differently, favouring the 'forward' and thus funnelling his multidirectional model into a singular, upward line. This tendency is evident in the ways Goethe describes 'irregular metamorphosis', which he also calls 'retrogressive metamorphosis' (1988: 77). During such changes, he writes, nature 'seems to grow slack, irresolutely leaving its creation in an indeterminate, malleable state often pleasing to the eye but lacking in inner force and effect' (1988: 77). Goethe may consider retrogression necessary, but his rhetoric of slackness and weakness contrasts tellingly with his account of 'regular' or 'progressive' metamorphosis:

> it can be seen to work step by step from the first seed leaves to the last formation of the fruit. By changing one form into another, it ascends – as on a spiritual ladder – to the pinnacle of nature: propagation through two genders. (Goethe 1988: 76)[4]

This account matches Rita Felski's précis of the *Bildung* plot, in which formation is 'gradual and accumulative, an irreversible process of development through successive stages. The unfolding of the text is directed toward this goal of retrospective self-knowledge, and all the aspects of the text gain their significance in relation to the developmental plot' (1989: 136). I hasten to repeat that nineteenth-century *Bildungsromane* are *not* simply linear but, rather, that epigenetic models of development encourage the simplifications Goethe could not avoid, over-reading and overstating the importance and primacy of 'progressive' change even as he acknowledges alternative modes.

Such simplifications are frequent for good reason. As a specific kind of change, development implies linear time. It assumes events occur 'in order, in sequence, or in succession, following each other in time in a causal and logical relationship. Time is unidirectional' (Meacham 1997: 43). For Kant, argues Jennifer Mensch, organic development was synonymous with 'linear advance': the 'path from an acorn to oak is not only linear, it is necessarily linear if it is ever to achieve the end toward which it was destined from the start' (2013: 140). Expressed through causal and cumulative continuity, development seems incompatible with anything but an irreversible temporality. As Friedrich Schlegel describes 'the course of the human spirit' in 'On Philosophy: To Dorothea', 'everything is in constant progress and nothing can disappear. Thus no step can be skipped, for the present step is necessarily connected to one before and after it' (1997: 433). Chronology is therefore not merely representative but constitutive of development; in developmental narratives, chronology is functional. As Hegel narrates his vision of *Bildung*, echoing Goethe's botanical conceit,

> The bud disappears in the bursting-forth of the blossom, and one might say that the former is refuted by the latter; similarly, when the fruit appears, the blossom in shown up in its turn as a false manifestation of the plant, and the fruit now emerges as the truth of it instead. These forms are not just distinguished from one another, they also supplant one another as mutually incompatible. Yet at the same time their fluid nature makes them moments of an organic unity. (Hegel 1979: 2)

Chronology is crucial in development because each stage must build synthetically on the previous one. A developmental story demands a parallel developmental discourse, without which it begins to be a different kind of story. To narrate a life out of order is to disarrange the events whose *succession* makes up the life.

Bildung is hard to extricate from linear time for another reason. As we have seen, the order of stages in individual development was thought to reflect a historical sequence. Individual development is thus only half the story of the *Bildung* plot. The other half is suggested by Goethe's *Urpflanze*, the archetype of all possible plant forms, and by Dilthey's appeal to 'that which is universally human in . . . a life-course' (1985: 335): the historical analogue of individual life. Time is the medium in which the individual gradually and successively realises itself as a specific instance of an archetypal pattern. For Hegel, then,

> the single individual must . . . pass through the formative stages on a way that has been made level with toil. Thus, as far as factual information in concerned, we find that what in former ages engaged the attention of men of mature mind, has been reduced to the level of facts, exercise, and even games for children; and, in the child's progress through school, we shall recognize the history of the cultural development of the world traced, as it were, in a silhouette. (Hegel 1979: 16)

The learning of each new 'age' supersedes and pushes back the learning of 'former ages' in developmental time; what my ancestors learned as youths I learned in kindergarten. Here are the unmistakable germs of the biogenetic law. What was ideal in Goethe and Hegel would be literal in Haeckel, but structurally their underlying narratives are identical.

Though rarely thematised, the historical analogue of the protagonist's development inheres in a *Bildungsroman*'s structure. Thus Joel Black claims that 'perceptions of a developmental parallel between individual and species are evident in Romantic "culture theories" and *Bildungsromane*' (2000: 124), while John Kadvany identifies 'the bildungsroman as the [biogenetic] law's literary analogue' (2001: 31).[5] If the genre's chronological plotting conforms to a distinctly modern understanding of change in time, it also more specifically reflects 'the beliefs in causation and chronology that became associated with the term "recapitulation"' (Mayr 1982: 472). As we saw in the Introduction, successful development meant a faithful recapitulation of evolutionary history; as Herbert Spencer put it, 'education should be a repetition of civilization in little' (1861: 76). It is time, then, to examine the mechanics of biological recapitulation, which help clarify the *Bildungsroman*'s narrative conventions and, thus, the significance of modernist experiments with the genre.

A Narratology of Recapitulation: Order and Progress

In recapitulation theory, the emphasis placed on the correct order of ontogenetic stages is directly linked to an underlying philosophy of universal progress. Both order and progress have correlates in narrative theory. Order corresponds to the parallelism of story and discourse in chronological narratives. Progress recalls the dynamic model of plot proposed by Peter Brooks, succinctly captured in the notion of 'the anticipation of retrospection' (1985: 23), which makes plot both progressive and teleological: the past and present are significant because we trust that their meaning will be clear in the end.

It was essential to recapitulation theory that developmental stages replicated the order of their evolutionary appearance. Deviations from this rule were gladly acknowledged by Haeckel, though he did so only to dismiss their relevance. He understood that to assign meaning to these deviations would undermine the universality of his law; what is more, it would threaten 'the fundamental principle of progressive differentiation which has dominated all of the concepts of embryology since Aristotle' (Oppenheimer 1967: 18–19). For this reason, 'the ultimate task of embryology and developmental physiology becomes the analysis of sequences of events in time' (Oppenheimer 1967: 18). This is also one of the basic tasks of narrative theory, which, implicitly or not, assumes chronology as an original or default condition. Thus the dual plot of recapitulation mirrors the chronological plotting of the *Bildungsroman*, an arrangement Meir Sternberg calls 'the immemorial cradle-to-grave formula of biography, real or fictional' (1990: 932).

Thus, in recapitulation as in the *Bildung* plot, each step in ontogeny or discourse matches a step in phylogeny or story: 1 (1'), 2 (2'), 3 (3'), 4 (4') . . . *n* (*n*'). I align ontogeny with discourse and phylogeny with story, rather than the other way round, because story, like Haeckel's phylogeny, is the purported true and original set of events, whereas discourse, like Haeckel's ontogeny, is viewed as a more or less faithful restatement of those events. The relation between ontogeny/discourse and phylogeny/story is linear (one-to-one) and easily graphed, as shown in Figure 1.1.

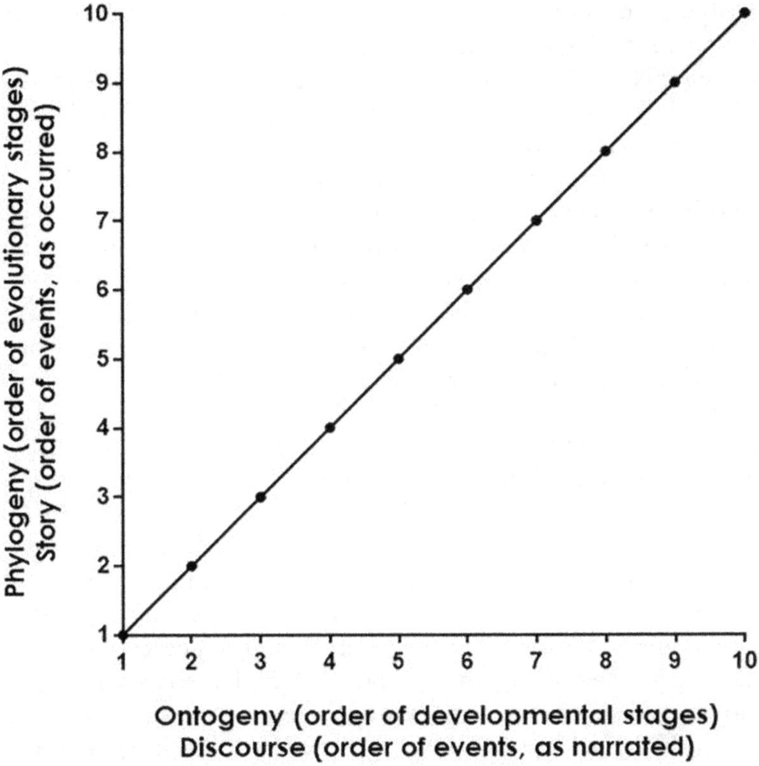

Figure 1.1 A schema of recapitulation (the linear relation between the order of ontogenetic stages and the order of phylogenetic stages), which doubles as a schema of chronological narrative (the linear relation between the order of events as narrated and the order of events as they purportedly occurred).

The progressive trajectory illustrated in Figure 1.1 was crucial to Haeckel. Like Goethe with plant metamorphosis, though more aggressively, Haeckel normalises and moralises linear development without denying that ontogenies often deviate from it. Explaining away such deviations, Haeckel distinguishes perfect recapitulation ('palingenesis') from corruptions of the proper order caused by omitted or displaced developmental stages ('caenogenesis'). Thus

> recapitulation is the more complete in proportion as the original *epitomized development (palingenesis)* is preserved by a constant heredity; on the other hand, it falls off from completeness in proportion as the later *disturbing development (cenogenesis)* is accentuated by varying adaptation. (Haeckel 1900: 142)

Though ubiquitous, caenogenetic 'modifications' were to Haeckel mere 'vitiations, strange, meaningless additions to the original, true course of evolution' (qtd in Churchill 2007: 75n56). Edward Cope, another prominent recapitulationist, dismissed deviations from 'exact parallelism' as accidents causing ontogeny to 'become inexact, or "falsified"' (1887: 200).

The stress laid on maintaining the correct ontogenetic order relates directly to recapitulation theory's vision of progressive evolution. If the appearance of new traits is to lead evolution forward and upward, it cannot occur at just any point in ontogeny; it must occur at the end of the ontogenetic sequence, after all ancestral stages have been recapitulated. Otherwise the parallelism of ontogeny and phylogeny would be broken. If ontogeny is 'to produce a "record"' of evolutionary history, writes Herbert Hurst, 'it is necessary that new chapters be added at the end of the pre-existing record' (1893: 197–8). This is the principle of 'terminal addition', explained as follows by Archdall Reid: 'progressive variation implies a prolongation of the parental development, a complete recapitulation with an additional step' (1910: 208). As terminal addition appends new traits onto the end of ontogeny, the complementary process of 'condensation' or 'acceleration' removes some traits from the beginning. Early ontogeny is therefore more fragmentary than later stages. Together, terminal addition and condensation produce evolutionary progress. The schema below, borrowing Haeckel's alphabetic analogy (1883: 7), shows how new developmental stages appear (for example, 'h' in generation 2) and how early stages can disappear (for example, 'b' in generation 2). As a result the middle stages are pulled, as it were, towards the beginning of ontogeny. Over several generations, ontogenies become more complex ('j' is more complex than 'i', which is more so than 'h'): in other words, there is progressive evolution:

1: a → b → c → d → e → f → g
2: a → c → d → e → f → g → h
3: c → d → e → f → g → h → i
4: c → e → f → g → h → i → j

Such simple progressivism was surely part of recapitulation's appeal. It confirmed a vision of the universe heading in a heartening direction, if not one dictated by a benevolent plan. 'Nothing so reenforces optimism as evolution', writes G. Stanley Hall, because 'development is upward, creative, and not de-creative. From cosmic gas onward there is progress, advancement, and improvement' (1904: ii.546). In Tennyson's *In Memoriam*, steeped in a pre-Haeckelian version of recapitulation, progress leads from primeval 'seeming-random forms' to 'the man'

> Who throve and branch'd from clime to clime,
> The herald of a higher race,
> And of himself in higher place,
> If so he type this work of time
>
> Within himself, from more to more . . .
>
> (Tennyson 1958: cxviii.13–17)

'From clime to clime' is literally geographical but the punning suggestion of ascent is hard to miss or to dismiss.

Recapitulatory progress, whether mechanistic or spiritual, was indeed used to justify existing hierarchies, even as it demanded an ethic of self-improvement and self-determination. From the historical pattern of progressive evolution, then, comes a moral injunction for the individual. It is a human duty to work through youth and animality in order to achieve spiritual maturity:

> Arise and fly
> The reeling Faun, the sensual feast;
> Move upward, working out the beast,
> And let the ape and tiger die.
>
> (Tennyson 1958: cxviii.25–8)

The sublation of youthful and primitive stages is a 'move[ment] upward' from our animal origins ('ape and tiger') and 'sensual' nature towards a spiritual being whose medium is the air ('arise and fly'). This notion of 'working out the beast' is a felicitous anticipation of Freud's concept of working through as a model for successful therapy. In recapitulatory development, likewise, the achievement of full humanity is contingent upon a successful run-through of the ancestral past. Peter Brooks supplies a parallel case in his account of repetition in *Great Expectations*:

> Whereas the model of the *Bildungsroman* seems to imply progress, a leading forth, and developmental change, Pip's story – and this may be true of other nineteenth-century educative plots as well – becomes more and more as it nears its end the working through of past history . . . The past needs to be incorporated *as past* within the present, mastered through the play of repetition in order for there to be an escape from repetition: in order for there to be difference, change, progress. (P. Brooks 1985: 134)

The past is not merely replayed; it is 'incorporated *as past*', transformed and thus rendered harmlessly *passed*. As Freud depicts 'bodily' development in *Civilization and Its Discontents*, 'the earlier phases of development are in no sense still preserved; they have been absorbed into the later phases for which they have supplied the material' (1961: 18). From a developmental perspective, this logic leads to an undervaluing of early life stages, a point to which I will return. From the analogous evolutionary perspective, it promotes indifference to the individual. Franco Moretti has noted that the *Bildung* plot inevitably curtails the protagonist's 'individuality' by asserting the higher needs of society and the nation (2000: 16). Similarly, models of progressive evolution tend to reduce individual organisms to mere stepping-stones on the way to the species' better future. Tennyson's 'man' is the mere 'herald of a higher race', useful insofar as he keeps the torches going.

This demotion of the individual leads to the contentious claims associated with the biogenetic law: the notion, expressed with typical bluntness by Haeckel, that 'Phylogenesis is the mechanical cause of Ontogenesis' (1883: 7). What is more, Haeckel insisted on making this 'causal-nexus of *biontic* (individual) and *phyletic* (historical) evolution' the keystone of his entire system, calling it 'the supreme law at the root of all biogenetic research' (1900: 142). Controversial even with fellow recapitulationists, Haeckel's phylogenetic causality raised major difficulties for recapitulation theory, most of them beyond the scope of this discussion. Suffice it here to say that 'Haeckel's causal arrow leading from phylogeny to ontogeny' (Churchill 2007: 58) gave philosophical ammunition to his critics, who saw it confused ultimate and proximate causality (Mayr 1994: 226). In the 1890s, Haeckel's erstwhile disciple Wilhelm Roux expressed doubts about historical causality because distinguishing cause from effect is empirically unfeasible when 'the organic processes of the *typical* or normal development of organisms are so incomprehensibly manifold and enigmatical' (Roux 1986: 118). Two decades later, Walter Garstang would completely turn the causal tables: 'ontogeny does not recapitulate phylogeny: it creates it' (1922: 82). As Gavin de Beer explains, ontogeny is more than 'an extrapolation into the future of a chain of events which happened in past and previous generations. Each ontogeny is a fresh creation to which the ancestors contribute only the internal factors by the means of heredity' (*EE* 17). This view of individual development, for de Beer, was reason enough to 'reject Haeckel's theory of recapitulation' (*EE* 102). Similar shifts are characteristic of modernist thinking. Garstang and de Beer follow William James who, in his early essay 'Great Men and Their Environment', attacks Herbert Spencer's historical determinism. A similar motive animates Bergson's own rebuttal of Spencer in *L'Évolution créatrice*. Freud's method, despite its recapitulatory foundations, similarly marks in its most innovative moments a 'shift of attention away from phylogenesis . . . to ontogenesis' (R. Brown 1985: 51).

Recapitulation and Its Discontents

Recapitulation's linear progressivism was conceptually elegant and satisfyingly universal. It was clear, however, that the realities of ontogeny and phylogeny were more complicated. What is more, certain logical corollaries of linear time were difficult to square with, even antithetical to, conceptions of progress as an increase in heterogeneity and adaptability. In this brief section, then, I outline two related paradoxes inherent in biological models of linear progressivism. Both equate thoroughgoing progress with the exhaustion of potentiality. The first, the problem of overspecialisation, is latent in all discussions of *Bildung* but especially central to my reading of *Eyeless in Gaza*. The second, the problem of entropy, restates overspecialisation in thermodynamic terms; it is most pertinent to my chapter on *Howards End*. In short, though linear progressivism seems to fit the general outline of the classical *Bildung* plot, its temporality proves inimical to the *Bildung* ideal itself.

The danger of specialisation worried early theorists of *Bildung*, particularly Wilhelm von Humboldt. A true education, for Humboldt, is more than training for a specialised career; it is the full and harmonious cultivation of multiple potentialities. In this context, specialisation is a perversion of *Bildung*, undermining it from within. In a distinctly post-war essay on 'Germany and Culture' in *The New Age*, Janko Lavrin argues that 'in spite of his enormous knowledge', a typical German

> lacks that inner 'style', that spiritual leaven without which even a great quantity of acquired culture is devoid of all flavour and charm . . . Hence he finds an outlet, not in a synthetic direction, but in devoting himself entirely to some 'specialism' or other. (Lavrin 1920: 384)

Becoming cultured in one area only may lead forwards along that particular line, but it also leads away from key qualities of *Bildung*: fullness, variety and openness.

Contemporary biologists similarly contrasted 'straight-line evolution' and 'true biological progress' (J. Huxley 1947: 175). Real progress, explains Julian Huxley, 'depends on all-round improvement, as opposed to the limited improvement or one-sided specialization which . . . automatically leads sooner or later to a dead end' (1947: 122). Huxley's account of evolutionary progress is strikingly similar to the ideal of *Bildung* described by Humboldt and Schiller – a developmental progress achieved without depleting the reservoir of potentiality. It is fitting, then, that Huxley should promote the pedagogic and ethical ideals of his brother, 'what Aldous Huxley calls many-pointed development, . . . this resolution of inner conflict to all his outwardly-directed activities – of knowledge and understanding, of love, of action, of emotional and aesthetic appreciation' (1947: 230).

Biological specialisation was often compared with entropy, a manifestation of the second law of thermodynamics whose inevitable increase will lead the universe to a state of inert homogeneity. In 1893, Louis Dollo suggested that evolution was 'the genealogical manifestation of the second law of thermodynamics' (Brooks and Wiley 1988: 103). What would become known as Dollo's Law considered evolution to be an entropic process because it is historical and therefore irreversible (Gould 1982: 38–9). Entropy is effectively synonymous with the arrow of time: 'time's arrow is a property of entropy alone', as Arthur Eddington puts it (1928: 80). Time-irreversibility is thus an inevitable correlative of entropic decay but also, as we have seen, of developmentalism. The second law of thermodynamics predicts the ultimate conversion of useable energy into useless dissipated energy; progressive specialisation in biological evolution seems to involve a similar exhaustion of primitive adaptability and morphological potential. Yet *Bildung* and entropy chart fundamentally different kinds of change. *Bildung* implies organic growth towards heterogeneity and complexity; entropy counters with the troubling notion that all energy will be exhausted, all motion stopped and all differentiation reduced to sameness. In *Embryology and Evolution*, an influential polemic against recapitulation theory, de Beer foregrounds the entropic implications of recapitulation, noting that it can account only for the exhaustion, and not the renewal, of potentiality in biological lineages. If evolution occurred solely by terminal addition, 'as Haeckel's theory of recapitulation would suggest, phylogeny would gradually slow down and become stationary', suggesting 'the dismal conclusion that the evolutionary clock is running down' (*EE* 95). Some lineages do run out of evolutionary steam, de Beer admits, but others diversify instead, disregarding 'the view that in the universe energy is always degraded' (*EE* 95).

It is important to note that neither de Beer nor any of his allies rejected recapitulation completely. Ontogeny does parallel phylogeny – sometimes. Nor do these cases of recapitulation describe whole organisms. Most confirmed cases, observes H. H. Swinnerton, are cases of 'localised recapitulation' (1938: 71), involving one or a few organs among many others developing along different lines, *reversionary* lines.

Reversions are processes which in one way or another counter the specialisation and entropy implicit in the recapitulation narrative. We have already seen that Julian Huxley posited alternatives to the evolutionary exhaustion produced by 'straight-line evolution' and overspecialisation (1947: 175). Entropy, too, could be reversed, if only temporarily and locally. The genetic and developmental theories emerging at the turn of the twentieth century made such reversals not merely conceivable but inevitable. After Mendel, Dollo's Law fails to account for the fact that, 'since organs and characters are genetically conditioned, and since any mutation may be reversed, it is not impossible for an organ or character which has disappeared to arise again' (Goudge 1961: 170). This insight would have been almost unthinkable before 1900: reversibility, as we have seen, challenges epigenetic understandings of development. One of the new biology's most radical effects was, indeed, to challenge the thoroughgoing epigenetic model of development and evolution epitomised by recapitulation theory.

Modernist Biology: Reclaiming Reversion in Development and Evolution

Writing in 1910, Louis Hussakof complains that biologists relied too heavily on recapitulation theory, 'invok[ing]' it like 'a sort of magic spell' in order to solve just about any outstanding problem (1910: 307). A decade later, hard-line recapitulationists were a besieged minority among biologists. What exactly precipitated the fall of recapitulation theory remains controversial (Churchill 2007: 39–41), but it certainly includes shifts in philosophical outlook, new perspectives enabled by new laboratory technologies and a growing archive of contradictory evidence. Recapitulation never disappeared completely from the biological landscape. As a master theory, however, it could not survive overwhelming evidence that 'recapitulation is only responsible for a certain fraction . . . of the relationships between juvenile and ancestral forms . . . [It is] neither a law, nor even a rule, but only one mode among many' (Viktor Frank, qtd in *OP* 206). It had become clear that reversions are normal phenomena, not mere deviations from perfect parallelism. As early as 1889, Carl Gegenbaur cited the ubiquity of reversions (caenogenetic characters) as grounds for doubting the universality of recapitulation theory:

> if we are compelled to admit that cenogenetic characters are intermingled with palingenetic, then we cannot regard ontogeny as a pure source of evidence regarding phyletic relationships . . . If it once be admitted that not everything in development is palingenetic, that not every ontogenetic fact can be accepted, so to speak, at its face value . . ., it follows that nothing in ontogeny is immediately available for the critique of embryological development. (Carl Gegenbaur, qtd by E. B. Wilson 1895: 104–5)

Thirty years later, stressing the same difficulties, Garstang would proclaim that 'recapitulation is dead, and need no longer limit and warp us in the study of phylogeny' (1928: 62).

Critics of recapitulation were a motley group, including some vitalists and other anti-Darwinian evolutionists. Those central to my study were the mainstream architects of today's Neo-Darwinian orthodoxy. Their models are dizzyingly complex, but for my purposes it suffices to show how each of the relevant processes is reversionary – how it counters the linear thrust of recapitulatory development. Some of them are quite broad. Atavism and interrupted development, examined in Chapter 2 and Chapter 6, are effectively synonymous and require just a brief introduction. Mendelian throwbacks, discussed in Chapter 3, require more explanation, especially because Mendelism also underlies the non-linear developmental processes examined in Chapters 4 and 5. The reversions foregrounded in these chapters are both consequences of *heterochrony* – temporal relativity in development rates – though they manifest differently as sex change (Chapter 4) and neoteny (Chapter 5).

Atavism and Interrupted Development

Atavism, a reversion to ancestral conditions, typically has negative associations. In 'Atavism Considered as a Conservative Agent in a State of Nature', Eugene Ringueberg does suggest it has 'the function . . . of serving as a restraining influence against what might otherwise be a too rapid divergence in any one direction' (1884: 544), but its usual connotations are pathology and regression. Max Nordau's degenerates and Cesar Lombroso's criminal types are atavisms, for example. In any case, atavism was known to be ubiquitous in nature, a fact difficult to reconcile with the purported universality of recapitulation. 'In a sense', admits Arthur Milnes Marshall, 'all the higher animals are degenerate; that is, they can be shown to possess certain organs in a less highly developed condition than their ancestors, or even in a rudimentary state' (1891: 843). (Witness Marshall's division of organisms into organs with independent developmental trajectories – a topic to which I will return.) Ashley Montagu would later go further, situating such 'so-called "atavisms"' as 'the occasional occurrence of a "tail" in man . . ., microcephaly, large canine teeth, the fourth molar, [and] supernumerary mammae' within the range of 'normal variability' (1938: 463).

In the context of recapitulation, where evolutionary ancestry corresponds to the early (embryonic or juvenile) stages of individual life, atavism is equivalent to arrested development. By implication immaturity itself, though a necessary step on the way to the goal of adulthood, is in a sense pathologically incomplete or at least not (yet) normal. Early stages are thus mere fuel for progressive change; a chick is just the hen's means of making itself. It is therefore unsurprising that 'so long as the study of embryology was dominated by the so-called biogenetic law, . . . the earlier stages of development were little heeded' (E. B. Wilson 1986: 67). But as new theories decoupled ontogeny from phylogeny, new biological fields such as ethology and ecology recognised juveniles as beings in their own right. 'As much as the adult', argues Peter Chalmers Mitchell in *The Childhood of Animals*,

> the young animal . . . has to be fitted to the special environment in which it lives. It is not merely a stage in development, but an independent living creature with its own needs and its own aptitudes, presenting characters

> that are neither a memory nor an anticipation, neither a relic of the past nor a preparation for the future, but suitable for its own purposes. (Mitchell 1912: 7–8)

Evolutionary theorists and developmental biologists were also revising the recapitulatory view of early life stages, as we shall see, and Gavin de Beer in particular insisted 'there are great biological advantages in remaining as little children' (1962: 66).

A similar shift characterises modernist *Bildungsromane* striving to render the experience of childhood rather than its recollection from a position of wise and ironic adulthood. If maturity is no longer idealised as the only significant part of life, its deferral may not be as problematic as some critics imply when they cite the modernist trope of delayed or arrested development. In Elizabeth Bowen's *The Last September*, for example, Lois experiences a 'sense of detention, of a prologue being played out too lengthily' (2000: 170), which may in fact be desirable, especially given her feeling that 'being grown up seems trivial' (2000: 140). As Oscar Wilde predicts in *The Soul of Man under Socialism*, anticipating de Beer, once 'the full expression of a personality' is possible, 'it will be as wonderful as the personality of a child' (1996: 21–2).

Mendelian Throwbacks

In *The Wonders of Life*, sensing threats to his biogenetic law, Haeckel insists that a truly scientific theory of evolution must be recapitulatory: 'Either there is or is not a direct and causal connection between ontogeny and phylogeny', he writes; 'either ontogenesis is a brief compendium of phylogenesis or it is not. Either epigenesis and descent – or pre-formation and creation' (1904: 401). To put the question so starkly was effectively to shut down debate: preformationism, where the embryo lies fully formed in its mother's egg, was evidently too absurd to entertain. But Haeckel was overlooking an important shift in thinking among embryologists. It was becoming clear that oppositions between preformation and epigenesis were less definite than Haeckel believed. The Mendelian revolution beginning in 1900 offered an entirely new way of conceiving of development and heredity, one which had been germinating since the 1880s: not a choice between 'either epigenesis . . . or pre-formation' but, rather, epigenesis for development and preformation for heredity.

This mixed model poses serious difficulties for recapitulation, which rests fundamentally on what Bowler calls 'the analogy between growth and evolution' (1988: 104). The importance of this analogy explains why recapitulation theory almost necessarily requires a model of heredity which blurs ontogeny and phylogeny: Lamarckian (or 'soft') inheritance, the transmission of acquired characteristics. If my experiences pass on to my children, the difference between me and my descendant is not qualitatively unlike the difference between my child self and myself now. Thus the great Lamarckian theorist Samuel Butler argues that

> the fish of fifty million years back and the man of to-day are one single living being, in the same sense . . . as the octogenarian is one single living being with the infant from which he has grown; and that the fish has lived himself into manhood, not as we live out our little life, living, and living, and living till we die, but living by pulsations, so to speak; living so far, and after a certain time going into a new body, and throwing off the old. (Butler 1890: 127)

In this model, 'living till we die' (development) and 'living by pulsations' (genealogy) differ merely in degree. It is easy to see why Lamarckians – the great majority of nineteenth-century biologists – saw recapitulation as a self-evident fact: the inheritance of acquired characters is just another way of expressing the process of evolution by terminal addition.

It was therefore only after a serious rival to Lamarckian inheritance emerged that recapitulation could be dethroned. This rival, Neo-Darwinian or 'hard' inheritance, was not strictly incompatible with recapitulation, and indeed the founding Neo-Darwinist August Weismann was committed to the biogenetic law. But the fit was far more tenuous, and by rejecting Lamarckian inheritance Weismann effectively signed a death warrant for recapitulation theory (Bateson 1913: 5). Where Lamarckism blurs ontogeny and phylogeny, Weismann's hard inheritance radically separates the development of the body (soma) from the transmission of genetic material (germ-plasm). The soma is the mortal stuff of individual development; the germ-plasm, carried unchanged through successive generations, is potentially immortal. In other words, development is epigenetic and heredity preformationist (de Beer 1938: 63). As the pioneering Mendelian geneticist Thomas Hunt Morgan would observe in 1916, the notion of preformed hereditary particles invalidated the central recapitulatory mechanisms of terminal addition and condensation; thus Weismann's evidence against Lamarckian inheritance 'played havoc with the biogenetic "law"' (1919: 19). Weismann himself did not see things quite so; Morgan's insight was possible because he interpreted Weismann with the benefit of hindsight, writing after the rediscovery of Mendel's breeding experiments with peas. Published in 1865 but ignored until 1900, Mendelism delivered the final blow against epigenetic conceptions of heredity and, thus, against the analogy of ontogeny and phylogeny. Its logic was so damaging that Ernest MacBride, an intransigent Lamarckian, rejected Mendelism *because* it 'is totally irreconcilable with the recapitulation theory' (1930: 884)!

Mendelism resembles Weismannism in the sense that both assume hard inheritance. Its most salient feature, however, differentiates it from Weismannism as well as from Lamarckism. Both of these, like nearly every other pre-Mendelian conception of heredity, assumed that parental contributions blend in the offspring, a process Richard Dawkins has helpfully compared to mixing paint colours – say blue and red in order to get purple. Logically, this type of inheritance tends irreversibly and inexorably towards homogenisation. In Dawkins's analogy, it is effectively impossible to recover the red and the blue from the purple (2009: 29). Such swamping or averaging is not how many heritable traits behave, however: a brown-eyed father and a blue-eyed mother, for example, do not have children with blueish-brownish eyes. This conundrum, which had so confounded Darwin, was resolved by the Mendelian hypothesis of atomistic, or non-blending, inheritance. As M. D. Eder explains in a 1909 review in *The New Age*:

> each germ cell is unique in regard to a large number of characters, called a unit character, and these unit characters are transmitted intact to the next generation. Tall and short do not give rise to an average kind of family; the children are exactly like one parent or the other in this respect. (Eder 1909: 192)

The corollary is spelled out further in another 1909 essay, 'Heredity and Variation in Modern Lights', by Britain's leading Mendelian William Bateson: because particles do not mix when they act together, 'the difficulty of the "swamping effects of intercrossing" is practically at an end' (2009: 223). There is thus no moral opprobrium in his claim that in a certain lineage 'impurity [c]ould be hidden in perpetuity' (Bateson 1913: 194).

If blending inheritance is like mixing paints, Mendelian inheritance is like shuffling cards: with each generation, genes are shuffled and recombined but like cards they retain their individual physical integrity (Dawkins 2009: 29). A trait is controlled by a gene whose effects and transmission are independent from the effects and transmission of other particles which control other traits. The gene controlling eye colour, say, is unlinked to the gene controlling earlobe attachment. This independence allows multiple genes to 'be recombined in various ways' (Bateson 2009: 223), producing a virtually infinite number of combinations of traits in the organism. Genes may have visible effects or not; some may lie latent for one or more generations. Either way, if they are transmitted to the next generation, they do so unchanged (barring a spontaneous mutation). Figure 1.2 demonstrates how Mendelism preserves variation over the course of generations. Transmitted whole even when they have no effect, genes 'can remain in storage indefinitely' and thus 'the variance of a species or population is conserved' (J. Huxley 1947: 160).

In this way, writes Julian Huxley, 'Mendelism at once explains the facts of reversion, which were at once so familiar and so puzzling to Darwin' (1947: 161). In Figure 1.2, the reappearance of light eyes in F2 is a reversion, the return of

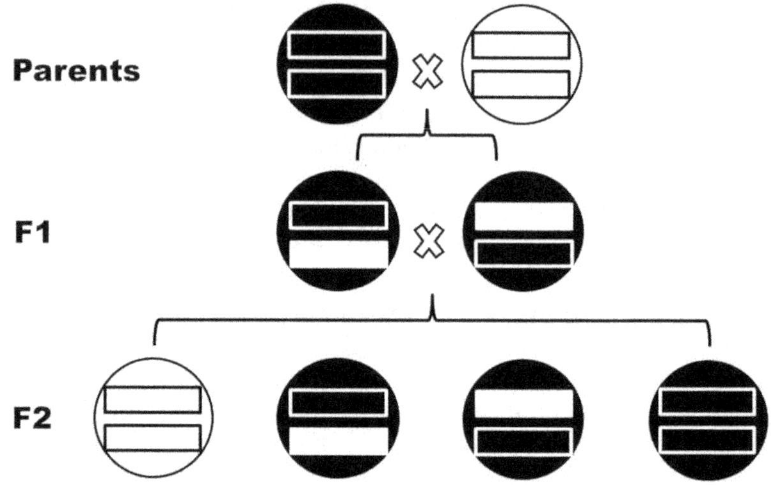

Figure 1.2 Diagram depicting non-blending Mendelian inheritance. Circles represent the individual's eye colour, which is either dark or light. Each individual carries two copies (alleles) of the eye-colour gene (represented by the rectangles), one inherited from each parent. Dark is dominant, so individuals with one dark and one light allele have dark eyes. Two 'pure' (homozygous) parents produce only 'impure' (heterozygous) offspring in Generation F1; their eyes are dark, though each carries a copy of the light allele. When two members of F1 are crossed, however, the alleles sort out in a predictable ratio: in F2, 75 per cent of the offspring are dark-eyed (of which 25 per cent are 'pure') and 25 per cent are light-eyed.

a character unexpressed in the immediate ancestry but present in more distant ancestors (in this case, a grandparent). Mendelism thus normalises atavism, by making it an unavoidable consequence of non-blending inheritance, and thus it avoids the progressive homogenisation predicted by blending inheritance. Rather than diluting difference with every cross, non-blending inheritance allows difference to recreate itself generation after generation. In *Heredity* (first published in 1908), J. Arthur Thomson illustrates this process in the inheritance of fur colour in domestic and wild ('wild type') rabbits. Wild rabbits have rich, multi-coloured fur, a mixture determined by multiple genes; through 'analysis' (physical sorting out of various gene combinations through selective breeding), farmers can produce domestic rabbits with pure white, brown, or black fur. Sometimes, however, domestic 'colour-varieties are crossed and the offspring are of the wild type' (J. A. Thomson 1912: 124), a reversion equivalent to the return of light eyes in F2 (Figure 1.2). This reappearance, explains Thomson, involves 'no mysterious re-awakening of long-latent characters', only the re-synthesis or 'repacking' of elements which had been separated in previous generations; thus 'colour-factors which have been separated out by analysis come together again and restore the wild form' (1912: 124–5). The return to the 'wild-type' exemplifies the reversionary logic E. M. Forster found so 'salutary' (1972b: 19), as we shall see in Chapter 3.

Heterochrony: Neoteny and Sex Change

We have seen how hard inheritance combines epigenetic development and preformationist heredity. More or less concomitantly with Weismann's work on heredity, a parallel change in perspective was taking place in the study of embryology. The embryologist Wilhelm His, who had rejected Lamarckism as early as 1874, pioneered the study of embryonic development as a causal and mechanical process, leading eventually to the rise of *Entwicklungsmechanik*, experimental embryology, at the end of the nineteenth century. His saw the developing organism as a mosaic of 'organ-building germ-districts' (*Organbildende Keimbezirke*). Instead of producing form epigenetically from original formlessness, His argued that from very early on in embryogenesis, individual cells or cell 'districts' were already destined to become a specific organ (Jenkinson 1909: 17). In other words, there was a certain amount of preformationism in development, though much of it was definitely also epigenetic. As John Wilfrid Jenkinson explains in *Experimental Embryology*, 'although the part of the embryo cannot be said to be preformed in the germ, the materials for those parts are already there, prelocalized, arranged roughly, at least, as the parts themselves will be later on' (1909: 17). While 'an old prejudice in biology' had favoured the 'perfect coordination' of the organism's parts as evidence of God's design, organic holism, or evolutionary superiority, *Entwicklungsmechanik* privileged the 'dissociability' of organismal parts (*OP* 234).

In His's view, then, morphology emerged not from the memory of ancestral form but from physical contact between adjacent cells, mechanical pressures which generate form by promoting and inhibiting growth and by forcing layers of cells to fold into complex configurations. Conceived in this way, the study of formation was less disposed to rely, explicitly or not, on mysterious form-giving impulses. Even extremely complex structures could be produced mechanistically, most notably by alternations in the speed and duration of growth in certain parts of the body – by a process called *heterochrony*. It is this kind of 'unequal growth', writes Jenkinson, which 'produces the form of the parts, and so of the whole body' (1909: 17), anticipating D'Arcy Thompson's ground-breaking 1917 book *On Growth and Form*. According to Thompson, a mathematician, the complex 'foldings' of cell-tissues involved in producing anatomical shape are 'the resultant of unequal rates of growth, – of local accelerations or retardations of growth, – in what to begin with was an even and uniform layer of embryonic tissue' (1917: 55). From a simple two-dimensional shape thus arises a complex three-dimensional morphology, a phenomenon

Thompson likens to 'a flat sheet of paper, parts of which are caused (as by moisture or evaporation) to expand or to contract, [and] the plane surface is at once dimpled, or "buckled", or folded, by the resultant forces of expansion or contraction' (1917: 55). Dispensing with historical causes or vital energies, Thompson shows that anatomical differences between related species can be represented as simple geometric transformations. To represent relations between three related crocodile species, for example, Thompson shows the skull of a saltwater crocodile (*Crocodylus porosus*) against a grid of regular squares (Figure 1.3). By compressing and stretching parts of the grid, he then produces the skull morphologies of two other crocodilians: the American crocodile (*C. americanus*), whose snout is relatively narrower and longer, and the long-extinct *Notosuchus terrestris*, whose snout is squatter and head much wider (D. Thompson 1917: 753). Thompson's innovation, then, was to 'equate our various magnitudes with time, and so to recognise that growth is essentially a question of rate, or of velocity' (1917: 155), translating developmental time into spatial form. What is fascinating about such transformations is often how minor they can be and still produce dramatically different shapes.

Thompson's approach recalls Bakhtin's notion of novelistic discourse as the interaction of multiple chronotopes: narratives combine multiple spatialisations of time, while a developing organism contains multiple organs developing at

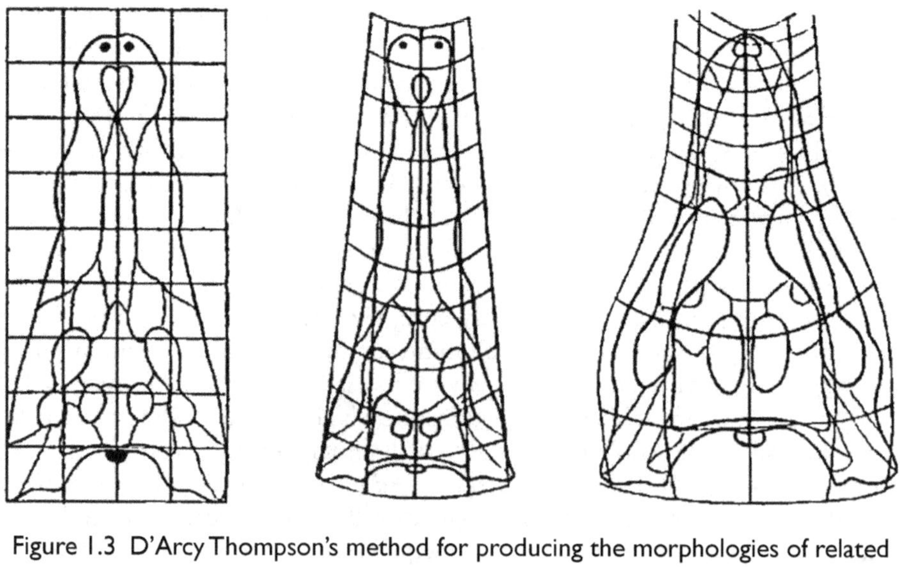

Figure 1.3 D'Arcy Thompson's method for producing the morphologies of related animals (in this case, three crocodile species) using geometric transformations. (Source: D'Arcy Wentworth Thompson, *On Growth and Form*, Cambridge: Cambridge University Press, 1917, p. 753.)

their own rates. Thompson's view of growth as a complex of variable rates and tempos suggests a mathematical counterpart to the modernist trope of multiple temporalities. Similarly, Gavin de Beer stresses the observed complexities of embryology in terms that a scholar of modernism must find irresistible: 'ontogeny', he writes, 'is a four-dimensional phenomenon in space and time, and . . . comparison between "stages", which are nothing but arbitrarily cut cross-sections through the time-axis, cannot always be expected to yield results of any significance at all' (1938: 61). Witness how closely de Beer limns to Édouard's complaint in Gide's *Les Faux-monnayeurs*: 'A slice of life – so said the Naturalist school. The major fault of this school was always cutting in the same direction, lengthwise. Why not in width, or in depth? Me, I'd prefer not to cut at all' (1975: 184).

Thompson had little interest in evolution; his view of development was largely ahistorical. It was easy, however, to incorporate his 'ratio[s] between rates of growth in various directions' (D. Thompson 1917: 54) into an evolutionary framework. The discovery of regulatory genes suggested an evolutionary explanation for dramatic changes in morphology such as those described by Thompson. While some Mendelian genes determine traits, such as eye colour, there is more to development than the presence or absence of discrete characters. By the 1910s it was clear, as A. C. Hardy explains, that some 'Mendelian genes can affect the *rates* of different developmental processes: accelerating or retarding the appearance of some characters or parts of the body in relation to others' (1958: 127). The implications were far-reaching because, as Julian Huxley explains, 'a single genetic change affecting a growth-gradient will automatically express itself in a changed relation in the size of a large number of organs' (1932: 3). If 'the biochemical effects of one gene may accelerate or retard the action of a whole group of others' (Haldane 1932: 20), then minute genetic variations can trigger major changes in morphology, thus resolving a once intractable opposition between biologists who insisted that evolution necessarily proceeds by small increments (Darwinists) and those who posited more sudden and dramatic changes (mutationists, including early Mendelians). Reflecting on this synthesis as early as 1918, the geneticist Richard Goldschmidt would proclaim with evident satisfaction that 'Darwin is right, after all' (1918: 49). In post-Mendelian biology, the pathways linking heredity and development, characterised by Richard Dawkins as 'tortuous indirect routes' (2006: 19–20), can accommodate both the gradual and epigenetic processes of *Bildung* and the abrupt and discrete alterations of metamorphosis.

The discovery of regulatory genes explained and naturalised the observation that various parts of the body develop differentially, in a biological counterpart of the Marxian notion of 'uneven development' (Esty 2012: 36–7). Such a model of growth clearly subverts the norm of linear development, as Beckett's Molloy well knows. Like a good recapitulationist, Molloy does not mind change as long as it occurs evenly and proportionately: 'when the two legs shorten at the same time, and at the same speed, then all is not lost, no. But when one shortens, and the other not, then you begin to worry' (*MO* 84). The term given to this process of differential growth, heterochrony, was coined by Haeckel to describe temporal displacements in the order of ontogenetic stages, one of the many caenogenetic processes which could corrupt perfect recapitulation (palingenesis). Now heterochrony became a significant player in the demise of recapitulation as biology's master narrative. Indeed, modernist biology would begin to find heterochronic operations everywhere. Unlike recapitulation, however, heterochrony is not a specific model of development; it is not a narrative structure but, rather, a relational dynamic whose narrative manifestations are innumerable. This way of thinking, explains Ernst Mayr, reflects a shift in focus from the end-points of development to its underlying mechanics, 'consider[ing] the manifestations of so-called recapitulation not as products but as indications of processes' (1994: 227).

As a result, recapitulation was demoted from its privileged role and was reconceived as just one of many possible relations between ontogeny and phylogeny. As Julian Huxley notes in his book devoted to the topic, *Problems of Relative Growth*,

> since rate-genes can obviously mutate both in the plus and the minus direction, so as to accelerate or slow down the processes which they control, it is clear that changes in rate-genes could as easily lead to the opposite of recapitulation as to recapitulation. (J. Huxley 1932: 237)

Nowadays, as Dawkins writes, it is generally accepted that heterochronic changes 'underlie many, if not all, evolutionary changes in anatomical shape' (2004: 325).

Recapitulation theory could not accommodate an understanding of development in which heterochrony was so central. In a 1932 review summarising the evidence against Haeckel's law, Waldo Shumway lays out the implications of heterochrony in a passage worth quoting at length. According to recapitulation theory, he writes,

> an ideal ontogeny is composed of a series of stages (a, b, c, d,. . . . . .) corresponding to a phylogenetic series of adults (A, B, C, D,. . . . . .). To this we may add new terminal stages (i, i, iii, iv,. . . . . .) corresponding to new types of adults arising in evolution (I, II, III, IV,. . . . . .). Unless the period of ontogeny is lengthened the series must be reduced by a shortening of the period allotted to each of its stages and eventually to the omission of some, e.g., c, e and h. The series now takes the form: (a, b, d, f, g,. . . . . .z, i, ii, iii, iv). (Shumway 1932: 94; ellipses in original)

Having thus described the principles of terminal addition and condensation, Shumway introduces the counter-evidence:

> But new characters may also appear by interpolation and without corresponding adult types. These caenogenetic characters may be represented individually (I, X, 3, 4, etc.). Their appearance will result in further abbreviations and omissions and we arrive at such a series as: (a, i, d,. . . . . .z, i, 8, vi). (Shumway 1932: 94; ellipsis in original)

Already disordered beyond recognition, the phylogenetic order now undergoes 'heterochrony' and 'become[s] thoroughly scrambled in the order: (a, i, p, 4, z, d. . . . . .8, z, i, vi). It will now require the services of an embryological cryptographer to decipher the evolutionary meaning in terms of A, B, C, and I, II, III' (Shumway 1932: 94; ellipsis in original). Beginning with palingenesis, Shumway successively deforms it through 'interpolation', 'abbreviations and omissions', and 'heterochrony'. Though parallelism remains a possible relation between ontogeny and phylogeny, the many ways in which parallelism can be broken suggest that other configurations are much more likely. This conclusion was already evident to Percy Davidson, who notes wryly in 1914 that ontogeny will 'present a "recapitulation" or chronological record of phylogeny, *except where suppression, consolidation, unequal acceleration, and retardation had incidentally prevented*' it from 'uniformly' repeating the order of historical changes (1914: 61). Expressed in this way, recapitulation is exceptional, not universal.

Heterochrony offered a welcome escape from 'the mental strait-jacket of recapitulation' (de Beer 1940: 97). Flexible and multivariate, it is congenial with the exuberance and diversity of life histories and morphologies observable in nature. Suggesting that 'heterochrony is the cause of most developmental alterations' and that 'heterochrony can cause major alterations', McKinney and McNamara marvel at 'the ease of creativity: the abundance of ways in which this process can be successfully perturbed to produce different, but viable, individuals' (1991: 47). If heterochrony seems to destroy recapitulation theory's promises of progress and human exceptionalism, it made some promises of its own.

While heterochrony can refer to relativity in developmental timing between any two (or more) parts of the body, its most dramatic consequences tended to involved differentials between sexual and somatic growth. Studying sex determination in gypsy moths (*Lymantria dispar*) in the late 1910s, Richard Goldschmidt found that when different varieties hybridise, their offspring begin life as one sex but eventually switch. A gypsy moth has both male and female genes, but the traits these genes control develop at different rates and degrees, resulting in either a male, a female, or a 'sex intergrade' (Goldschmidt 1917: 433). Within a single variety, the rates of gene expression are well coordinated, so the moth is only ever a male or a female. In hybrids, however, the rates are decoupled, off-phase as it were, and the actions of the initially faster and dominant female gene, say, are later overtaken by those of the male gene, resulting in 'developmental intersexuality' (J. Huxley 1922d: 197). This incredible phenomenon also affects the uneven development of various body parts, so that at a given stage 'one organ is already say completely male, another still female, a third female at the base, male at the end' (Goldschmidt 1917: 440). The notion of 'intersex' individuals as 'sex-mosaics . . . in time' (J. Huxley 1922d: 198) recalls Virginia Woolf's depiction of development in *Orlando*, a novel whose challenges to the recapitulatory *Bildung* plot are examined in Chapter 4. For now, suffice it to note that sex change from male to female is a reversion, since recapitulationists universally ranked maleness over femaleness in their developmental hierarchies.

Heterochrony explains another oddity of sexual development. When sexual organs develop relatively faster than the rest of the body, the organism becomes sexually mature in a juvenile or even embryonic body. This condition, known as *neoteny*, is exemplified by domestic dog breeds such as spaniels, which have pup-like features all their lives, and, as we shall see, humans and axololts. 'Such "Peter Pan" animals discard their old-fully grown forms and become adult in a condition similar to that of early stages of development in their relatives and ancestors' (de Beer 1962: 62). Neoteny was, de Beer notes, one of the primary 'flies in the Haeckelian ointment of recapitulation' (*EE* 102). Indeed, as the result of developmental processes, neoteny is 'the exact reverse of recapitulation' (de Beer 1962: 61). Neoteny is not, therefore, 'a corollary of recapitulation', as Joel Black incorrectly claims (2000: 124). Recapitulation involves adding new traits at the adult end of ontogeny (terminal addition) and accelerating development through earlier stages (condensation); neoteny involves retarding development so that it never reaches the adult end.

Recapitulation theory viewed neoteny as a form of degeneration or incomplete development. For recapitulation's critics, neoteny was an engine of evolutionary creativity, an 'escap[e] from the blind alleys of specialization' (J. Huxley, qtd in Montagu 1989: 254). De Beer, one of neoteny's great champions, argues that it is 'generally recognised that the most successful lines of evolution have been those in which exactly the opposite happened; those in which the recent descendant resembles his ancestor not when adult but when young, by failing to grow right up' (1962: v–vi). 'Instead of being rejected as caenogenetic exceptions', then, 'embryonic and larval variations or persistencies may become the leading features of subsequent evolution' (de Beer 1938: 58–9). In the evolutionary struggle to remain adaptable, an animal which recapitulates its phylogenetic history is 'irreversibly committed to specialisation and differentiation, . . . and can no longer alter [its] prospective fate' (*EE* 83). Consequently, 'the real winner is the animal which only goes a short way up the trunk of its family tree, and branches off as early as possible along a brand new line of its own' (de Beer 1962: 66). Neoteny could reverse 'racial senescence' through what de Beer called 'clandestine evolution' (*EE* 30) and later 'Peter Pan evolution' (1962: vi). This fascinating phenomenon is discussed in Chapter 5. First, however, we turn to a more generalised form of modernist reversion in Joyce's *Portrait of the Artist as a Young Man*.

Notes

1. For more comprehensive treatment of topics covered in this chapter, see the fine historical studies of Frederick Beiser (2011), Peter Bowler (1984, 1988), W. H. Bruford (1975), Denise Gigante (2009), Jennifer Mensch (2013), Michael Ruse (2009), Helmut Müller-Sievers (1997) and Robert J. Richards (1992, 2002, 2008), as well as the more technical works of Jane Oppenheimer (1967), Stephen J. Gould (1977), Ernst Mayr (1982) and E. S. Russell (1982).
2. On biology and the *Bildungsroman*, see Hartung (2016: 51–69) and Lehleiter (2015: 13–14, 282–4).
3. Beckett neatly illustrates how one object's movement is forward or backward relative to the movements of other objects:

   > The moon was moving from left to right, or the room was moving from right to left, or both together perhaps, or both were moving from left to right, but the room not so fast as the moon, or from right to left, but the moon not so fast as the room. (*MO* 40)

4. Goethe's notion of 'regular metamorphosis' leading to 'propagation by two genders', and his inability not to pathologise 'irregular metamorphosis' (1988: 76), prefigure Freud's notion of perversion as a *necessary* deferral of reproductive heterosexuality as the goal of psychosexual development (Roof 1996: xx).
5. Kadvany's mention of the 'biogenetic law' in relation to Goethe, Hegel and others is anachronistic; the term was coined by Haeckel in the 1860s.

2

A PORTRAIT OF THE ARTIST AS A 'BIOLOGIST IN WORDS': LANGUAGE, EPIPHANY AND ATAVISTIC *BILDUNG*

> A developing organism is . . . a system struggling with the help of its ancestral tendencies to survive and to convert itself into successive viable shapes.
>
> – Gavin de Beer, 'Embryology and Evolution' (1938: 63)

'In the history of words there is much that indicates the history of men', writes James Joyce as a student at University College. This history, he continues, is forged by a vanguard of literary masterpieces, 'landmarks in the transition of a language, keeping it inviolate, directing its course straight on like an advancing way, widening and improving as it advances but staying always on the high road' (1959: 28–9). Joyce's enthusiastic rhetoric of national destiny, perfectibility and imperialism may seem surprising in light of his later writings, which would so playfully yet forcefully attack notions of historical progressivism. But these are the words of a youth seventeen or eighteen years old, written for the approval of a schoolmaster. Anyhow, Joyce would soon disavow them, submitting the parallels between development, evolution, history and philology to increasingly byzantine travesties and parodies.

'Oxen of the Sun' offers a stark case, with its overdetermined parallelism of fertilisation, embryological development, parturition, biological and linguistic evolutions, and progressive inebriation. Its seemingly linear structure conceals numerous reversions, which produce a humorous yet urgent critique of recapitulation theory. Though Joyce models 'Oxen' on 'the natural stages of development in the embryo and the periods of faunal evolution in general' (*U* 907), the relations between individual and evolution as he depicts them are hardly parallel. If the debates constituting the episode are 'the epitome of the course of a life' (*U* 397), it is a topsy-turvy life indeed, for as Mary King argues, 'Oxen' is 'a multilayered contrapuntal score, a fugal canon with aleatory characteristics, in which a disrupted pseudolinear mimesis of the movement of English prose and its validating texts is a simulacrum for the development of a male fetus' (*U* 350). If recapitulation theory requires the embryo's successive passage through increasingly perfect forms, Joyce offers 'abortions', 'monstrous births', 'swine-headed . . . or doghaired infants', and 'cases of arrest of embryonic development at some stage antecedent to the human' (*U* 372, 391). Revelling in such failures of recapitulation, 'Oxen' exemplifies the reversionary dynamics I examine throughout this book.

Superimposing the history of English prose and the growth of 'Stephen the embryo' (as Joyce put it to Frank Budgen; *U* 906), 'Oxen of the Sun' is a condensed rewriting of Joyce's earlier *Bildungsroman*. Like 'Oxen', if less outrageously, *A Portrait of the Artist* uses gestation as an ordering principle and likewise uses a stylistic progression to formalise its thematic focus on development. Overlap between *A Portrait* and 'Oxen' has already been noted, most notably by Anthony Burgess. In 'Oxen,' he writes, 'a history of English Literature – which is a good enough record of the spiritual history of a nation – is used to symbolise embryonic growth; in *A Portrait*, embryonic growth is used to symbolise the spiritual history of a young poet' (Burgess 1988: 44). Both texts use stylistic shifts to mimic the process of development; both use reversions to disrupt the linear succession of styles. In 'Oxen', the reversions include historical anachronisms, such as the recurring 'double-thudding Anglo-Saxon', and the final 'tailpiece', which muddies the ostensible progressivism of English history with nonstandard forms such as 'Pidgin English, nigger English, Cockney, Irish, Bowery slang and broken doggerel' (*U* 906). *Portrait*'s corresponding reversions include epiphanic returns to the past of childhood or history; the repetitions of motif and verbal echo; and the final shift from narration to diary.[1]

These parallels suggest that *A Portrait* engages covertly with the embryological and evolutionary biology more visibly exploited in 'Oxen'. Several critics who have likened Stephen's growth to larger historical patterns have indeed noted *A Portrait*'s recapitulatory structure. 'The principle, ontogeny repeats phylogeny, provides', according to William Fitzpatrick, 'insight into Stephen's growth as an artist. It seems that the artist must . . . run through the racial history of his language so that he may create a new mode and language of art' (1974: 131). More broadly, William Hutchings finds that 'the structure of all of Joyce's fiction' reflects the view 'that the experience of an individual . . . reiterates and epitomizes the history of his race' (1978: 339). Christine Froula argues that 'Joyce simulates an ontogenesis that bodies forth his theory of cultural phylogenesis' (1996: 3). Theodore Spencer describes the novel as a progression through five 'themes', evoking the sublative mechanism of recapitulation: 'Stephen's development as an individual may be described as a process which sloughs off the first four [themes] in order that the fifth may stand clear' (1969: 19). In these and other cases, however, recapitulation serves as a metaphorical rather than literal connection between the novel and biological theories of development. It is in an anagogical rather than evolutionary sense that Hugh Kenner links Stephen's youth to 'the childhood of the race' (1948: 365). As Mark Gaipa complains, 'critics may agree on the presence of recapitulation in Joyce's texts, but few are willing to see it as more than a metaphor or framing device' (1995: 197).[2] Most scholars are indeed simply too uninterested in biology to try exploring what insights the science might have to offer. Thus Clive Hart can write of *Finnegans Wake* that 'the process of writing the book was analogous to the recapitulation of ontogenesis in phylogenesis' (1993: 437n7), when he surely means the recapitulation of *phylogenesis in ontogenesis*! The critical readiness to overlook biology's potential interpretive contributions has obscured some of Joyce's crucial manoeuvres in his modernist reformulation of *Bildung*.

Though most recent critics read *A Portrait* as a critique or reformulation of the genre, it is sometimes read as a straightforward *Bildungsroman*. In structure and theme, indeed, the novel rather closely follows the generic outline of the classical *Bildung* plot. Stressing this conservatism in an essay reading *A Portrait* against *Jacob's Room*, Karen Lawrence finds that Joyce's novel ultimately accepts the genre's 'central notions of identity and vocation' by endorsing 'the basic idea of growth and development' (1986: 32). Joyce's *Bildungsroman* is certainly more traditional than Woolf's, but *Jacob's Room* is a very inventive text indeed; the contrast inevitably leaves *Portrait*'s relatively modest innovations underexposed. Lawrence also overstresses the linearity of Stephen's 'journey towards identity', which is, she argues, paved by sequential 'moments of revelation' (1986: 32). In my view, these epiphanies puncture rather than propel the linear *Bildung* plot, allowing the past (personal, historical, evolutionary) to check the momentum of Stephen's progressive development. The implications of these checks are neither simply psychoanalytical nor merely antiquarian: they put Joyce's formal strategies into inextricable relation to his thematic treatment of literary history, colonialism and racial origins.

There are, in this sense, more affinities between *A Portrait* and the later novels than critics of earlier generations might have believed. As most commentators now agree, *Portrait* is not an apprentice novel whose traditionalism and legitimation techniques would be parodied or deconstructed in *Ulysses* and *Finnegans Wake*. Instead, as Margot Norris so persuasively argues, *Ulysses* and *Finnegans Wake* exaggerate ironies and critical energies already present in the first novel, 'revisiting and re-exploring some of the more glaring gaps and dissonances in *A Portrait*' (Norris 1992: 183). In this light, the travesties of recapitulation so evident in 'Oxen' amplify and clarify, rather than revise or upturn, *Portrait*'s developmental vision and formal strategies. The same is true of 'The Mime of Mick, Nick and the Maggies' in *Finnegans Wake*, an explicit parody of the notion of childhood as a recapitulation of ancestral animality. With 'promptings from Elanio Vitale' (Bergson's *élan vital*), the children's game is announced as 'the Pageant of Past History worked up with animal variations' (*FW* 221), but despite three attempts the allegorised courtship fails to secure the sexual pairing which would symbolise the end of youth and the beginning of social and reproductive maturity. To read 'Oxen' and the 'Mime' as rewritings of Stephen's childhood is to recognise how profoundly *Portrait* already torqued the classical *Bildung* plot. Despite its apparent linearity, the narrative is riddled with reversions, many of them triggered by Stephen's epiphanies. The seemingly chronological plot is crossed-stitched with what Kevin Ohi calls 'queer atavism – by unrealizable worlds, reticulated and nonsubordinated developments, and non-communicating cells' (2015: 91) – though I might generalise it here as modernist atavism. If Joyce's novel endorses the ideal of *Bildung*, the form it generates in order to narrate Stephen's development nevertheless abjures the chronology, gradualism and recapitulatory structure of the classical *Bildung* plot.

In progressivist models of history, the past serves as anchor and spur for the individual's forward development, but this past must be past. The retention or return of past forms is thus a pathological reversal, an atavism. And such reversals are exactly what happen, time and again, to Stephen's development. Throughout *A Portrait*, Stephen experiences what he interprets as setbacks in the fulfilment of the artistic 'end he had been born to serve' (*PA* 165). These checks less often come from the external world than most theories of the *Bildungsroman* would predict; though not unaffected by familial and social realities, Stephen rolls rather well with the world's punches. What really frustrates his aspirations are internal events, almost all of them involving a private encounter with sexuality and reproduction, at the locus of convergence between the artistic mind and 'the bestial part of the body able to understand bestially and desire bestially' (*PA* 139–40).

This convergence occurs in and through language. For Stephen, verbal mastery in speech and in art amounts to a transcendence of 'the sensible world', to an ascension to a pure and spiritual 'inner world of individual emotions' (*PA* 167). In classical theories of *Bildung*, language plays a central role in channelling development from the body upwards to the successively higher levels of mind and spirit; the child's growing linguistic competence therefore evidences a growing capacity for disembodied abstract thought and aesthetic and spiritual experience. Max Müller famously argued that 'language is the Rubicon which divides man from beast' as part of his anti-evolutionary belief that 'the science of language will yet enable us to withstand the extreme theories of the Darwinians, and to draw a hard and fast line between man and brute' (qtd in Fitch 2010: 395). As Tecumseh Fitch puts it, 'Müller effectively substituted "language" for the soul that played the key distinguishing role in earlier religion and philosophy' (2010: 395). Other post-Darwinian linguists incorporated language acquisition into the great system of recapitulation, starting with Hippolyte Taine's seminal observations on young children learning the rudiments of speech. The psychologist William Stern similarly insisted that 'child language is to fully developed language as the language of primitive people is to that of civilized peoples' (Stern, qtd in Jakobson 1968: 65). Because language acquisition was one of many parallel ontogenetic processes according to leading nineteenth-century philologists and psychologists, the progressive complexification and abstraction of the growing child's language seemed to confirm the validity of recapitulation in other domains as well. For Haeckel, language acquisition was in fact more than just another proof of his biogenetic law: the apparent fact that language acquisition recapitulates glossogeny (language evolution) supplied a keystone for his monistic philosophy, bridging animal morphology with human culture.

There is thus a specific logic behind Stephen Dedalus's ambition to use a *verbal* art to 'forg[e] . . . out of the sluggish matter of the earth a new soaring impalpable imperishable being' (*PA* 169). Language, as he sees it, will propel him to maturity and purity, away from childhood, animality, the body and sexuality. As we saw in the Introduction, however, Joyce had his doubts about recapitulation and wished 'to attack with drawn sword' (1977: 19). His *Bildungsroman* consequently ensures that language never sheds the materiality which Stephen so fervently denies. Try as he might to isolate language from the body, words persist in mediating between the realm of art and the sexual, reproductive body.[3] Given the Manichean linkage of body with gross animality and language with mind and spirit, the intercalation of bodily and linguistic stages of Stephen's development effectively confuses the parallel lines of progressive change demanded by recapitulation.

Throughout *A Portrait* and his oeuvre, Joyce exults in transgressing boundaries between the primitive and the civilised, merging human and animal, sacred and secular, high and low, Symbolist and Naturalist, beautiful and ugly. Joyce deploys language against Stephen's idealistic notions of development, staging his experience with words not as stepping-stones to the future but as reversions 'back into the perambulator' (*PA* 237) – and back into ancestry. The medium of Stephen's chosen art puts paid to the comforting belief that 'the past was past', as he tells himself after his climactic confession (*PA* 146). The past survives actively in the present, either in literal remainders or in displaced form. While the text of *A Portrait*, tightly focalised through Stephen, is good at concealing the marks of the body and its foetal, historical and animal residues, these are ironically preserved in their linguistic analogue.

Rather than moving inexorably and irreversibly from body to mind to spirit, Joyce's *Bildung* plot is grounded in a language encrusted with reversions. Ironically, the modern form of expression sought by Stephen is atavistic.[4] Within the framework of recapitulation theory, atavism is the result of an incomplete ontogeny, one which has failed to work through its full phylogenetic itinerary. Atavism is thus inimical to the classical *Bildungsroman* as a chronicle of modern subject formation. Cannon Schmitt observes that while recapitulation theory enables faculties of racial memory which can 'give coherence to a human . . . subject' embedded in a larger national, racial, or familial community, 'they only do so . . . in and through faculties of recall that are, at best, equivocal' and liable to fragmentation (2009: 27). Among other challenges, the notion of evolutionary memory problematises the emergence of a modern subject. Though not discussing the *Bildungsroman* specifically, Dana Seitler clearly identifies the threats atavism poses to the modes of identity formation which structure the genre. As a 'mixed temporal entity', the atavistic body 'produces modern subjectivity as less certain, less determinedly structured by the idea of continual progress'; as a remainder of the 'unenlightened, uncivilized, stateless time of human prehistory' (Seitler 2008: 66), atavism confounds the individual's movement towards 'enlightenment', defined by Kant, in the language of *Bildung*, as 'man's emergence from his self-immaturity' (Kant 2003: 54). Though Stephen Dedalus writes in his diary that 'the past is consumed in the present' and thus 'brings forth the future' (*PA* 251), Joyce's novel models a radically different relationship between past and present.

A Portrait resists the recapitulatory structure of the classical *Bildungsroman*, as well as Stephen's desire to transcend the bodily, by forcing the archaic and animal to coexist, albeit tensely, with the modern and artistic. Rather than rejecting the ideal of *Bildung*, however, the novel's unsettling marriage of sexuality, language and artistic self-cultivation represents one of modernism's most pointed reminders that the body participates in and throughout the process of self-formation. Its participation manifests as a reversion in *A Portrait* nonetheless because it must contend throughout the narrative, but especially in the later chapters, with a philosophical tradition and generic expectations which view the body as a primitive precursor to the emergence of civilised, spiritual maturity. From this perspective, the body's active part in Stephen's development continues long after it should have been abandoned in favour of more grown-up concerns.

These reversions manifest primarily in two closely related forms. The first is in Stephen's response to language, which far from striking him as pure, abstract or spiritual, affects him erotically and carnally. The second is the epiphany, an aesthetic response whose effect on the narrative is to put the plot on hold. Various critics have variously named the resulting pauses. Tobias Boes, like me, calls them epiphanies (Boes 2012: 132), but they have also been called markers of cyclical time (Levenson 1985: 1020), Freudian regressions (Brivic 2006: 284–5), anti-realist eruptions of 'a lyrical, repetitive, Paterian mode' (Attridge 2000: 74) and 'Rimbaudian' interruptions of 'a Flaubertian field' (Moretti 2000: 244). Whatever they are called, these epiphanies are consistently triggered by language (thus the two forms of reversion mentioned above are in fact one). This fact seems to have escaped critical attention. Nor have critics noted that Stephen's epiphanies involve various forms of temporal regression, awakening his cultural and animal memories from 'the slumber of centuries' (*PA* 100). For despite what Stephen implies in his aesthetic theory, epiphanies may arrest movement but they are not timeless. As the narrator describes them, epiphanies drag Stephen's thoughts or emotions back in time, either into personal flashbacks or into visions of the historical or pre-historical past. Thus Stephen sees through the 'strange eyes' of his younger self and of his forebears, both human and 'infrahuman' (*PA* 19, 167). A fascinating corollary emerges from this interpretation: Stephen's epiphanies have a material origin (in the senses and the body) but an apparently transcendental effect – a seamless merger of Symbolist and Naturalist ideas producing a distinctly modernist aesthetic.

My interpretation of words as a reversionary force suggests a partial solution to the problem of ironic distance which has long troubled readers of *A Portrait*. It is only from Stephen's perspective that the flesh represents entrapment and the frustration of *Bildung*; Joyce's text, by contrast, celebrates the sexual body which connects 'the history of words' to 'the history of men' (1959: 28). While Stephen envisions his artistic development as a forward and upward line from flesh to spirit, the narrative stages his encounters with words as a series of atavistic returns to the animal body. As the Newmanian narrator in 'Oxen of the Sun' suggests, maturation is not simply progressive and linear because 'there are sins' in the individual's past which assert their presence in his development. There are, the narrator continues,

> evil memories which are hidden away by man in the darkest places of the heart but they abide there and wait. He may suffer their memory to grow dim, let them be as though they had not been and all but persuade himself that they were not or at least were otherwise. Yet a chance word will call them forth suddenly and they will rise up to confront him in the most various circumstances, a vision or a dream. (*U* 400)

Throughout *Ulysses* 'a chance word' can trigger the return of Stephen's repressed, especially through visions of his dead mother. The passage above also explains exactly how words subvert Stephen's desired developmental trajectory in

A Portrait. Figured as a large embodied archive, language refuses to be mastered in the service of Stephen's artistic destiny or reduced to a 'progress' from 'lyric' through 'epic' to 'dramatic' modes (*PA* 214–15). Language pulls his growth as an artist off the rails of any predetermined historical template.

Language Acquisition and *A Portrait*'s Ontogenetic Structure

A Portrait's structure mirrors Stephen's developing consciousness,[5] and because his sense of reality is primarily linguistic, the clearest marker of his development is language. Stephen's consciousness emerges from the stream of language with which he interacts, privately in his mind, in dialogue with others and in literature. As in most *Bildungsromane*, Stephen's ontogeny unfolds over the course of the story's duration spanning infancy to young adulthood. But Joyce, who offers few objective markers of passing time, allows this progression to be expressed – and, by readers, experienced – mainly through stylistic changes in the discourse. As Campbell and Robinson put it, 'the style matures with the growth of the hero' (1968: 357).

Because the narrator's syntax and style grow ever more complex, Stephen may seem to be maturing progressively, irreversibly, as expected given the narrative grammar of *Bildung* and, as we have seen, of recapitulation. Yet the maturing style also provides the best record of the ongoing embodied nature of Stephen's development. Language implicates the body from the very beginning of the novel and, despite Stephen's pretensions, does so to the end. In the opening vignette, the toddler Stephen tries to sing '*O, the wild rose blossoms*' only to produce '*O, the green wothe botheth*' (*PA* 7); his lack of verbal control marks the written text as a production of still clumsy oral organs. This emphasis on embodied language is all the more striking in comparison with the beginning of *Great Expectations*: 'My father's family name being Pirrip, and my Christian name Philip, my infant tongue could make of both names nothing longer or more explicit than Pip' (Dickens 1996: 3). Pip and Stephen are both introduced as infants struggling to speak, but Pip's struggle is recounted in adult retrospective and adult language. It is *told*, in what Joyce calls in 'A Portrait of the Artist' (1904) the 'iron, memorial aspect'. Seeking direct access to 'the features of infancy', by contrast, Joyce *shows* the fumbling productions of Stephen's infant tongue, presenting the passage of time not teleologically but as 'a fluid succession of presents' (*PA* 257).

Painting a series of experiential portraits, Joyce couples development and thus narrative structure with Stephen's sensory and perceptual world (that muddy zone between mind and body) and with his anatomy (his immature vocal apparatus). The opening passage's sensuousness reflects a mind almost wholly constituted by perception. Stephen soon masters speech enough to hide its patent link with his mouth and throat, but whenever he tries to express himself, to forge an identity and destiny for himself, the language he has inherited dampens his forward momentum with a contrary impulse, as if to 'revert at once to its physiological and its cultural roots' (Attridge 2000: 66). His fascination with language remains ineluctably embodied, either directly through its vocal production or indirectly through its impact on the emotions and physical desire. Stephen cannot help but connect language with excremental and sexual functions, through which it consistently marks the presence of the flesh. Joyce was a 'biologist in words' long before Beckett coined the epithet in 1929 (Beckett 1961: 19).

Decisive moments in Stephen's development are consistently marked by the turbulent convergence of language and biology. Just before accepting his artistic destiny, Stephen sees some schoolfellows bathing in the sea. He is pained to see 'the signs of adolescence' revealed by 'their pitiable nakedness' because they mirror his own physical transformation, reminding him 'in what dread he stood of the mystery of his own body' (*PA* 168). Such reminders are inconvenient for a budding artist who cannot fathom art in the bodily realm. To neutralise the physical affinity with his peers, then, Stephen appeals to his linguistic superiority. Yoking the bathers' bodies to their 'banter', he uses his own 'formal[ity] in speech' (*PA* 180) as a fulcrum for distinguishing himself. His speech is so different that the bodily likeness can only be deceptive! Having established this difference, he can smugly reflect on 'how characterless they looked' (*PA* 168) compared with his own self-conscious individuality. Thus de-individuated, viewed 'collectively', the boys and their 'banter' confirm 'his mild proud sovereignty' (*PA* 168). Stephen can then reconceive his physical puberty as a spiritual metamorphosis from puerile body to mature spirit: 'His soul had arisen from the grave of boyhood, spurning her graveclothes' (*PA* 170). As Joyce presents it, however, this developmental vision is unmistakably one of Stephen's protective delusions.

Immediately after the swimming boys, he sees a girl and imaginatively transforms her 'into the likeness of a strange and beautiful seabird' (*PA* 171). She resists his spiritual vision, however, with an overdetermined reminder of her bodily reality: 'her long slender bare legs were delicate as a crane's and pure save where an emerald trail of seaweed had fashioned itself as a sign upon the flesh' (*PA* 171). Stephen tries to refine the girl's 'boldly' exposed thighs out of existence, anticipating his thoughts 'on the correspondence of birds to things of the intellect' and, in the figure of ibis-headed 'Thoth, the god of writers' (*PA* 171, 224, 225), on the rarefied realm of literature. But the seaweed mars the illusion of sexual purity and pure language, demonstrating that language may conceal the body like clothing but, like clothing, cannot erase it and may even emphasise its sexual allure.

Throughout the novel, the carnality of language fuses the novel's form and content. The changing prose styles literally incorporate its developmental plot. The novel's structural mechanics are therefore visible in the behaviour of individual words and motifs – some words and motifs more than others. Though Stephen finds all words 'mysteriously alive' (Budgen 1960: 57), the liveliest are those relating to sex and reproduction. In this context, the encounter with 'foetus' is catalytic; more than any other moment in the novel, it reveals the interpenetration of developmental and reproductive dynamics, a permeability which unsettles his aspiration to follow the classical route to *Bildung*. From the moment of the encounter onwards, Stephen will consistently translate language into sexual thoughts and reactions. This translation is unbidden and disturbing, laying bare the sensuality and materiality of the medium he strives to spiritualise. Stephen's reaction to 'foetus' is visceral, betraying the body's oneness with the mind: thus the word 'startled his blood', and Stephen is 'shocked'

> to find in the outer world a trace of what he had deemed till then a brutish and individual malady of his own mind. His monstrous reveries came thronging into his memory. They too had sprung up before him, suddenly and furiously, out of mere words. (*PA* 89–90)

'*Foetus*' is the objective correlative of his adolescent fantasies: it expresses what his animal body sensed only dumbly, and it answers his 'wondering' about where – 'from what den of monstrous images' (*PA* 90) – his lust originates.[6] Though he will later admit that true art can excite sexual emotions, acknowledging that 'I also am an animal', he nevertheless persists in quarantining his animal nature in favour of 'a mental world' (*PA* 206) where language is purified and disembodied. Being 'monstrous', however, the images elicited by 'foetus' refuse to cooperate with Stephen's dualism. Linked three times to 'foetus' (*PA* 90, 92) and once to his atavistic 'dreams, peopled by ape-like creatures' (*PA* 116), the word 'monstrous' suggests both animality and the 'mental world': a reader of Skeat's *Etymological Dictionary*,[7] Stephen would know that 'monster' has cognates in 'mental' and 'mind' (Skeat 1884: 363, 376). His sexual 'thoughts', 'reveries', and 'dreams' may be in the mind, but they bear the mark of the flesh and the beast. Stephen founds his mythic identity on the invention of human flight, but Daedalus was also responsible for the monstrous hybrid Minotaur.

'The letter! The litter!' puns Joyce (*FW* 93), linking writing with both waste and offspring. Likewise, if less wittily, *Portrait* ties dirty words to the sexual body and, in spite of Stephen, to art. Readings of a novel, *The Count of Monte Cristo*, frame his visits to Nighttown and his tendency to connect lust with utterance: 'a cry for an iniquitous abandonment, a cry which was but the echo of an obscene scrawl which he had read on the oozing wall of a urinal' (*PA* 100). He seeks an outlet for 'the wasting fires of lust' which figure as 'soft speeches', 'verses pass[ing] from his lips', 'inarticulate cries', 'unspoken brutal words' and a 'murmur' (*PA* 99). Though these vocal and verbal manifestations of lust might suggest Freudian displacement, they do not protect him from unconscious desires or from his 'humiliating sense of transgression' (*PA* 99). Rather than transcending the sexual body, his language is mired in it. This reversionary dynamic recalls Joseph Valente's reading of the Nighttown passage, which links Stephen's conflicted feelings about dirty water to the novel's resistance to the '*bildungsmythos* of a young man's self-conscious graduation from homosexual play to heterosexual maturity and (re)productivity' (1998: 60). In its place Joyce stages 'a progressive overlapping and interfolding of sexual preferences' which 'exerts a subtle yet potent pressure on the subsequent course of Stephen's development' (Valente 1998: 60). My focus on embodied language suggests that the complicating effects of same-sex desire on the *Bildung* plot, so persuasively diagnosed by Valente, are only one manifestation of the novel's reversionary dynamics; according to recapitulation theory, homosexuality is one of many forms of developmental arrest at a pre-mature, atavistic stage.

'Foetus' has obvious reproductive associations, and the spectre of reproduction, as Stephen seems to intuit from a very young age, complicates self-formation. The *Bildung* plot, Moretti argues, is dependent on 'dismantling the continuity between the generations' (2000: 4), so it is fundamentally threatened by the 'anastomosis of navelcords' linking mother to child and forcing the linear, cumulative process of *Bildung* into cycles of successive *Bildungs*. If the *Bildung* plot must begin anew in the child, the parents' own *Bildung* becomes belated, even obsolete – perhaps especially for the male parent. In *Ulysses*, Stephen appears to view reproduction in exactly these terms, musing that 'the son . . . is a male: his growth is his father's decline, his youth his father's envy, his friend his father's enemy' (*U* 199). Though relevant to Stephen's strained relationship with Simon Dedalus, it is the possibility of another father–son configuration which gives him existential vertigo: 'Am I a father?' (*U* 199). For the hero of a *Bildungsroman*, a son's 'growth' is the herald of personal 'decline'. Of less concern to Stephen, but clearly important to Joyce, is the strain of reproduction on female development. The disruptions of *Bildung* in 'Oxen of the Sun' are localised in the primary albeit offstage action: Mina Purefoy's three-day struggle to deliver her ninth child. As Bloom's sympathies suggest, Mrs Purefoy suffers more than labour pains; her whole life, her individual potentialities, have been diverted into the business of childbearing and rearing. Stephen views his mother and her 'nine or ten' children similarly (*PA* 241).

Stephen's encounter with '*Foetus*' is formative. It fuses word and lust, cementing the bonds between reproductive flesh and creative mind which inform the rest of the narrative. From now on, his mind will insistently excavate traces of the sexual body from words and literature. Wandering Nighttown 'like some baffled prowling beast', he seeks to release his bodily needs but also 'the unspoken brutal words rush[ing] forth from his brain' (*PA* 99). The prostitute's 'softly parting lips' touch him physically but also press upon 'his brain . . . as though they were the vehicle of some vague speech' (*PA* 101). In the guilty aftermath his lips feel tainted by the 'lewd kiss' but also by the 'foul and shameful words' (*PA* 105). During his cathartic confession, word and body merge as 'his sins trickled from his lips, one by one, trickled in shameful drops from his soul, festering and oozing like a sore' (*PA* 144). Like 'foetus', other words which intrigue or perplex Stephen have obvious sexual or reproductive significances. 'Kiss' is clearly erotic, whether it is his mother's controverted bedtime kiss, the kiss he withholds from Emma or the prostitute's 'lewd kiss' (*PA* 14, 70, 105). A kiss, for Stephen, is more than just a kiss; it always carries the danger of 'the contact of her sex' (*PA* 242) – a pun Joyce is unlikely to have scorned. There are also clear sexual connotations to 'suck', the novel's first 'queer word' (*PA* 11). Its etymology, moreover, adds a procreative suggestion: 'suck', notes Skeat, means 'imbibe, esp. milk', and derives from the Sanskrit root '*SU*, to generate' (1884: 608). Joyce surely knew, though Stephen seems not to know, that 'tundish' (*PA* 188–9) is a euphemism for penis in Shakespeare's *Measure for Measure*, where the context is Juliet's pregnancy.

Other words which arrest Stephen's attention are less evidently sexual. These are '*Lotts*', 'detain', 'ivory' and the fragments of literary prose and poetry he hears, reads or recalls. This language too, however, is sexualised – through etymology, intertextuality or circulation in the Joycean network of motifs. Indeed, of all the words which markedly strike Stephen, only '*home, Christ, ale, master*' (*PA* 189) lack any detectable sexual association. The words affecting Stephen are often sexualised not by denotation or even connotation but by textual memory. '*Lotts*', a surname painted on a stable wall, mysteriously cures Stephen of his 'baffled desire' for Emma with its redolence of 'horse piss and rotted straw' (*PA* 86). No need here to invoke Joyce's notorious sexualisation of excrement and waste: '*Lotts*' will recur in the risqué lyric '*Lott*ie Collins lost her drawers' (*PA* 197; emphasis added). 'Detain' seems chaste enough – Stephen quotes it from Newman's description of the Virgin Mary when he differentiates aesthetic and mercantile language. Mary, however, is never quite pure to Stephen. Even when 'used according to the literary tradition', words cannot be extricated from 'the tradition of the marketplace' (*PA* 188) – literally, a pornographic economy. It is after the prostitute puts 'her hand on his arm to detain him' that Stephen loses his virginity (*PA* 100). The act of manual detention echoes in Emma's touch when her 'hand had lain in his an instant, a soft merchandise' (*PA* 219); then in his rapturous reaction to 'Mulier cantat', whose 'soft beauty' touches him 'with a touch fainter and more persuading than the touch . . . of a woman's hand' (*PA* 244); and finally in his 'thrilled' homoerotic reaction to Cranly 'seiz[ing] his arm' (*PA* 247).

Yet Stephen persists in imagining the 'stages of his spiritual progress' (*PA* 148) as the progressive mastery of words and the transcendence of the flesh. In his religious phase, he finds solace in 'the simple fact that God had loved his soul from all eternity, for ages before he had been born into the world, for ages before the world itself had existed' (*PA* 149) – that is, when he was bodiless, all soul. After baring his body to the pleasures of Nighttown, the devotional Stephen pictures his 'spiritual progress' as a different kind of undressing. Rather than expose his flesh, he imagines casting it off

> as if his very body were being divested with ease of some outer skin or peel. He had felt a subtle, dark, and murmurous presence penetrate his being and fire him with a brief iniquitous lust: it, too, had slipped beyond his grasp leaving his mind lucid and indifferent. (*PA* 149)

Likening spiritual awakening to the metamorphosis of a butterfly, which emerges from the chrysalis having completely reabsorbed and reorganised its larval body, Stephen deludes himself that he is unconnected to his own childhood self. Later in the novel, when he notes his mother 'remembers the time of her childhood' (*PA* 250), he admits only doubtfully that she also remembers 'mine if I was ever a child' (*PA* 251). For all his desire to cordon off the past in the past, Stephen faces opposition from a text whose distinctive use of motif supplies not only the forward momentum generated from the accumulation of repetitions (Boes 2012: 132), but also a reciprocal backward impulse. After his confession, Stephen's 'lucid and indifferent' state may flatter his sense of having progressed beyond the temptations of the flesh, but a textual déjà vu suggests otherwise. When he was a habitual visitor of Nighttown, a strikingly similar 'cold lucid indifference reigned in his soul' (*PA* 149, 103). Together, the two instances of lucid indifference, the debauched and the devotion, generate a rather hybrid aesthetics in which the artist is simultaneously disembodied and embodied, 'within or behind or beyond or above his handiwork, invisible, refined out of existence, indifferent, paring his fingernails' (*PA* 215). In theory Stephen refines all sensuousness from aesthetics, but his *experience* of artistic creation as 'the word . . . made flesh' 'in the virgin womb of the imagination' (*PA* 217) is hilariously sexual. Writing his villanelle may have 'kindled again his soul', but its generation in the afterglow of a wet dream also 'fulfill[s] all his body' (*PA* 223).

Given his attempt to master and spiritualise language, Stephen is irritated when words spontaneously self-organise into a nonsense poem ('*the ivy whines upon the wall . . .*'), as if art were a bodily product rather than the result of mental distillation. Stephen therefore discounts the mindless poem as 'drivel', preferring to read it as bodily waste (saliva or mucus running from the mouth; *OED*) than as poetry. But the occasion of dismissing the poem makes another key word, '*ivory, ivoire, avorio, ebur*', 'sh[ine] in his brain' (*PA* 179). Nothing in *A Portrait* better demonstrates the reversionary power of language, whose sexuality emerges from Joyce's elaborate use of motifs; every echo sends the narrative curling back to earlier sources. 'Ivory' is thus bestialised and feminised in association with 'Tusker Boyle' alias 'Lady Boyle because he was always at his nails, paring them' (*PA* 42). The memory of Boyle saying 'an elephant had two tuskers instead of two tusks' leads Stephen's mind back to Eileen Vance's 'long thin cool white hands . . . like ivory' (*PA* 42). Covering his eyes with 'white and thin and cold and soft' hands, Eileen, Stephen's first potential wife (*PA* 8), helped him understand why Mary is called 'the Tower of Ivory' (*PA* 36). 'Ivory' has, beyond this personal association, no evident sexual signification, but its entry in Skeat encourages a fruitful game of cross-referencing. 'Ivory' leads to the Sanskrit '*ibha*, an elephant' (Skeat 1884: 304) and from there to the Hebrew '*aleph*, an ox' (Skeat 1884: 187). And the ox, a beast central to Stephen's personal mythology, is despite its castration associated with fertility. 'Co-radicate with humid', the word 'ox' derives from '*ukshan* . . . a Vedic epithet of the Maruts ["storms"] who, by bringing rain . . . impregnate the earth like bulls' (Skeat 1884: 412). Oxen and water meet in Stephen's iconography of both artistic production and sexual arousal and orgasm; together they supply the associative conduit from Eileen's 'cold white' hands to the 'corpse-white' bodies of the schoolboys in the 'cold seawater' who call Stephen 'Bous Stephanoumenos! Bous Stephaneforos!' (*PA* 168). Linking him to the sacrificial bull (*Bous*), these epithets trigger Stephen's first conscious identification with Daedalus, the 'hawk-like man' who also designed fertile artificial bulls. Stephen the bull is ready for an epiphany. When it comes, it is aptly triggered by the birdgirl with thighs as 'soft-hued as ivory' (*PA* 171). It is one of Joyce's abiding ironies that Stephen persists in his distrust and disgust of the flesh: the more the budding poet engages with words, the more insistently they lead back to the body.

Epiphany as Atavism

Stephen builds his future on words, but those words force him back into the past. When he hears 'kiss' and 'suck', he relives his mother's bedtime kiss and the hotel lavatory. 'Ivory', as we have seen, has a similar effect. Such flashbacks, being personal, require no appeal to evolutionary theory; they resemble Proust's or other kindred models of unconscious memory. Other words bring Stephen deeper in time, back before his birth, his historical era or even his species. In these cases memory is an insufficient explanation. 'Foetus' reveals a past Stephen never saw: in the empty anatomy theatre 'he seemed to feel the absent students about him . . . A vision of their life, which his father's words had been powerless to evoke, sprang up before him out of the word cut in the desk' (*PA* 89–90). In the pub afterwards, Stephen feels older than his father's peers (*PA* 95), as if his epiphany had tapped him into 'the conscience of [his] race' (*PA* 253). Soon after, Stephen's mind, still ruffled by 'foetus', appears to harken back even deeper into the past, to a prehistorical moment. Seeing 'a maid in a white cap and apron . . . watering a box of plants on a sill' (*PA* 91), Stephen notes that the 'sill . . . shone like a slab of limestone' (*PA* 91), evoking

Cork's Carboniferous limestone deposits, evidence of an ancient seabed whose fossilised inhabitants were subject to considerable geological research at the time (J. Douglas 1909). Fittingly, then, the sea (as well as watery words) has an especially intense effect on him, as if it prompted 'the powerful recurrence of the tides within him' (*PA* 98). 'Foetus' and the other words 'epiphanized' by Stephen (*SH* 218) may trigger 'an esthetic stasis' (*PA* 206), but they have histories. The simultaneously static and historical nature of Stephen's epiphanies finds structural expression in narrative pauses which contain vast tracts of time which exceed the span of his biography, merging the ages going back to the origins of language in bodily gesture (J. Cope 1962: 73). The developmental plot structuring the novel is troubled repeatedly by reversionary digressions, narrative eddies which recirculate and muddy distinctions between progress and repetition, sequence and network, desire and epiphany.

To investigate the reversionary power of language and its effects on Stephen's *Bildung*, let us turn to a long passage in the fifth chapter. Having just observed how his friend Cranly reacts to a 'gross name' ('ballocks'), then watched his love interest Emma pass by, Stephen recites to himself a line of sixteenth-century verse, misremembering Thomas Nashe's 'Brightness falls from the air' as 'Darkness falls from the air' (*PA* 234, 232). The misquotation initiates a narrative pause, and in the long description which follows Stephen experiences a vivid and multi-staged immersion into Elizabethan times. At first the words evoke a 'trembling joy, lambent as a faint light', but they inevitably grow monstrous with 'the darkness of desire': 'What was their languid grace but the softness of chambering?' he wonders (*PA* 233). Earlier in the same chapter, the thought of 'chambering' had 'stung his monkish pride' and spoiled the 'pleasure' he seeks in lyrics such as Ben Jonson's 'I was not wearier where I lay' (*PA* 176). A seemingly innocent distraction from the 'spectral words of Aristotle and Aquinas' (*PA* 176), the pleasure Stephen finds in 'the dainty songs of the Elizabethans' is a slippery slope, leading inexorably to the 'shadow under the windows of that age' (*PA* 176), to 'a phrase, tarnished by time, of chambering and false honour' (*PA* 176). From Nashe's lyric the immersion into Elizabethan times is more intensely sensorial:

> he tasted in the language of memory ambered wines, dying fallings of sweet airs, the proud pavan, and saw with the eyes of memory kind gentlewomen in Covent Garden wooing from their balconies with sucking mouths and the pox-fouled wenches of the taverns and young wives that, gaily yielding to their ravishers, clipped and clipped again. (*PA* 233)

Though 'dainty' (*PA* 176), the Elizabethan lyrics are infected by (and infectious with) the sordidness and sexual obsessions of their age. Language may be 'fossil poetry', as Emerson believed, but the philologist Richard Chenevix

Trench would reply that words also 'embody facts of history, or convictions of the moral common sense' and thus, 'so far as that moral sense may be perverted, they will bear witness and keep a record of that perversion' (1853: 13). Stephen's lovely 'ambered wines' are perverted by the 'pox-fouled wenches' whose sexuality and allure are fossilised along with the beauty in the lyrics he admires.

The passage takes a remarkable turn when Stephen's increasingly sexual vision of Elizabethan times combines with the lingering smell of Emma: 'Vaguely first and then more sharply he smelt her body. A conscious unrest seethed in his blood. Yes, it was her body he smelt, a wild and languid smell, the tepid limbs over which his music had flowed desirously' (*PA* 233). Nashe's song has ineluctably led Stephen's mind to sex. His sensitivity to Emma's odour, harkening back to his mother's 'nicer smell' (*PA* 7), is also a reversion to a deeper, pre-human past. Olfactory arousal was in Joyce's time frequently listed as an atavism, and as Havelock Ellis argues in *Sexual Selection in Man*, 'the grosser manifestations of sexual allurement by smell belong, so far as man is concerned, to a remote animal past which we have outgrown' (1905: 110). Nevertheless, Ellis adds, 'the latent possibilities of sexual allurement by olfaction . . . still remain ready to be called into play', especially in 'exceptional and abnormal persons' (1905: 110–11) who include, as he notes earlier, 'poets and novelists' (1905: 73).

Perversion begets perversion: the associations triggered by Nashe snowball and grow ever more bestial. As Emma's smell fades, leaving the image of 'the secret soft linen upon which her flesh distilled odour and a dew' (*PA* 233), a louse appears on Stephen's neck. As though generated by his arousal, or by the allusion to 'dew' (a Joycean euphemism for semen), the insect reminds Stephen that lice were once thought to be 'born of human sweat' (*PA* 233), products of the body which

> were not created by God with the other animals on the sixth day. But the tickling of the skin of his neck made his mind raw and red. The life of his body, ill clad, ill fed, louse-eaten, made him close his eyelids in a sudden spasm of despair and in the darkness he saw the brittle bright bodies of lice falling from the air and turning often as they fell . . . He had not even remembered rightly Nash's line. All the images it had awakened were false. His mind bred vermin. (*PA* 233–4)

So close on the heels of Emma's odorous passage, mere hours after the composition of the Symbolist villanelle, the louse and its association with Nashe's poem is the novel's ironic riposte to Stephen's opposition of sex and art. The louse further bestialises Stephen's initially idyllic vision of Elizabethans, lending a vampiric and entomological allure to the 'kind gentlewomen . . . with sucking mouths' (*PA* 233), and reminding us that Nashe's song, 'In Time of Pestilence', is a report from a time of plague (a disease transmitted by fleas, another insect with sucking mouthparts, one with a long history in erotic poetry). Steven Connor, in his wonderful essay on flies in Beckett, calls the louse an 'anomaly-animal' (2014: 60) along with other 'imperfect creatures' which confound philosophical systems, taxonomies and moral hierarchies because they 'do not belong to created nature' (2014: 48). Joyce's louse enables reality to counteract Stephen's bias towards the idealist aspect of *Bildung* with its dialogic counterpart in bodily existence – what Michael Minden calls 'the body's insistent refusal to coincide with the products of the mind, of social, historical or philosophical consciousness' (1997: 217). 'Lice', notes Jean-Michel Rabaté, 'embody the stubborn resistance of nature or the body to ideas' (2001: 86). It is indeed thanks to the louse on Stephen's neck that we catch a glimpse of his suffering, malnourished body. Like ageing in *The Picture of Dorian Gray*, tuberculosis in *The Magic Mountain*, or Paul Morel's triumphantly loveless sex with Clara in *Sons and Lovers*, the louse on Stephen's neck typifies the modernist celebration of the flesh and its purported pathologies.

Stephen's 'mind bred vermin': uncreated by God, born of the body, the louse travesties his ideal conception of language and art. It therefore worries him that the insects are self-begotten – it is a quality he reserves for artistic 'postcreation' (*U* 373). As an ironic rejoinder to Stephen's perspective, the louse joins Lynch in exposing the 'scholastic stink' of Stephen's aesthetic theorising, which includes such questions as '*Can excrement or a child or a louse be a work of art?*' (*PA* 214). Louse and Lynch both counter Stephen's Manicheism by accepting the body's excretions – dung, offspring or vermin alike – into the larger Joycean realm of art. Because Stephen sees art as refined or transmuted nature, as 'life purified in and reprojected from the human imagination' (*PA* 215), he has good reason to worry about language's bodily origin.

Also ironic is the fact that Stephen's most intense aesthetic experiences coincide with a state of sexual exhaustion. After his wet dream, Stephen completes his villanelle overcome with 'languorous weariness' and the certainty that 'soon he would sleep' (*PA* 222). 'The languor of sleep' he felt after his birdgirl epiphany (*PA* 172) is retrospectively revealed as similarly if less literally post-orgasmic. Nowhere is the reversionary power of the epiphany clearer than in the moments following his vision of the birdgirl. The drowsiness following the intensely personal 'profane' or 'quiet' joy (*PA* 171, 176) is an awakening onto a strangely expansive vista which is geological, evolutionary, even astronomical in scope: 'his eyelids trembled as if they felt the vast cyclic movement of the earth' (*PA* 172). Removed from his self, thrown into 'some new world, fantastic, dim, uncertain as under sea, traversed by cloudy shapes and beings' (*PA* 172), he seems to re-experience an earlier visit to 'another world' under 'the vapoury sky' of Nighttown.

Like the birdgirl encounter, Stephen's vision of Nighttown blends elements of Naturalism and Symbolism, and it similarly manifests as a return in time, an 'awaken[ing] from the slumber of centuries' (*PA* 100):

> From the foul laneways he heard bursts of hoarse riot and wrangling and the drawling of drunken singers. He walked onward, dismayed, wondering whether he had strayed into the quarter of the Jews. Women and girls dressed in long vivid gowns traversed the street from house to house. They were leisurely and perfumed. A trembling seized him and his eyes grew dim. The yellow gas-flames arose before his troubled vision against the vapoury sky, burning as if before an altar. Before the doors and in the lighted halls groups were gathered arrayed as for some rite. He was in another world. (*PA* 100)

Drifting from the sordid realities of modern Dublin into myth and history, the passage evokes Canaan, Ancient Greek rituals and the perfumed prostitutes of Stephen's Elizabethan reveries. His sexual initiation is less rite of passage than encounter with the archaic, 'some dark presence moving irresistibly upon him from the darkness . . . Its murmur besieged his ears like the murmur of some multitude in sleep; its subtle streams penetrated his being' (*PA* 100). The murmur seems to be a physiological but also a genealogical reaction – 'his blood . . . in revolt' (*PA* 100). These aestheticised and sexualised experiences of the past both stop and open up time, derailing the train of verbal and thematic associations which drive the developmental plot. Time collapses: 'Was it an instant of enchantment only or long hours and years and ages?' (*PA* 217). In Stephen's mind, the 'instant' contains 'ages', a vague quantity ranging from a period of human history, real or mythical, to a geological era. The notion of ages compressed into an instant would be compatible with recapitulation theory if Stephen's epiphanies did not so persistently take him *back* in time. As it is, the reversionary tendency mirrors his frustrated attempts to purify language. Achieving an epiphany for Stephen is indeed often just a matter of hearing or saying the right word, and the past floods in.

The archaeology of Stephen's aesthetic apprehension disproves Jeanne Delbaere-Garant's claim that 'words impress themselves on the Lockean white sheet of his young mind' (1977: 132). His mind is anything but a *tabula rasa*. What Joyce models is much closer to Ernest Fenollosa's belief that 'every word, a metaphor, perhaps several degrees deep, still has the power to flash meaning back and forth between apparently divergent and intractable planes of being' (qtd in Kenner 1971b: 105–6). Words call up old memories, images and emotions from the great cultural and animal repository of the body and mind. Fenollosa was obviously familiar with recapitulation theory, which offers any number of such 'planes of being'. Linking extant words to their history, he is convinced that 'we should find the whole theory of evolution . . . lying concrete in our etymologies' (qtd in Kenner 1971b: 106). Fenollosa's philological perspective suggests the mechanism by which words can so powerfully affect Stephen's growth, and by extension the reversionary structure of *A Portrait*. Language, as Trench argues, is an archive of cultural and biological memory:

> just as in some fossil, curious and beautiful shapes of vegetable or animal life, the graceful fern or the finely vertebrated lizard, such as now, it may be, have been extinct for thousands of years, are permanently bound up with the stone, and rescued from that perishing which would else have been theirs, – so in words are beautiful thoughts and images, the imagination and the feeling of past ages, of men long since in their graves, of men whose very names have perished, these, which might so easily have perished too, preserved and made safe for ever. (Trench 1853: 13)

Hardly new in Trench's time, this view of language gained traction only in the mid-nineteenth century, after 'converging lines of evidence . . . from geology, from archaeology, from biology forced on men's minds the idea of Prehistory' (Kenner 1971a: 46). Only then could philology produce projects like Skeat's dictionary, the *New English Dictionary* and Pound's theory of the ideogram. Philology and biology trace back similar histories from different data. As Kenner writes, 'we are joined – this is the theme of Comparative Philology – as much to one another as to the dead by continuities of speech as of flesh' (1971b: 96). Language in *A Portrait* thus has a bodily immanence overlooked in Seamus Deane's claim that, at the end of 'The Dead' and in all Joyce's subsequent fiction, 'what is buried in the past can only rearrive in the present in a spectral form' (2000: 35).

As we have seen, words, phrases and literature trigger *A Portrait*'s numerous reversionary epiphanies by calling Stephen's 'mental world' back to its unwelcome seat in the 'flesh' (*PA* 206). From infancy to exile, Stephen finds that 'words . . . str[ike] some deep chord in his own nature', and this chord entraps him ever more firmly in 'the sluggish matter of the earth' (*PA* 247, 169). This 'chord' evokes the umbilical 'cords [which] all link back' to the beginning of time, the 'strandentwining cable of all flesh', which will later remind Stephen of his embodied materiality (*U* 37). This linkage, so inconvenient to Stephen's way of seeing his self and destiny, suggests a further explanation for his extreme reaction to 'foetus' (*PA* 89). In Maud Ellmann's most recent analysis of Stephen's disproportionate response, he is unsettled by 'foetus' because the word forces upon him the direct connection between mother and embryo, a connection embodied during gestation by the umbilicus and later memorialised in the umbilical scar (2010: 169). Both navelcord and navel mark Stephen's maternal connection and, by extension, his direct if broken physical link to the deep past 'through the successive anastomosis of navelcords' (*U* 374).

Two moments in particular demonstrate how Joyce deploys deep-time reversions against Stephen's own overly idealistic conception of progressive *Bildung*. In both moments, Stephen's ontogeny and phylogeny visibly interact, but they do not run parallel in accordance with recapitulation theory. When his bathing friends call him 'Dedalos' and 'Bous', Stephen suddenly sees history before his eyes: 'all ages were as one to him' (*PA* 168). Linked to Daedalus,

> he seemed to hear the noise of dim waves and to see a winged form flying above the waves and slowly climbing the air. What did it mean? Was it a quaint device opening a page of some medieval book of prophecies and symbols, a hawk-like man flying sunward above the sea, a prophecy of the end he had been born to serve and had been following through the mists of childhood and boyhood . . .? (*PA* 169)

Stephen's journey from 'the mists of childhood and boyhood' towards 'the end he had been born to serve' – the vocational *telos* of the *Bildungsroman* – is also a return to the mythic past of Daedalus. Where recapitulation demands parallelism (embryo → adult : ancestor → descendent), Joyce supplies a chiasmus (childhood → maturity : ancient Crete ← modern Dublin). Chiasmus, as Elliott Gose has shown, is one of *A Portrait*'s ruling figures, characterising everything from phrases and sentences to chapters and, indeed, the novel as a whole (1985: 261). Through its mirroring structure, chiasmus exposes Stephen's delusion that 'the past [is] past' (*PA* 146); the past is the very substance to his prophetic visions.

Directly before his vision of Daedalus, Stephen crosses a group of Christian Brothers, recognises the wisdom of not taking orders and once again 'dr[aws] forth a phrase from his treasure': 'A day of dappled seaborne clouds' (*PA* 166). Savouring and analysing the affective and aesthetic power of the phrase, he makes another ancestral return. In yet another visceral reaction to water and smell, he recoils as 'a faint click at the heart, a faint throb in his throat told him once more of how his flesh dreaded the cold infrahuman odour of the sea' (*PA* 167). Then, turning his gaze against the current 'along the course of the slow-flowing Liffey' (*PA* 167), he sees medieval Dublin:

> like a scene on some vague arras, old as man's weariness, the image of the seventh city of christendom was visible to him across the timeless air, no older nor more weary nor less patient of subjection than in the days of the thingmote . . . He heard a confused music within him as of memories and names which he was almost conscious of but could not capture even for an instant . . . (*PA* 167)

Stephen reverts to Norse Dublin, experiencing the lives of its inhabitants. On the same beach in 'Proteus', the sight of midwives dumping 'a misbirth with trailing navelcord' (*U* 38) induces a similar communion with his ancestors: 'a horde of jerkined dwarfs, my people . . . Their blood is in me, their lusts my waves. I moved among them on the frozen Liffey, that I, a changeling, among the spluttering resin fires' (*U* 45). In the first-person pronoun, Stephen is both self-divided ('I, a changeling') and united with another, historically remote Dubliner ('I moved among them'), as though he were both himself and his lineage, his whole culture.

The phrase which precipitated this reversion, 'a day of dappled seaborne clouds' (*PA* 166), is another one of Stephen's misquotations. The correct phrase, 'a day of dappled breeze-borne clouds', is from Hugh Miller's *Testimony of the Rocks* (1857: 277), a pre-Darwinian attempt to reconcile the Biblical Creation story with geological evidence of deep time – an eminently apt trigger for Stephen's ancestral memories. It comes from one of Miller's phenomenally long sentences, and it is effectively a thought experiment designed to imagine prehistory. '[L]ooking back upon myriads of ages' and 'calling up in memory what once had been' (H. Miller 1857: 277), the reader sees the geological and faunal development of the earth through the eyes of the fallen Lucifer. This Lucifer is an evolutionary eschatologist, deciphering the future from the bodies of primitive organisms: 'like some old augur looking into the inner mysteries of animal life, with their strange prophecies', he sees, 'after the dynasty of the fish had been succeeded by the dynasty of the reptile, and that of the reptile by the dynasty of the sagacious mammal', that 'man was fast coming to the birth' (H. Miller 1857: 277). There is much here to please Stephen, not least Miller's 'lucid supple periodic prose' (*PA* 167) and its celebration of humanity as the end of an evolutionary creation. There is also Stephen's sense of identification with Lucifer, a connection strengthened by the fact that he, like Miller's Lucifer, also plays the role 'of an augur' by looking, as men have 'for ages', for 'symbols and portents' in animals (in Stephen's case, the animals are birds outside the national library) (*PA* 224).

Stephen's response to 'a dappled day of seaborne clouds' is a rewriting of an even clearer reversionary moment in *Stephen Hero*, when his artistic sensibility drives him

> to pierce to the significant heart of everything. He doubled backwards into the past of humanity and caught glimpses of emergent art as one might have a vision of the plesiosauros emerging from his ocean of slime. He seemed almost to hear the simple cries of fear and joy and wonder which are antecedent to all song, the savage rhythms of men pulling at the oar, to see rude scrawls and the portable gods of men whose legacy Leonardo and Michelangelo inherit. And over all

> this chaos of history and legend, of fact and superstition, he strove to draw out a line of order, to reduce the abysses of the past in order by a diagram. (*SH* 37–8)

Through Stephen's futile attempts to tame the 'chaos of history', Joyce ironically puts forward a more expansive vision of artistic progress, one in which reversions play a crucial role. Stephen, as we have seen, prefers to sever his future from his 'antecedent[s]'. To this end, Stephen offloads the faculty of memory, whether personal or historical, to women. 'Certainly she remembers the past', he writes of his mother; 'all women do. Then she remembers the time of her childhood – and mine if I was ever a child' (*PA* 250–1). To Cranly he insists he 'was someone else' when he was in school, as if his own history were immaterial to his goal: 'I was not myself as I am now, as I had to become' (*PA* 240). 'I cannot answer for the past', he adds (*PA* 243), echoing his question to Davin: 'My ancestors threw off their language and took another . . . Do you fancy I am going to pay in my own life and person debts they made?' (*PA* 203). Male artists, Stephen implies, look ahead and move forward, echoing Hegel's and Haeckel's view of development as successive outgrowths from primitive stages; the past prepares for but ideally disappears from the fully developed soul. Stephen then tries to formalise his vision of development as a constant transcendence of the past: 'the past is consumed in the present and the present is living only because it brings forth the future' (*PA* 250–1). But like earlier attempts to move only forwards, this is feeble posturing. The novel counters with a messier developmental picture, which gives voice to the histories Stephen tries in vain to silence. Complicating Stephen's naïve historical and biographical formula, Joyce plays on the digestive and gestational valences of Stephen's words 'consumed' and 'brings forth', suggesting that the present incorporates the past rather than transcending it. The opposing biological processes of breaking down and engendering organic matter parallel the novel's dialogic tension between plot and epiphany, progress and reversion, recapitulation and 'this chaos of history' (*SH* 35), and this systemic tension and dialogism cannot be reduced to any linear or teleological narrative.

Stephen feels words most strongly when their history, etymological, literary or personal, is sexual, but he is disposed to ignore this fact by his sense of 'destiny' and his Catholic education. Only rarely does Stephen appear receptive to their embodied nature. When Davin tells him about the woman of the Ballyhoura Hills, Stephen's haunted response is produced or at least intensified by the fact she is shirtless, pregnant and offering milk. As usual, Stephen tries distilling his response to sexualised or reproductive language into a spur for *spiritual* self-development: the 'soul waking to the consciousness of itself' (*PA* 183). But the body is intransigent. Thoughts remain stuck on 'the figure of the woman . . . calling the stranger to her bed', and the 'soul' he extricates from Davin's tale is not angelic but animal, 'batlike' (*PA* 183). Every movement forward and upward is thus marbled with reversion. Even in the cathartic moments following his confession, when Stephen thinks 'life lay all before him' (*PA* 146), his sense of destiny is undercut by a pun which situates his future in the past: 'before him'.

This dual temporality, which structures the plot of *A Portrait*, recurs finally in Stephen's famous and famously perplexing vow to 'go to encounter for the millionth time the reality of experience' (*PA* 252–3). There is a paradox in the notion of experiencing something for the millionth time, and while the expression may reflect the muddle of Stephen's youthful romanticism, it also cuts to the heart of the novel's reversionary *Bildung* plot. Pericles Lewis has argued that when Stephen vows to 'forge in the smithy of [his] soul the uncreated conscience of [his] race' (*PA* 253), Joyce articulates a modernist nationalism that 'places an emphasis on the role of the race in shaping the individual's experience' (P. Lewis 2000: 1). Ingenious as it is, Lewis's portrait of Stephen as a messianic embodiment of the Irish nation seems questionable. Concluding that 'the racial conscience is the sort of god that Stephen plans to serve through his writing and his personal experience' (2000: 2), Lewis's explanation may be logical, but it is markedly at odds with Stephen's character, with his vow not to 'serve that in which [he] no longer believe[s] whether it call itself [his] home, [his] fatherland or [his] church' (*PA* 247) and with Joyce's stated scepticism concerning nationalism and myths of national identity. More problematic is Lewis's implication that the artist must submit to national history by replaying it (2000: 2), just as the organism in Haeckel's biogenetic law is a mere effect of phylogenetic causes. The notion of experiencing reality 'for the millionth time' suggests a more complex historical engagement than the recapitulatory dynamic implied in Lewis's claim that 'the racial conscience is the source of all Stephen's experiences, but, as a great soul, Stephen in turn transforms the racial conscience' (2000: 2). Aside from the dubious claim that Stephen is 'a great soul', this explanation overlooks the many ways in which the past, including the non-Irish past of English language and literature, detains Stephen in his attempts to 'forge ahead' and 'go forth to encounter reality' (*PA* 12, 159).

The relation between past, present and future which emerges from Stephen's encounters with verbal and corporeal reality are too kaleidoscopic and indeterminate to fit Lewis's effectively palingenetic model of national conscience. The narrative dynamic of *Bildung* in *A Portrait* is not recapitulatory; it is simultaneously forward and backward or, to quote one of the novel's recurrent phrases, 'hither and thither' (*PA* 111, 137, 138, 157, 161, 171, 224). Stephen's vow to 'forge in the smithy of my soul the uncreated conscience of my race' (*PA* 253) may suggest finality – but not closure. It has the same unnerving indeterminism of an earlier cry, 'on and on and on and on!' (*PA* 172), in which, Michael Levenson avers, 'there is perhaps one "on" too many' (1985: 1020). Indefinite movement forward is progress without teleology, and progress without an end is anathema to the classical *Bildung* plot (Moretti 2000: 90). This may be why Stephen feels so threatened by genealogy and procreation: he feels himself, as an individual with a quasi-divine vocation, diminished by the unbearable, inescapable corporeality of 'the long lane . . . of generations, more generations and still more generations' (*FW* 107). No wonder he is at a loss for words when his friend Temple alerts him to 'the law of heredity': 'Reproduction is the beginning of death' (*PA* 230–1).

Against the self-annihilating prospect of reproduction and genealogy, however, stands the open-endedness of creative activity. The individual may well be constrained by 'the influence of collective tradition upon the individual' (*FW* 268) and limited by 'gnosis of precreate determination' (*FW* 262), but against such determinism is the potential freedom of the undetermined future, the 'agnosis of postcreate determinism' (*FW* 262). As we have seen, *Finnegans Wake* often revisits *A Portrait*'s 'zulugical' experiment with the *Bildungsroman* ('this genre of portraiture of changes of mind') (*FW* 165), stressing the unexpected possibilities of reversion: 'these modes carrying us back to the superimposed claylayers of eocene and pleastoseen formation and the gradual morphological changes in our body politic which Professor Ebahi-Ahuri . . . neatly names a *boîte à surprises*' (*FW* 165). One of these surprises occurs, fittingly, in Book II, Chapter 2, devoted to 'the study hour of the children' (Campbell and Robinson 1968: 162). Concerned with individual education, which it constantly parallels with cultural and biological history, the chapter is a kind of meta-*Bildungsroman* examining its own relationship with recapitulation theory, among other forms of 'imaginable itinerary through the particular universal' (*FW* 260). The relationship is fraught, as it is in *A Portrait*, and explicitly framed by recapitulation theory when Professor Jones supplies this cryptic note: 'From cenogenetic dichotomy through diagonistic conciliance to dynastic continuity' (*FW* 275). Caenogenesis, deviation from perfect recapitulation, hints at how Joyce portrays 'the relation of the peculiar idiosyncrasies of the individual to the vast and general scheme', as Campbell and Robinson put it, adding that 'there are processes in the development of the individual which do not recapitulate the development of the race. Through these an element of novelty is introduced into the great picture' (1968: 173). *Finnegans Wake* offers two ways of reading the progression from caenogenesis to continuity, shedding retrospective light on the plot dynamics of *A Portrait*. For the humourless Professor, responsible for the notes in the right-hand margins, 'cenogenetic dichotomy' is ultimately corrected through procreation ('dynastic continuity'); but this interpretation is irreverently challenged in the left-hand margin by Joyce's avatar Shem, who scoffs at the promise of dialectic synthesis ('diagonistic conciliance') and favours the unnatural involutions and mismatched gestational temporalities of 'superfetation' (*FW* 308). Superfetation is a condition in which a foetus is conceived by an already-pregnant female, resulting in simultaneous gestations at different stages of development. Few biological phenomena more literally embody the notion of uneven development. Through the reversionary process of caenogenesis, then, Joyce counters the progressivism of palingenesis, a linear movement in which constant improvement becomes richer by embodying into its progressive trajectory a countervailing movement – yielding 'impovernment' (*FW* 273).

Notes

1. The shift to the diary invites contradictory interpretations. Pericles Lewis, among others, reads it as a move towards self-consciousness and agency, calling it Stephen's 'ascension to the role of narrator' (2000: 13). Others see the diary as a form more liable to betray Stephen's immaturity (and thus the novel's irony) than the preceding figural narration; Jessica Berman, for example, reads the diary as an ironic document, the individual's 'inability to transcend his linguistic embeddedness or to retain his authority in and through the language that surrounds him' (2011: 126). My reading is closest to Nels Pearson's assessment of the diary as a failure 'to totalize Ireland', a document 'full of withdrawn conclusions and frustrated revisions of previous attempts to summarize Irishness' (2015: 6).
2. The biogenetic law, claims Scarlett Baron, 'would have appealed to Joyce as a structuring trellis' (2013: 184), but his use of recapitulation is critical and opportunistic rather than programmatic. The main source of embryological information in 'Oxen of the Sun' is Giulio Valenti's *Lezioni Elementari di Embriologia*, a textbook steeped in the biogenetic law (Benzenhöfer 1989: 610); yet it is significant that Joyce borrowed disproportionately from Valenti's accounts of 'embryological monstrosities' and 'curiosities from the history of embryology' (Benzenhöfer 1989: 611), suggesting a desire to pervert and parody rather than perpetuate recapitulatory thinking. In *Joyce and Jung*, Hiromi Yoshida interprets 'the phylogenetic pattern of development in *A Portrait*' as a parody of the Jungian idea that 'psychic development is primarily phylogenetic rather than ontogenetic' (2007: 23). This reading, like mine, sees the novel's plot as a frustration of the classical *Bildungsroman*'s aspiration towards 'the highest level of consciousness' (Yoshida 2007: xvi). Yoshida, however, mostly overlooks the biological aspect of ontogeny and phylogeny. In *Joyce and Reality*, John Gordon relates Stephen's growth to the organic developmentalism of Goethe, Darwin, Haeckel and Spencer (2004: 3–32).
3. In 'Language, Sex, and the Remainder in *A Portrait*', Derek Attridge stresses 'the relation between implicit sexuality and overt attention to language, especially to single words' (2000: 64). Brook Miller (2013) devotes a chapter to Stephen's inability to grasp the hylomorphism of body and soul. These readings, and mine, are consistent with Jessica Berman's view that *A Portrait*'s 'intensely heteroglossic' narrative consistently exceeds and ironises the limitations of Stephen's individual perspective (2011: 122).
4. In *Stephen Hero* Stephen calls himself 'modern', prompting Cranly to dismiss the difference between 'ancient' and 'modern' (*SH* 190). When Stephen counters that 'the modern spirit is vivisective' whereas 'the ancient spirit' accepted ideas on faith,

Cranly significantly asks, 'I suppose you do know that Aristotle founded the science of biology' (*SH* 190–1).

5. The correlation between style, psychic development and gestation was first noted by Stanislaus Joyce (2003: 17) then developed into a critical framework by Sidney Feshbach (1967) and by Richard Ellmann (1965: 307). Critics of all theoretical stripes have followed suit, including Gerald Doherty (2008), Breon Mitchell (1976), Gerald Peters (1993) and Fritz Senn (1978/1979, 1987).
6. Maud Ellmann claims that Stephen's reaction to '*Foetus*' resists explanation (1982: 95), as does Attridge (2000: 75), but their readings overlook a simple cultural explanation. Stephen's shock is perfectly consistent with his Irish-Catholic upbringing. Jonathan Bolton, for example, links sexual ignorance to the fact that 'protagonists in Irish *bildungsromane* often mature too quickly' or else 'remain immature and inexperienced' (2010: 10).
7. In *Stephen Hero*, Stephen 'read Skeat's Etymological Dictionary by the hour' (*SH* 32); see Whittaker (1987).

3

MENDELIAN INHERITANCE, 'ETERNAL DIFFERENCES' AND ENTROPY IN *HOWARDS END*

> The garden of a shepherd's cottage swallowed up in a deer-forest lost all trace of its previous cultivation and became a weed-ground. After many years it was delved, and soon there appeared many different kinds of old-fashioned flowers whose seeds had lain dormant for several generations. So may ancient flowers and weeds now and again reappear out of latency in that garden which we call our inheritance.
>
> – J. Arthur Thomson, *Heredity* (1912: 124)

Proponents and antagonists of recapitulation theory agreed that the link between development and evolution is heredity, but their agreement ended with the question of hereditary mechanisms. Recapitulation theory almost inevitably assumes Lamarckian inheritance, which, as we saw in Chapter 1, makes development and genealogy coextensive; Mendelism, by contrast, radically separates them. In theory, the difference between the two hereditary paradigms should have profound implications for the *Bildung* plot. In practice, novelists rarely have a genetic vision fine-grained enough to affect narrative dynamics in any detectable way, even when heredity plays an important thematic role.

A significant exception is E. M. Forster, whose fiction repeatedly pits hereditary transmission against *Bildung*, as the protagonists of *The Longest Journey* and *Maurice* learn the hard way. Similar issues mark most of Forster's fiction.

If this claim seems counterintuitive, it is because modernist and queer studies, which have so productively mined the complexities of Forster's fiction, tend to favour affiliative over filiative dynamics. Forster's focus on reproduction, meanwhile, enjoys little attention, though it is evident even to casual readers. 'Birth' was one of Forster's theoretical concerns (*AN* 36) and a recurrent theme and structuring principle in his fiction. *Where Angels Fear to Tread*, *The Longest Journey*, *A Passage to India* and *Howards End* all include or anticipate the arrival of babies, but this feature tends to be overlooked or dismissed as an aspect of his heterosexist surface plots. As John Beer puts it, 'homosexuality gave [Forster] an "outsider's" view of things, making him look at the world from a point of view which did not regard marriage or the procreation of children as central' (qtd in Martland 1999: 20). What is central, according to such interpretations, is the 'struggle for heirs of same-sex lovers' (Malik 1997: 230), 'the problem of continuity without physical begetting' (Martin 1997: 257). Arthur Martland alone allows that for Forster 'procreation . . . was an important issue' (1999: 20).

Claims to the contrary neglect how often his novels feature 'physical begetting', and how significantly it participates in their queer plotting. Part of the oversight stems from the rightfully influential double-plot model proposed by Judith Herz. Forster's stories and novels, she suggests, have a manifest heterosexual plot and a more or less concealed homosexual plot. This dual structure, Herz argues, emerges less from the operations of Forster's unconscious desires than from authorial 'strategies invented to contain [sexual energy] – not necessarily to disguise it' (1978: 254). For Herz and many others, then, the aesthetic and political complexity of Forster's narratives derives from the 'tensions generated by the collision of the surface plot and the under plot' (1978: 255). It has proved easy for critics to read the two plots in contradictory terms, as Herz does when she suggests that 'often one [plot] is true, the other a lie. Finally one or the other is displaced' (1978: 257). If this were the case, Forster's recurrent use of procreation would signal diversionary tactics or false consciousness. But is that how reproduction actually functions in his novels? In fact, fertility often mediates between heterosexual surface plot and homosexual under-plot, enabling rather than concealing or displacing queer dynamics. In *Where Angels Fear to Tread*, to cite only the clearest case, Gino inhabits a homoerotic social space but also fulfils 'his one desire' to 'become the father of a man like himself' (1975: 52). So much depends on his 'divine hope of immortality: "I continue"' (1975: 52). Without it his son's death would not be tragic – and nothing less than tragedy will do to spark Gino and Philip's homoerotic bond. Gino is a Forsterian ideal, the rare man 'who comprehends that physical *and* spiritual life may stream out of him for ever' (1975: 109; emphasis added). The same case could be said of Stephen Wonham, George Emerson and Alec Scudder, perhaps also of Dr Aziz.

The fact that Maurice 'wanted children' (1999: 137), then, is neither trivial nor contradictory. The sense of contradiction is, after all, the product of heterosexist binaries which view homosexuality as the pathological antithesis of healthy reproductive heterosexuality. By interweaving reproductive surface plots with queer under-plots, Forster debunks the myth of homosexual sterility, in both negative form (as deviance from a biological necessity) and positive form (as a protest against compulsory heterosexuality), and thus refuses to divide conventional from true love along the line of sexual orientation. The scandalous, fertile heterosexual unions between Lilia and Gino, Mrs Elliot and Robert, and Helen and Leonard resemble the same-sex, cross-class love of Maurice and Alec far more than they resemble Charles and Dolly Wilcox's bourgeois marriage. In Forster's fiction, as Herz puts it, 'the heterosexual/homosexual distinction is quite artificial' (1978: 254). Refusing easy oppositions, his plots recall Edward Carpenter's philosophy of 'nonheterosexual evolutionary democracy' (Bredeck 1997: 32). Carpenter saw homosexuality as a positive mediating force in humanity's survival, for if 'homogenic love' is 'non-child-bearing love' (1918: 67, 69), it is nevertheless needed for the successful 'generation' of 'bodily children' (1918: 70). In Carpenter's view, homosexuals ensure humanity's future by reconciling differences between heterosexual males and females who would otherwise 'drift into far latitudes and absolutely cease to understand each other' (1918: 17).[1] Only connect, indeed!

Howards End may lack the homoeroticism of the earlier novels, but it is still a queer narrative, upending even as it reimagines the marriage and *Bildung* plots. It is true that the potentially erotic triangle involving Leonard Bast and Henry Wilcox is rerouted onto the 'safe heterosexual path' of manly competition over Margaret or Jacky (Miracky 2003: 50), and that the Forsterian homosexual Tibby Schlegel remains pointedly quarantined from the plot. Still, there is a close analogy between the double plot of *The Longest Journey*, which uses covert homoeroticism to queer its manifest heterosexual story, and the double plot in *Howards End*, whose progressive and reversionary impulses dialogically queer each other. Queer form may emerge from procreative content; indeed, *Howards End* has many formal and thematic parallels with the overtly homosexual stories of *The Life to Come* (Herz 2008: 606–7), deploying a similar interplay of progressive plot and reversionary counter-plot. What Stephen da Silva has said of the posthumous stories is also true of *Howards End* – that the favoured characters, by 'moving back in time at an ontogenetic level, . . . also move back in history' (1988: 252). This reversionary dynamic is subtler in *Howards End* than in 'The Other Boat', but subtlety is not complacency or complicity. If anything, *Howards End* casts its critique wider. The 'developmental narrative which can . . . only see homosexuality as a failed, immature version of heterosexuality' (da Silva 1988: 241) – as recapitulatory accounts of sexual development assumed – would similarly damn most characters in the novel, albeit for other reasons. Most notably, Helen is an unmarried mother and, as her relationship with the Italian Monica suggests, bisexual; Margaret is a childless wife. Both sisters are blue-stockings and thus, to many contemporaries, masculine. Leonard and Jacky, meanwhile, are working class. Though I certainly do not equate various sexual, gender, race and class identities, each of which has its peculiar social struggles, they would all have been diagnosed as immature based on classical conceptions of *Bildung* and recapitulation theory alike. Homosexuals, the working class, non-whites such as the colonial subjects working offstage for the Wilcoxes, and women were routinely ranked lower than the ideal adult white man in recapitulatory classifications.

As I read it, then, *Howards End* repurposes the Forsterian dual-plot structure, reconfiguring the collision of hetero- and homosexual plots as the entwinement of two different forms of inheritance plot. Each is invested with its own values; each is inadequate if it is not connected to (which is not to say synthesised with) the other. This perspective dispenses with the need to draw firm oppositions between heterosexuality, filiation and reproduction on one hand and homosexuality, affiliation and friendship on the other. Forster was always wary of such stark binaries. Thus when the narrator asks if 'passion' for non-material things might 'be transmitted where there is no bond of blood' (*HE* 96), he only *seems* to privilege culture and personal relations over genealogy. In fact the novel holds them in dialogic interrelation, and indeed it is only after a 'bond of blood' has been forged through marriage and procreation that the house and other 'such things' become available for transmission.

In an early revisionist reading of Forster's novels, Alan Wilde suggests that seeing Forster's narrative innovations requires 'forgoing some of our assumptions about the novels' and stories' aesthetic coherence', for only then can we 'discover heretofore unrecognized levels of complexity, which make of the books, if less perfect and autonomous creations, at any rate a more authentic record of Forster's (and modernism's) struggles' (1991: 52). Wilde risks stating that incoherence is itself the form of Forster's fictions, and though there is certainly some value in this suggestion, I prefer to take his words as an injunction to find new formal logics behind the apparent chaos.

Herz's notion of the Fosterian double plot is the result of such a readerly receptiveness to new formal arrangements. Building on her model, I read *Howards End*'s messy narrative in relation to Mendelian genetics, a new scientific paradigm whose influence on Forster is detectable, as I have shown elsewhere, as early as *The Longest Journey* (Newman 2016a). *Howards End* can thus be read as a *Bildungsroman* disrupted and reinvented by Mendelism. If its plot seems clunky and hard to reconcile with the *Bildung* plot, it is because *Bildung* had emerged alongside a completely different understanding of how development relates to heredity, an epigenetic developmentalism that makes individual growth and inheritance co-extensive, part of a single process. A model of 'hard inheritance', by contrast, Mendelism isolates heredity from lived experience (Mayr 1982: 687) and therefore requires different narrative formats and temporalities – different chronotopes – for the distinct processes of development and genealogy. In *Howards End*, birth and death interrupt and undo development; the progressive *Bildung* plot clashes with a genealogical plot which appears to undo the work of 'acquir[ing] culture' (*HE* 37). From this clash emerges the 'discordant creaks in the mechanism of the plot' (Daleski 1985: 119), the 'discrepancies, disharmonies and disturbing shifts . . . in mode and convention' (Leavis 1952: 264–5) which have long frustrated the novel's readers. Particularly important in this respect is the Mendelian account of reversion, an explanation Forster would later call Mendel's 'salutary principle' (*TC* 19). The 'principle' suits his aesthetics and politics for two related reasons: first, it so thoroughly naturalises reversion that the concept of atavism as a pejorative term for abnormal development loses all meaning; second, its vision of non-blending inheritance counters the homogenisation Forster feared in individual, sexual and civic life. By embracing Mendelian reversion, then, *Howards End* seeks to resolve the paradoxical correlation between progress and entropy, thereby rehabilitating the ideal of *Bildung* in its 'battle against sameness' (*HE* 336).

Mendelian inheritance offers a new perspective on *Howards End* as a modernist *Bildungsroman* peculiarly invested in both the genealogical imperative and the queer strategies of what Scott Nelson calls 'narrative inversion' (1992: 311). My point is not that genetics resolves the 'contradictions, gaps, and inconsistencies' James Miracky identifies in *Howards End* (2003: 26), but that it helps define those seeming failures as manifestations of a specific narrative logic and suggests why Forster would enlist that particular kind of narrative muddle. This genetic framework clarifies how Forster adapts the *Bildung* plot to the realities suppressed by the neat parallelisms of recapitulation theory and its allied narratives of self-formation. Thus he seeks to make the *Bildungsroman* more welcoming to 'the chaotic nature of our daily life, and its difference from the orderly sequence that has been fabricated by historians' (*HE* 104).

Inheritance and Forster's *Bildung* Plot

'Inheritances change destinies and instigate stories', writes Allan Hepburn (2007: 3), and few novels illustrate his claim as well as *Howards End*. Its plot is triggered by the short-lived promise of Helen's marriage to Paul Wilcox; thickened by Ruth Wilcox's death and surprising bequest to Margaret; partially resolved by Margaret's marriage to Henry Wilcox; brought to twin climaxes by the conception of Helen's son and by Leonard's death; and resolved when Mr Wilcox's makes Margaret and the baby legal heirs to the house. At the heart of this jumble is Helen's illegitimate child by a married, working-class man, a scandal which offends the sensibilities of the Wilcoxes and provokes the novel's crisis of generic identity. The baby's arrival disrupts the self-fulfilment plots focused on Margaret and Leonard (which would traditionally have found closure in the equilibria of marriage and death, respectively), leaving in their wake an open-ended plot of genealogical continuity. The narrative is quite literally a tangle of family trees, intermingling the Schlegel paternal with the English maternal line and both with the Wilcox, Howard, Mosebach, Cahill and Fussell lines.

Family trees are plots, after all. Their nodes and branches – marriages, matings, births, deaths – are the constitutive events of a story; in sequence, they constitute the chain of actions Barthes associates with the proairetic code (1970: 26). Reading family trees as plots reveals how the structure of *Howards End* complements its thematic concerns, including concerns that might seem more congenial with affiliative rather than filiative relations. Genealogies, indeed, provide a substrate for non-biological networks of transmission, canalising the flow of money, property, gifts, ideas and, textually, verbal echoes and motifs.[2] If I largely pass over these affiliations, it is not because I find them unimportant but only because their importance has been amply demonstrated elsewhere. Even stripped of affiliative connections, moreover, the novel's conflicting genealogical structures are byzantine and interesting enough to warrant specific attention to genetic linkages. In any case, the central conflict of *Howards End* is not between blood and spirit or biology and culture, but between alternative forms of filiation – one of which, favoured by Forster, rescues the ideal of *Bildung* from the homogenising and entropic forces of cultural and biological sameness.

At this point, I should address the question: is *Howards End* a *Bildungsroman*? My answer is clearly yes, but my reasons may not be as clear. Besides its stated concern with Margaret's 'growth' and Leonard's 'development' and struggle 'to acquire culture' (*HE* 275, 313, 37), the novel bears few of the structural or characterological features of the genre. It does not chart the growth of a central protagonist from infancy or childhood to maturity; indeed, there is no evident focal character. More significantly, its inheritance plot is problematic, shifting the focus from individual formation to the inter-generational transmission of biological traits, culture and property. Reproduction sits uneasily with *Bildung*, though, as Bakhtin argues, all biographical novels 'embryonically' contain traces of the hero's lineage (1984: 18). Some novels, like *Sons and Lovers* and *The House in Paris*, showcase this 'prehistory of Bildung' (Castle 2006: 105), but to expose the generational context of self-formation is to no small degree to diminish its significance. A single birth suffices to challenge, as Gillian Beer writes of Darwinism, 'the single life span as a sufficient model for understanding experience' (2000: 11). Though producing heirs is the duty of a good citizen, reproduction in the post-recapitulatory context of Mendelian inheritance shatters

Bildung's implicit parallelism between individual and historical progress because it cancels the progress accrued by the parent. As Reginald Punnett explains in his popular book *Mendelism*, the new genetics severed the link between heredity and personal experience: 'Education is to a man what manure is to the pea. The educated are themselves the better for it, but their experience will alter not one jot the irrevocable nature of their offspring' (1907: 80–1). The result, in Forster's novel, is a generic collision between *Bildungsroman* and family novel, two genres with different though overlapping temporalities. Most family novels foreground one member of one of its generations (Imogen in Rose Macaulay's *Told by an Idiot*), while several *Bildungsromane* spill over into the generation before or after the protagonist's (*The Longest Journey*, *The Rainbow*). Such novels generate modernist forms by embracing rather than concealing the structural contradictions between the genealogical and developmental plots.

A *Bildungsroman* which features procreation, such as *The Longest Journey*, differs radically from more traditional texts such as *A Portrait of the Artist* because its protagonist Rickie is part of a genealogical story beginning before his birth, with his parents' courtship, and ending, as he sees it anyway, with the death of his daughter. *The Longest Journey* is one of those modernist *Bildungsromane* Gregory Castle describes as 'ensemble narratives in which Bildung plots are embedded and thereby re- or decontextualised by a larger narrative structure that contains them' (2006: 192). Straddling three generations, *The Longest Journey* cannot cohere around one protagonist, though Rickie is undeniably the centre of what is primarily a developmental narrative. In *Howards End*, the generic outlines are stretched beyond recognition by the dominance of its genealogical operations.

Strangely, though, it is because of its genealogical plot that I consider *Howards End* a *Bildungsroman*. Because Margaret and Leonard are already grown-up at the beginning of the story, their development in the novel is moral and social but not ontogenetic – their youth is not part of the narrative. And a *Bildungsroman*, as I have been defining it, must span at least one transition between the more or less distinct ontogenetic stages of childhood, youth and maturity. In the absence of Margaret's or Leonard's childhood, then, the novel supplies the crucial formative life-stage by proxy, as it were, in the form of Leonard's son by Margaret's sister Helen. The *Bildungsroman*'s defining ontogenetic arc is therefore completed not by an individual but over the generational divide. The *Bildung* plot thus spans multiple bodies and minds, proceeding backwards from adulthood to infancy – a reversion in the biological, narrative and legal senses of the word.[3] Shifting in focus from individual to lineage, Forster decouples the process of self-cultivation from the span of a life, distributing it across characters and generations linked by hereditary transmission. Instead of self-realisation coming with maturity, it is achieved only when maturity spawns a new infancy, in the next generation.

This unusual take on the genre depends on the Mendelian logic of 'throw[ing] back', a form of reversion which 'pick[s] up the pieces' of Margaret's and Leonard's fragmented *Bildung* plots and reconstitutes them in the baby (*HE* 320, 336). Mendelism is never mentioned outright in *Howards End*, though it is named in Forster's nearly contemporaneous unfinished novel *Arctic Summer* (1980: 148). Yet *Howards End* does repeatedly suggest a genealogical vision rooted in a Mendelian understanding of inheritance, most tellingly in its allusion to 'throw[ing] back to a nobler stock' (*HE* 320). In this respect, the novel seems almost designed to test the Mendelian notion of non-blending inheritance, especially in its formal and thematic insistence on maintaining differences despite connection.

The most obvious manifestation of this principle, which hardly requires a Mendelian lens, is the novel's notoriously flimsy way of linking characters who seem constitutionally incompatible. The meetings and matings of the Wilcoxes, Schlegels and Basts have perplexed generations of readers, none of them more than the unions of Margaret with Henry and of Helen with Leonard. The novel's resolution, which finds the Schlegel sisters, Mr Wilcox and the baby happily or at least resignedly gathered at Howards End, has likewise been deemed pat or implausibly triumphant. These judgements, though understandable, reveal a fixation on ideal unions and resolutions which *Howards End* simply does not attempt. It resists them, in fact, by ending not with a successful unification but with an emphasis on the coexistence of differences. Leslie White has claimed the novel ends not in harmony but in the 'salutary disconnection of disparate sensibilities' (2005: 44). This is surely correct, but I would quibble that White goes too far with the term 'disconnection', with its implication of separation or fragmentation. What *Howards End* favours is a form of connection which does not result in synthesis. The novel's mantra, 'only connect' (*HE* 183), may stress the adverb as much as the verb: connect only. Falling between separation and union, Forsterian connection is relation which bridges difference without erasing or flattening it out, just as Mendelian inheritance combines genes without blending them, allowing them to be reshuffled in the next offspring, or the next generation. Rather than 'the anodyne of muddledom, by which most men blur and blend their mistakes' (*HE* 315), the novel stages a 'battle against sameness' (*HE* 336).

In opposition to the threat implied by the entropic 'daily gray', Forster looks hopefully to the logic of Mendelism. Thirty years later, in an attack on Nazi race science, he would appeal more explicitly to 'the civilizing figure of Mendel' (*TC* 19), embracing the possibilities for heterogeneity, impurity and reversion which he perceived in the new genetics. Yet this appropriation of Mendelian genetics is already evident in *Howards End*, with its distinctly modernist vision of individual *Bildung* decoupled from larger narratives of national history and biological progress. The England of *Howards End*, like its muddled inheritances, is too mixed to sustain the myth of an individual archetype; the soul-nation allegory is an inadequate answer to the question, 'who shall inherit England[?]' (Trilling 1962: 118). As the novel's contrast between rainbows and greyness suggests, heterogeneity is the ideal of Forster's developmental vision and the goal of his reversionary *Bildung* plot. His politics and aesthetics are therefore most clearly aligned in his protest against entropy, understood as the dissipation of energy (physical but also spiritual), the dissolution of affections and the blending of differences. In 'What I Believe', he expresses his distrust for 'Great Men' who 'produce a desert of uniformity' (*TC* 70). In an early essay on Dryden, he denounces Milton's successors for reducing the poet's luxuriance to 'a world of murky grey', an image echoed in Forster's poem 'Incurious at the Window', in which a regiment of identical soldiers symbolises 'death's universal grey' (2008: 142, 730). In *Howards End*, 'universal gray' is the terrifying outcome of various homogenising forces: capitalism, imperialism, urban sprawl, stereotyping, 'esprit de classe', and the genealogical imperative to 'breed like rabbits' (*HE* 125, 18, 271). Against these grey entropic forces, Forster recruits the 'differences . . . planted by God in a single family, so that there may always be colour' (*HE* 336). These differences, whose explicit linkage to family and metaphorical association with plants suggest Mendel's pea-breeding experiments, rebuff the 'universal gray' through the reversionary return of past variety – a necessary corollary of non-blending inheritance.

Non-blending Inheritance versus the Entropic Grey

A model of non-blending inheritance is a precondition for reading *Howards End* as a *Bildungsroman*, albeit one which allocates parts of the developmental plot to more than one individual in more than one generation. If individuals are merely 'the expression of a particular aggregation of such [heritable] characters' (1907: 74), as Punnett argues in *Mendelism*, then their constituent parts can be combined and recombined in innumerable arrangements. There is then no *genetic* reason to prioritise the self-consistency of an individual organism during its lifetime over the continuity of an individual gene across generations (Dawkins 2008: 4–8). Perverse as this logic might appear, it can paradoxically promote aspects of development and selfhood which, for Forster anyway, come closer to the *Bildung* ideal than does the notion of blending inheritance, with its blurring of boundaries between individual and genealogy.

Finding 'comfort' in 'eternal differences' (*HE* 336), Margaret would appreciate William Bateson's 1909 claim that Mendel finally explained 'the process by which a polymorphic race maintains its polymorphism' (2009: 223). As outlined in Chapter 1, pre-Mendelism models of inheritance assumed that parental genetic materials blend during fertilisation; they therefore failed to explain the observed maintenance of variation generation after generation. Francis Galton gave the wonderful name 'regression towards mediocrity' to his observation that very tall parents tend to have children of closer-to-average height. This is a real phenomenon, but blending models could see inheritance in no other way, even when facts were uncooperative. Parents with blue and brown eyes do not have babies with blue–brown blends; bulls and cows generally produce either male or female calves, not offspring of intermediate sex.

Non-blending inheritance preserves difference, while its blending precursors envision intergenerational transmission as an irreversible advance towards 'universal gray' (*HE* 125). Though congenial with recapitulation, then, blending inheritance reveals the entropic underside of its progressivism, a tendency towards sameness. For this reason Darwin, who dimly imagined a non-blending alternative, struggled to explain how heredity could produce novelty instead of homogeneity (Olby 1985: 47). Relative to the inexorably entropic implications of blending inheritance, Mendelism permits a kind of time-reversibility which would seem to violate the second law of thermodynamics (though only on a local scale). Though its genetic mechanism is conservative at a molecular level, the transmission of non-blended genes produces constant novelty at the level of the organism. The inheritance of a single Mendelian trait, say blue and brown eyes, is a rather simple affair, but organisms inherit not one but myriad traits. As Forster's contemporary M. D. Eder writes in *The New Age*, 'complications ensure, for the child may be exactly like one parent in one unit character, say size, and exactly like the other parent in another unit character, say form' (1909: 192). Because each individual comprises thousands of 'unit characters', the number of possible combinations is practically infinite. An individual is a mosaic, and a mosaic model does offer means of rescuing inheritance and evolution from the tyranny of irreversible time and entropy. If 'living things [are] cheats in the game of entropy', writes Gilbert Lewis in *The Anatomy of Science*, Mendelian inheritance is one mechanism by which they can 'breast the great stream of apparently irreversible processes . . . While the rest of the world seems to move toward a dead level of uniformity, the living organism is evolving new substances and more and more intricate forms' (1926: 178).

Forster was not alone in finding aesthetic and political comfort in Mendelism. In 'Mankind in the Making', a polemic against the eugenic desire to 'breed a homogeneous docile herd' (1904: 40), H. G. Wells demonstrates a remarkably early awareness of the Mendelian revolution. Wells disputes the vague hereditary models on which eugenicists pin their hopes of propagating such complex qualities as '"ability", "capacity", "genius", and "energy"' (1904: 41). On the elusive topic of 'beauty', which is not a trait but 'a miscellany of synthetic results compounded of diverse elements in diverse proportions' (1904: 45–6), Wells states that 'there is no science yet, worthy of the name' (1904: 50). At this point, however, he inserts a footnote lauding 'the very striking researches of the Abbé Mendel' (1904: 50n), hinting that Mendelism might offer a scientific perspective more attuned to the complexities of inheritance. In his earlier discussion of beauty, indeed, his logic and notation are strikingly reminiscent of Mendelism. If 'human appearance' were

> made up of certain elements, a, b, c, d, e, f, etc., then we might suppose that beauty in one case was attained by a certain high development of a and f, in another by a certain fineness of c and d, in another by a delightfully subtle ratio of f and b.
>
> A, b, c, d, e, F, etc.
> a, b, *c*, *d*, e, f, etc.
> a, *b*, c, d, e, *F*, etc.,
>
> might all for example represent different types of beauty. Beauty is neither a simple thing nor a constant thing, it is attainable through a variety of combinations. (Wells 1904: 43)

Unexpectedness is central to Wells's model: beauty composed of *A–F* together may well vanish in the next generation if *A* is partnered with *f* or *a* with *F*. Conversely, the beautiful *c–d* combination may unexpectedly arise from crossing two unprepossessing parents (*c–D* and *C–d*). Hardly rigorous, this model nevertheless approximates Mendelism by generating a huge range of possibilities from the combination of a few independently mobile 'elements'.

This Mendelian perspective reminds us that Margaret's 'only connect' (*HE* 183) is a call not for union or agreement, but for the coexistence of difference as difference. Connection, as the narrator reports Margaret's vision, is

> the building of the rainbow bridge that should connect the prose in us with the passion. Without it we are meaningless fragments, half monks, half beasts, unconnected fragments that have never joined into the man. With it love is born, and alights on the highest curve, glowing against the gray. (*HE* 183)

This oft-quoted passage is rarely identified as a theory of the novel – or at least a theory of the novel in which it occurs. But it articulates nicely *Howards End*'s complicated, incommensurable plot lines and genealogies. Unconnected differences are 'meaningless fragments', but blended differences produce an equally meaningless 'gray'. The 'rainbow bridge' is an apt ideal, recalling how white light disperses through a prism into its separate constitutive colours. In *Unities*, H. M. Daleski complains that the 'late appearance of a rainbow in the daily gray is novelistic legerdemain' (1985: 125). Closer inspection, however, reveals the logical and structural inevitability of Forster's rainbow metaphor, which beautifully suits his putting of genealogy and Mendelism in service of a modified *Bildung* plot. Indeed, the narrator explicitly ascribes the ability to build 'the rainbow bridge' to those who are truly mature, unlike Mr Wilcox, 'mature as he was' (*HE* 183). At the moment of closest contact between Margaret and Leonard, who are the primary foci of the novel's developmental plot, Margaret distils self-cultivation into an anti-entropic 'struggle against life's daily grayness' (*HE* 140). Leonard's attempts 'to acquire culture' (*HE* 37) are similarly described as an effort to 'push his head out of the gray waters and see the universe. He believed in sudden conversion, a belief which may be right, but which is peculiarly attractive to a half-baked mind' (*HE* 47). Unfortunately for Leonard, his ambition cannot be realised in his lifetime: the necessary 'conversion' is so 'sudden' that it will require a genealogical reboot which he is fated not to survive. All he can hope for in his lifetime, as Helen fears, is just enough money to perpetuate his 'gray life' (*HE* 120) and to 'mak[e] the gray more gray' (*HE* 251).

In this respect, however, Leonard is still better off than his foil Mr Wilcox. It is in the hopeless expectation of connection that Margaret seeks to spur her husband's development. Initially, having found him incomplete, she had put her faith in the prospect of self-cultivation, his *Bildung*:[4] 'she would only point out the salvation that was latent in his own soul, and in the soul of every man' (*HE* 183). To her disappointment, Henry's 'soul' is poor soil indeed for hosting further growth, for in it 'all had reverted to chaos' (*HE* 183). The undifferentiated state of his 'soul' expresses itself as a blindness to detail and distinction; Margaret cannot help him because 'he never noticed the lights and shades that exist in the grayest conversation, the finger-posts, the milestones, the collisions, the illimitable views' (*HE* 184).

The many other allusions to the entropic empire of grey are diagnostic of *Howards End*'s developmental narrative as a struggle to resolve conflicts without solving them, to combine without mixing the colours of 'the rainbow bridge' (*HE* 183). A classical *Bildungsroman*, with its single protagonist and its ideal of hegemonic culture, would be unequal to the task. In order to preserve the diversity Forster valued in England's classes and individuals, the Schlegel plot must be linked with the plots of other families in different social circumstances: 'the world would be a gray, bloodless place were it entirely composed of Miss Schlegels' (*HE* 25–6). For *Howards End* as a *Bildungsroman*, this connective dynamics offers a vision of *Bildung* founded on a muddled but, in contrast with the idealised hero as national archetype, more ethically and politically responsible allegory – not an isomorphism of soul and nation but, rather, a diffuse nation made up of innumerable and various souls. If the nation cannot accommodate the plurality and variety of souls inhabiting it, Forster suggests, too bad for the nation; doubts about human types, a recurrent theme in *Howards End*, are central to its capacious nationalism, its embrace of England and Europe as 'mongrel for ever' (*TC* 19).

What *Howards End* suggests, then, is a form of *Bildung* quite unlike the individualistic striving exemplified by Stephen Dedalus and Paul Morel. It is social and genealogical. When Margaret defends Leonard's potential, even as she admits its failure, she praises interpersonal connection and the status of Howards End as a physical place and spiritual home: 'either some very dear person or some very dear place seems necessary to relieve life's daily gray, and to show that it is gray. If possible, one should have both' (*HE* 142). Margaret does not specify what makes a person 'very dear', though her sister Helen is the obvious referent. Companionship, friendship and other such horizontal personal relations are of course also eligible (especially given the bond between her and the first Mrs Wilcox), but insofar as Forster charts the realisation of potential, it is through vertical, intergenerational relations. The fundamental narrative function of the Schlegel sisters is to channel the ownership of the titular house from the Wilcoxes, who gained it through marriage, to the son of Leonard Bast. It is a tortuously indirect trajectory for returning the house to the earthy, spiritual 'aristocracy' (*HE* 19) embodied by Ruth Wilcox and Miss Avery but also latent, genetically, in Leonard. In other words, *Howards End* is a genealogical drama designed to restore Howards End to its original yeoman stock. It is also a *Bildungsroman*, but in a reversionary, modernist sense because the 'nobler stock' (*HE* 320) inherits the house through the sacrifice of full individual development. Leonard dies young. Margaret marries, Helen has a child: each sister completes half of the traditional plot of female development, but neither completes both halves. Henry Wilcox saves his honour and his marriage but ends up diminished. Charles Wilcox and his offspring lose their title to Howards End. The success of Forster's genealogical *Bildung* plot depends on the arrested developmental plot of every major player in the novel.

The novel's premises make any other end unimaginable. Leonard could never acquire culture or Howards End on his own. As 'colourless, toneless' as his own life, he is viewed (by Margaret) as the victim of hereditary entropy or degeneration:

> One guessed him as the third generation, grandson to the shepherd or ploughboy whom civilization had sucked into the town; as one of the thousands who have lost the life of the body and failed to reach the life of the spirit. Hints of robustness survived in him, more than a hint of primitive good looks, and Margaret, noting the spine that might have been straight, and the chest that might have broadened, wondered whether it paid to give up the glory of the animal for a tail coat and a couple of ideas. (*HE* 113)

To Mr Wilcox, Leonard is the epitome of unfitness. His death confirms the Social Darwinist creed that when 'the shoe pinch[es]' (*HE* 188) the weak step aside in order to ensure 'the survival of the fittest' (*HE* 189). Leonard does cut a sorry figure; his charms are relics, ancestral rather than actual.[5] Individual failure aside, however, he has 'robustness', 'primitive good looks' and 'glory' which promise a future denied to Wilcox posterity. Leonard is therefore not 'an evolutionary disappointment', as David Medalie has it, though he may be 'a *eugenic* disappointment' (2002: 18) – which is not at all the same thing. His unfortunate 'exclusion from the happy ending' (Medalie 2002: 20) is mitigated, if not compensated for, by the genetic paradigm *Howards End* deploys as a rejoinder to the eugenic ideal of purity and the conservative fear of degeneration. First, it strongly suggests that Leonard's deplorable condition is environmental, the result of social rather than genetic causes. As J. Arthur Thomson points out in his explanation of 'arrests of development', many cases of degeneration are 'peculiarities of pre-natal or post-natal nurture' (1912: 126). Such apparent atavisms 'may be congenital, but they are not germinal' (1912: 126), Thomson argues, because it is

> through defective nutrition or other untoward conditions of nurture [that] the expression of the inheritance is inhibited. The organism is not able to perfect itself in all its parts; not, we suppose, through any germinal defect (as subsequent generations may show), but simply because it was not sufficiently fed . . . (J. A. Thomson 1912: 125)

Howards End bolsters its attack on eugenic ideals with a post-Mendelian scepticism about the notion of genetic purity. As William Bateson writes in *Mendel's Principles of Heredity*, mosaic heredity means 'that an organism may be pure-bred in respect of a given character though its parents were cross-bred in the same respect' and 'that an individual may be pure in respect of one character and cross-bred or impure in respect of others' (1913: 17). What is more, the mechanisms of Mendelian heredity ensure that the past conditions idealised by degeneration alarmists can easily reappear. These biological perspectives help make sense of Leonard's reduced circumstances and diminished figure, and offer the double-edged promise that his offspring might revert to a more healthy form. At the end of the novel, then, when Leonard travels to Howards End and to his death, he finds himself far from the 'the gray tides of London' (*HE* 106) in the land of his ancestors. These shadowy figures are, according to the narrator, 'England's hope', for they 'carry forward the torch of the sun, until such time as the nation sees fit to take it up. Half clodhopper, half board-school prig, they can still throw back to a nobler stock, and breed yeomen' (*HE* 320).

The allusion to 'throw[ing] back' anticipates Forster's explicit praise for 'the civilizing figure of Mendel' in the 1939 broadcast 'Racial Exercise'. By showing that pea plants 'keep throwing up recessive characteristics' as if turning back the genealogical clock (*TC* 19), Forster's Mendel 'embodies a salutary principle', 'a valuable weapon' for 'civilized people', who are wary of the doctrines of purity, 'only know[ing] that we are all of us mongrels' (*TC* 19–20). 'Racial Exercise' highlights the urgency of Forster's genealogical vision, representing Nazi racial doctrine as an extreme form of family snobbery. It begins whimsically enough: 'If I go the right way about it, I come of an old English family, but the right way is unfortunately a crooked one' (*TC* 17). It takes a 'zigzag course' to arrive at a family with roots, the Sykes, but 'if I take a wrong turning and miss the Sykes, darkness descends on my origins almost at once. Mrs. James is a case in point, and a very mortifying one . . . I am directly descended from her' (*TC* 17). Most explicit in 'Racial Exercise', the same argument about heredity, purity and genealogy is recognisable as early as *Where Angels Fear to Tread*, and in *Arctic Summer*, written in 1911 and 1912, it is fully formed: 'A genealogical tree that *is* genealogical would be valuable', says Venetia, but 'people are so apt to make a fuss about their eminent ancestors . . . and to hush up those who aren't' (1980: 151). It is also Venetia who mentions 'Mendelism' (1980: 148).

Forster sees great ethical potential in an atomistic theory of inheritance which normalises atavism, not least because it offers a genetic solution to evolutionary entropy, reversing progressive homogenisation by shuffling and reshuffling old elements into novel arrangements. A kindred procedure guides the unlikely genealogical contacts between members of *Howards End*'s various families, a form of outbreeding that ensures the right heirship for the house. Like Darwin, Mendelians recognised the advantages of outcrossing; unlike Darwin, they had a hereditary mechanism that could explain its benefits. By 'reshuffling' our constituent 'units' (genes) into 'new arrangements', writes Julian Huxley, 'sexual reproduction gives the opportunity for . . . separate useful characters to be combined in a single breed' (1920b: 203). Such enriching combinations are less likely when like breeds with like, and to be 'pure', as Leonard is said to be at the novel's end, is to be 'enfeebled' and incapable of 'regeneration' (*HE* 313). By the same logic, though, Leonard's son is blessed, combining the latent nobility of his patrilineage with his Anglo-German matrilineage, itself the productive hybrid of 'two supreme nations, streams of whose life warmed [Margaret's] blood, but, mingling, had cooled her brain' (*HE* 198). The house, after all, belongs not to the pure but to the noble.

Idealising the return to 'a nobler stock' might sound rather conservative. Yet conservative is surely not the right word for reversions which are, throughout Forster's fiction, so evidently suffused with homoeroticism, paganism and fantasy. And his quasi-mystical, homoerotic plot dynamics frequently do involve questions pertaining to biological inheritance. In *Arctic Summer*, 'Mendelism' is invoked to explain Clesant March's uncanny likeness to a blond soldier in a sixteenth-century fresco – as it turns out, an ancestor (1980: 148). Significantly, the likeness is visible only to Clesant's male admirer Martin Whitby. The notion of 'carry[ing] forward the torch of the sun' (*HE* 320) is not evidently related to homosexuality in *Howards End*, but that relation is suggested intertextually, for similar expressions serve to entwine queerness with procreation in an early draft of *The Longest Journey* (1984: 376) and in *Maurice* (1999: 78). Leonard Bast's procreative transmission is queered not by literal homosexuality (latent or overt) but by the scandalous nature of an affair conducted across class boundaries, against his marriage and despite Helen's unmarried status. His fatal trip to Howards End thus symbolically anticipates his posterity's reversion to 'nobler stock' and provides the conditions for the final and necessary scandal.

The queerness of Leonard's rural return is therefore not held in opposition to reproductive futurism *per se*. The counterpoint is, instead, a particular manifestation of reproductive futurism which views genealogical descent as a blind, entropic progression into sameness. As Leonard contemplates the rural scene an automobile, symbol of the Wilcox clan, passes and reveals

> another type, whom Nature favours – the Imperial. Healthy, ever in motion, it hopes to inherit the earth. It breeds as quickly as the yeoman, and as soundly; strong is the temptation to acclaim it as a super-yeoman, who carries his country's virtue overseas. But the Imperialist is not what he thinks or seems. He is a destroyer. He prepares the way for cosmopolitanism, and though his ambitions may be fulfilled, the earth that he inherits will be gray. (*HE* 320)

This passage, together with the preceding vision of 'England's hope' in the 'half clodhopper, half board-school prig' (*HE* 320), refutes claims that Forster rejected procreation outright. To be sure, the disagreeable Imperial type, apparent winner in the 'battle of life' (*HE* 187), exudes reproductive vigour and promises to 'breed like rabbits', as Miss Avery mocks the Wilcoxes (*HE* 271). Yet what differentiates the Imperial from the yeoman is not fertility. The yeoman, after all, 'breeds as quickly . . ., and as soundly' (*HE* 320). The contrast rests, therefore, on distinctions between alternative reproductive narratives. Moving ever forward, the Imperial colonises and homogenises. Following 'the tendency of civilization . . . upward' (*HE* 188), his mission resembles the misguided, dehumanised philanthropy Margaret abhors, 'the many-coloured efforts thereto spreading over the vast area like films and resulting in a universal gray' (*HE* 125). By contrast the labourers, though not 'men of the finest type', could counter irreversible entropy by 'throw[ing] back' to a past form (*HE* 320).

This reversion is the novel's best evidence of Foster's Mendelian framework, but there is at least one other intriguing clue. It is concealed in the humorous description of a central though effaced character, whose indispensability to the plot contrasts starkly with her wasted developmental and reproductive potential in the story. 'Awesome' in her dishevelment (*HE* 48), Jacky is a veritable aggregation of fragments, recalling Punnett's portrayal of 'the individual' as 'an aggregate of unit-characters' whose 'individuality' is merely 'the expression of a particular aggregation of such characters' (1907: 74). Jacky is 'all strings and bell-pulls – ribbons, chains, bead necklaces that clinked and caught – and a boa of azure feathers hung round her neck, with the ends uneven' (*HE* 48). There follows a memorable description of Jacky's hat:

> her hat, which was flowery, resembled those punnets, covered with flannel, which we sowed with mustard and cress in our childhood, and which germinated here yes, and there no . . . As for her hair, or rather hairs, they are too complicated to describe, but one system went down her back, lying in a thick pad there, while another, created for a lighter destiny, rippled around her forehead. (*HE* 48)

Does Forster pun on 'punnets' and Punnett? It seems unlikely, and yet Jacky's hat so strongly hints at the novel's concern with reproductive success (not all seeds germinate). And the portrait of her 'hairs' mirrors the fluvial imagery which provides a thematic counterpart to the novel's elaborate 'system' of hereditary streams, imagery to which I return below. Finally, Jacky most poignantly embodies the anti-*Bildung* plot which *Howards End* combines, tenuously and sometimes awkwardly, with its *Bildung* plot. 'On the shelf' (*HE* 49), she is the novel's most pathetic victim of developmental entropy; she is indeed 'descending quicker than most women into the colourless years' (*HE* 48).

Showing Jacky 'past her prime' (*HE* 48), Forster offers a microcosm of *Howards End*'s structure as a *Bildungsroman* astride on both ontogenetic and phylogenetic plots. A similar moment occurs when Margaret disputes Helen's self-diagnosed developmental defeat. Helen claims to be 'ended' because she will 'never marry' (*HE* 335), mirroring Jacky's fate but also the fall of Mr Wilcox, marked by very similar words: 'I'm ended' (*HE* 331). Margaret takes a larger view of development, allowing the next generation into her ken:

> Develop what you have; love your child. I do not love children. I am thankful to have none. I can play with their beauty and charm, but that is all – nothing real, not one scrap of what there ought to be. And others – others go farther still, and move outside humanity altogether. A place, as well as a person, may catch the glow. Don't you see that all this leads to comfort in the end? (*HE* 335–6)

This 'end' is exactly what Margaret has found 'to relieve the daily gray': 'some very dear person' (Helen), 'some very dear place' (Howards End) (*HE* 142). Bringing people and place together has been a complicated business, however, requiring the combination of various kinds of genealogies and the supplement of various non-biological modes of inheritance.

Stream Counter Stream

In *Howards End*, the conflict of inheritances occurs between alternative models of genealogy and culture embodied on the one hand by the Wilcoxes, on the other by the Schlegels. Of the two Forster evidently prefers the Schlegel model, and yet it is, on its own, as insufficient and flawed as its opposite. The narrative does not then chart a conflict between models from which one emerges victor; instead, the narrative emerges from the interaction of the two models, a complex messy *Bildung* plot which Margaret does well to call, repeatedly, a 'tangle' (*HE* 141, 334, 337). It is a rhizomatic mess of biological and other forms of inheritance, nothing like the unified developmental line which 'moves forward' in step with 'the tendency of civilization [which] has on the whole been upward' (*HE* 188). Nothing less than a 'tangle' is needed to ensure the transmission of Mrs Wilcox's gift to Margaret, then to Helen and Leonard's son. It takes many, often implausible twists and turns to move the house, against the obstacles set by family, social convention and the law, from one Mrs Wilcox to the next. For the Wilcoxes, letting the house 'pass out of the family' is to 'dislocate Society' (*HE* 123). But standing above a 'society [which] is based on the family' (*HE* 315), Ruth, the genial plot-master, guarantees that the plot does her will.

The tension at the heart of *Howards End* results from the collision of two types of family tree, descendant and ascendant. Both family trees have a branching structure, but descendant trees branch out towards the future, chronologically, fanning out from one ancestor to many descendants; naturally they are linked to the Wilcoxes. Ascendant trees branch out towards the past, against the clock, fanning out from one descendant through two parents and four grandparents to its eight great-grandparents and so on. This reversionary perspective on genealogy, which is of course associated with the Schlegels, is one Forster would recommend to the audience of 'Racial Exercise', suggesting that a clear-eyed view of one's ancestry is the best way 'to combat the pompous and pernicious rubbish' (*TC* 20) of family snobbery and, by extension, the 'ridiculous doctrine of Racial Purity' (*TC* 18).

Linked to descendant trees, then, the Wilcoxes' social, professional, ideological and reproductive activities are future-oriented. Their primary representative, Henry Wilcox, is a patriarch, generator of all succeeding Wilcoxes (Charles, Evie and Paul, then Charles's four children). The novel charts his descent – in two senses, as it turns out. Margaret and Helen are anchored by 'their origin' and resemble Ruth Wilcox by 'worship[ping] the past' and by caring more for 'ancestors' than for descendants (*HE* 19, 26). The two families are both marked, in fact, by their contrasting attitude to what has come and gone: for the Wilcoxes, the past is 'savagery' from which we have progressed (*HE* 172), and for the sisters, it is the Golden Age of 'Esterház and Weimar'

(*HE* 26), the cradle of *Bildung*. By foregrounding the alternative perspectives on genealogy, Forster complements the thematic oppositions embodied in the two central families with a structural conflict between two plots with opposing temporal orientations.

As I have already suggested, both genealogical perspectives are entropic if taken alone. Forward looking, the current of the Wilcoxes is progressive and ever expanding. 'Without their spirit life might never have moved out of protoplasm' (*HE* 172), admits Margaret, and yet 'the energy of the Wilcoxes' is largely 'wasted energy' (*HE* 21, 174), for it simply increases the need for further exertion. Representatives of efficiency, capitalism, empire and reproductive futurism, the Wilcoxes are doomed by success. The increasingly ramified structure of descendant trees nicely illustrates this kind of dissipation over time. Henry's successes appear to confirm his faith that 'the tendency of civilization' is 'upward' (*HE* 188), but the future promises decline. Ever more capital and territory is required to maintain his family's standard of living. This entropic narrative reveals the structural and ideological similarities between capitalism, imperial expansion and 'marriage settlements' (*HE* 25). Advising Mr Wilcox to 'divide his income into ten parts' and distribute it among his children (*HE* 177), Margaret exposes an uncomfortable fact: his resources cannot sustain so much partitioning. Paul, who 'hasn't a penny' (*HE* 18), must therefore participate in colonial exploitation – a project many British commentators, liberal and conservative alike, saw as an entropic dissipation of national vigour (McDuffie 2009: 79). Evie's wedding, meanwhile, is resented by Henry and Charles as a financial drain on family resources. Charles may believe in '"everyone for himself"', but this doctrine threatens 'to leave his children poor' (*HE* 213). In both imperial and marital contexts, 'breed[ing] like rabbits' may 'keep England going' (*HE* 271), but the going is ineluctably towards homogeneity and sameness: Charles's sons are aptly called 'edition[s] of Charles' (*HE* 182). This headlong advance into entropy is unmistakably linked to the Wilcoxes as embodiments of the 'Imperial' type, who 'cares too much about success, too little about the past' (*HE* 171).

Meanwhile, the backward-looking Schlegel plot is nostalgic, idealist, artistic and uneasy with modernity. Hating 'plans' and 'lines of actions' (*HE* 6), the sisters think as little about the future as their fruitful investments allow. Their father Ernst dreamed of turning back the clock on modern German 'Imperialism', hoping to 'rekindle the light within' in the old Germany of 'Hegel and Kant' (*HE* 27, 26). The longing persists in Ernst's daughters, linking them superficially to Ruth's more earthy sense of history, yet their nostalgic ideal of culture is just as dissipative as the Wilcox cult of efficiency. Margaret protests too much when she denies being 'a barren theorist' (*HE* 7), and Helen despairs that 'it makes no difference thinking things out. They come to the same' (*HE* 172). The sister's exalted 'personal relations', Margaret fears, will 'lead to sloppiness in the end' (*HE* 25). The Schlegel plot's shape as an ascendant tree is a temporal mirror image of the progressive Wilcox plot. On their own, then, the Wilcox and Schlegel streams – descendant and ascendant – lead to exhaustion and sameness.

Descendant and ascendant trees are abstractions, but the novel gives them concrete expression in the figures of rivers and trees, both common metaphors for lineage. The wych elm plays a key symbolic role in *Howards End*, its fate coupled to the future of the house (*HE* 334) and of England (*HE* 203). But rivers more often and more clearly incarnate for the novel's concerns with time, entropy and inheritance. Rivers connect characters, especially Margaret and Helen, and ground characters at Howards End. Fittingly, rivers can resemble either (or both) descendant or ascendant genealogies, depending on whether we trace them with or against the current. Thus they play double symbolic duty in the novel, presenting a recurrent image of its key conflict between Schlegel and Wilcox. The Wilcox stream is evident in Evie Wilcox and Percy Cahill's robustly heterosexual and conventional courtship, whose 'habitual course' repulses Margaret as an oppressive 'torrent of . . . love' (*HE* 149). She prefers 'her backwater, where nothing happened except art and literature' (*HE* 149). To read *back-water* literally, Margaret is more comfortable going against the current, if not moving upstream than staying still as time rushes by. It is a tonic to 'the continual flux of London', in which 'all the qualities, good, bad and indifferent, [are] streaming away – streaming, streaming for ever' (*HE* 179). Yet 'backwater' also hints at a stagnancy consistent with the Schlegel version of entropic motionlessness. To reverse the entropic tendencies of Wilcox fecundity and Schlegel barrenness requires bringing together the opposite currents – the descendant and the ascendant.[6]

'All genealogies, perhaps, are reticulated' rather than 'linear', writes Kevin Ohi, 'if one views them from "above" and not from any governing perspective (oneself, for example)' (2015: 213). While Forster's two central families privilege one linear genealogy over the opposite one, the omniscient narrator offers a more detached glimpse of the 'reticulated' reality. Connecting the two streams requires a mediating intervention, so the narrative supplies one in the form of Leonard Bast. As an individual, of course, Leonard is a model of *Bildung*'s entropic failure, and yet he forges an invigorating connection between the Wilcox and Schlegel plots, reinfusing genealogical and development energy into the streams of the two declining families. In the language of plant breeding, Leonard cross-pollinates two enfeebled lineages, revitalising them through 'hybrid vigour' (the hybrid offspring of two inbred lines often exceeds both parents in fitness; Bruce 1910: 627–8).

It seems significant, then, that the result of Leonard's transgression and then sacrifice – Helen and Margaret's reconciliation at Howards End – should occasion a passage which merges arboreal and fluvial imagery: 'The present flowed by them like a stream. The tree rustled. It had made music before they were born, and would continue after their deaths, but its song was of the moment' (*HE* 312).

Coupling stream-like time with the wych elm signals a moment of connection between the novel's contending genealogical plots; it also concretises the chronotopic collision of the *Bildungsroman*'s individual temporality ('of the moment') with the family novel's multigenerational span ('before they were born . . . after their deaths'). Again, rivers are more frequently figures of connection than trees.[7] In his bird's-eye views of England, a frequent device in Forster's fiction including *Howards End*, the emphasis is generally on the flow of rivers descending to the sea but, now and then, running the other way. In *The Longest Journey* 'streams do divide' against their usual tendency to converge (1984: 272); in *Howards End* 'the Thames . . . run[s] inland from the sea' (*HE* 158). This bi-directionality recalls Bergson's claim that 'there is in reality but a certain current of existence and its antagonist current: hence the whole evolution of life' (2007: 186). Neither current alone can produce 'evolution', which is generated by the productively turbulent contact zone between the two opposing streams. It is no wonder that Forster situates Howards End on the edge of London's approaching sprawl, in a liminal land where, as he writes in *Arctic Summer*, 'all the alluvial complexities of the Thames valley, merg[e] into one another, differentiating, pushing out tongues of meadowland or wood, creating clear yet countless subtleties of blue and green' (1980: 249). In 'Arthur at Ampelos', too, streams are entangled, multidirectional, though in this case the rivers are metaphorical, made of

> yellow marigolds, streaming in dazzling beauty down towards the sea. At the further corner of the field, where an outcrop of volcanic rock terminated the alluvial land, there began a counter-stream of crimson poppies, which spread in fan formation far into the mass of gold. Not in the rainbow did tints mingle more imperceptibly, and there was no point where the eye could decide that the field had passed from one colour to the other (Forster 1980: 243)

The aesthetic exuberance of the collision between floral stream and counter-stream suggests the generative connection between divergent world views – not exactly those of the Schlegels and Wilcoxes but nevertheless structurally analogous to them. Arthur, an archaeologist studying the 'prehistoric civilization of Crete . . . in the hope of not merely discovering its offshoots, but also its origins', charts value along a temporal axis; his aunt, who admits that 'origins . . . bored her' and loves the 'beautiful' regardless of its age, ranks value on an aesthetic axis (1980: 242). The axes meet in 'the rainbow' of colliding floral streams, which mix but whose individual marigolds and poppies remain distinct – like Mendel's genes. In *Howards End* Margaret's great insight, prompted by Leonard's tragic intervention, is that both streams are necessary. What matters are not the streams themselves but their connection, not progress or origins but 'the future as well as the past' (*HE* 337).

Leonard connects current with counter-current by means of procreation. If Charles's fertility enlarges the empire of grey, Leonard's restores a bit of the lost 'colour' (*HE* 336). Though downtrodden, Leonard heralds the possibility of 'a nobler stock' (*HE* 320), whereas each Wilcox generation seems to bleed nobility. Henry's 'nature', states the narrator pointedly, 'was nobler than his son's' (*HE* 95). For Leonard, as for Rickie Elliot in *The Longest Journey*, forging the crucial connection comes at a heavy price. Only after 'Leonard lay dead' (*HE* 327) can the narrator answer his earlier questions about transmission 'where there is no bond of blood' (*HE* 96):

> life was a deep, deep river, death a blue sky, life was a house, death a wisp of hay, a flower, a tower, life and death were anything and everything, except this ordered insanity, where the king takes the queen, and the ace the king. Ah, no; there was beauty and adventure behind, such as the man at her feet had yearned for; there was hope this side of the grave; there were truer relationships beyond the limits that fetter us now. (*HE* 327)

This passage exemplifies what readers often dismiss as Forster's 'sentimental' and 'vague gesturing' (Leavis 1952: 271). It does indeed fire off a rather muddled set of images and clumsy metaphors: how can life be a river and a house, and death both sky and hay? And yet 'ordered insanity' (*HE* 327) is the structuring principle of *Howards End*. The passage just quoted is the vital node where the novel's many plots and symbolic threads converge on the figure of Leonard. His death, 'a wisp of hay', connects him rhythmically to Ruth Wilcox, whose death had provoked the question: 'a wisp of hay with dew on it – can passion for such things be transmitted where there is no bond of blood?' (*HE* 96). Leonard's death suggests a positive answer. The 'deep, deep river' of 'life' once again suggests the two currents he paid so dear a price to connect: one moving towards 'beauty and adventure behind', the other towards 'truer relationships' ahead (*HE* 327). His death enables Schlegel, Bast and Wilcox lines to meet. As a result, the inheritance of Howards End is directed into a new channel. Before Leonard's intervention, the house was transmitted from Ruth to Henry, who planned to bequeath it to Charles along the entropic Wilcox line.[8] Inheritance along the Schlegel line has followed the equally entropic transmission of culture, which for the offspring of Ernst Schlegel takes the form of spinsterhood: 'old-maidish' Margaret (*HE* 157), the 'old maid' Helen (*HE* 189), and of course 'Auntie Tibby' (*HE* 40). This tendency is marked by an increasingly desperate search for housing which leaves the three siblings separated if not fully estranged. Checking the two entropic tendencies is the scandalous genealogical event of Helen and Leonard's fertile union. Leonard dies by the Wilcox sword and under the Schlegel books, yet by prompting

Charles's arrest and Henry's moral collapse, he reroutes the house from Charles to Margaret and, ultimately, to her nephew – Leonard's son.

This crucial connection is rather more complicated, however, because it is in fact an effect of an unwitting collaboration between Leonard and his structural double: Paul Wilcox, of all people. Before Margaret even knows why Helen has gone into exile, she intuits her sister's pregnancy by tracing the tangled plot back to the brief romance with Paul. 'Can human nature be constructed on lines so insignificant?' wonders the narrator, before explaining that

> the blundering little encounter at Howards End was vital. It propagated itself where graver intercourse lay barren; it was stronger than sisterly intimacy, stronger than reason or books . . . Paul had faded, but the magic of his caress endured. And where there is enjoyment of the past there may also be reaction – propagation at both ends. (*HE* 275)

This passage is a microcosm of Helen's plot in *Howards End*. With unsubtle reproductive metaphors, it begins by rehearsing the genealogical imperative, the 'tiny mishap' of heterosexual attraction overcoming those things Margaret holds dearest: 'sisterly intimacy', 'reason' and 'books' (*HE* 275). The kiss propels the plot; it is 'vital' and overcomes 'barren[ness]'. But to Margaret's eye its propagation is entropic, 'the growth of morbidity' (*HE* 275). Soon, though, the counter-current intervenes, as it tends to do when the Schlegels mention 'the past': 'where there is enjoyment of the past there may also be reaction' (*HE* 275) – that is, there may be what we might call downstream effects, consequences in the future. The implication is that loving the past enriches the future by virtue of going 'contrary to the prevailing current' (Forster 1972a: 196), against the impulsion of the genealogical imperative. The result is reversionary *and* progressive all at once. The novel's developmental plot is thus bidirectional, charting 'propagation at both ends' (*HE* 275). One end tends towards development, following the forward but catabolic drive associated with Paul and the *Bildung* plot, a movement in which 'man . . . digest[s] his own soul' (*HE* 275). The other end tends backwards, towards the real but hidden cause of Helen's exile, the gestation of a new soul, associated with Leonard and the family novel.

Helen's pregnancy, significantly, reverses yet another case of entropic dissolution: her estrangement from Margaret. Like the Wilcoxes, who drift apart after Ruth's death (*HE* 157), and the Basts, who become estranged after Leonard's marriage (*HE* 234), the sisters are from the start 'beginning to diverge' (*HE* 28). 'The widest gulf' separates them by the time Margaret accepts Mr Wilcox's proposal (*HE* 171), and the gulf yawns widest after Mr Wilcox hastens Leonard's ruin. Seeing Helen pregnant by Leonard recalls Margaret to their bond:

> they never could be parted because their love was rooted in common things . . . All the time their salvation was lying round them – the past sanctifying the present; the present, with wild heart-throb, declaring that there would after all be a future, with laughter and the voices of children. (*HE* 296)

The temporality suggested by this passage is not that of time's entropic arrow – the chronology which would dictate the individual's recapitulatory progress from infancy to maturity. It is a 'tangle' in which the past (*HE* 334), not simply left behind by the present and future, can return like the 'old gap' in 'the hedge that divided' Howards End from its neighbour, a gap 'Mr. Wilcox had filled up' but which has now 'reappeared' (*HE* 311). This is the gap which allows Miss Avery to ignore decorum and cross property lines towards Howards End, leaving a 'track through the dew [that] followed the path that [Mr Wilcox] had turfed over' (*HE* 311), on her way to prepare the house for Helen's arrival. The re-emergence of the buried path overlays the house's past with its current state, 'sanctifying' it and preparing it for 'the voices of children' to come (*HE* 296). There is an unmistakable analogy here between Miss Avery's earthy aristocracy and the Mendelian reversion 'to a nobler stock' awaiting Leonard in the person of his son (*HE* 320).

A Final Contretemps

Working this Mendelian logic into *Howards End*, Forster bridges physical and spiritual inheritance. Ruth 'believed so in ancestors' (*HE* 97), though not in a way her husband or children comprehend. For them, her act of dissociating blood and property is 'Treachery' (*HE* 97). They value ancestry and houses financially or sentimentally, and though they think 'home life is what distinguishes us from the foreigner' (*HE* 257), they are always 'on the move' (*HE* 134). In this Henry's 'children have all taken after him' (*HE* 73), joining the 'nomadic horde' which 'accrete[s] possessions without taking root in the earth' (*HE* 146). Ruth's idea of succession, by contrast, has more to do with place than with blood: if she 'cared about her ancestors' (*HE* 19), it is because they went 'back to the land' (*HE* 205). She recognises her 'spiritual heir' in Margaret (*HE* 96) because Margaret too deplores the modern 'craze for motion' (*HE* 337) and longs for a return to the grounded ways of the past. In choosing her heir, Ruth apparently takes the long view, for it is Leonard who must 'get back to the Earth' (*HE* 115) – literally in death, figuratively by 'breeding yeomen' (*HE* 320).

Ruth's leitmotif is hay, and the novel's final words – 'it'll be such a crop of hay as never' (*HE* 340) – hint that the house will revert to the Howards even as it shelters Schlegels, Wilcoxes and Basts. Strictly speaking, the Howards are dying out. The survivors (Ruth's children and grandchildren) are barred from the house by biological inheritance (hereditary hay fever) and inheritance law (Henry's new will). But the Howards will survive, non-genetically, thanks to other kinds of connection. Almost all we know of them, including their link to Miss Avery, is revealed by the endearingly tactless Dolly Wilcox: 'Hadn't Mrs. Wilcox a brother', she muses, 'or was it an uncle? Anyhow, he popped the question, and Miss Avery, she said "No." . . . Tom Howard – he was the last of them . . . I say! Howards End – Howard's Ended!' (*HE* 201). In her laboured wordplay, Dolly unwittingly reveals a truth her in-laws could not have imagined: the Howard line and Howards End are one. She also uncovers crucial non-genetic links between Ruth, Miss Avery, Margaret and Leonard's son.[9] There is more joining Ruth and Margaret than marriage to the same man; they have the same 'way of walking', and Miss Avery finds them interchangeable (*HE* 199, 267–8). Margaret is also symbolically of Miss Avery's family: who first leads her to Howards End but Miss Avery's niece Madge, a diminutive Margaret?

These non-genetic connections come closest to cohering at the novel's end. The hope raised by Leonard and Helen's son is partly genealogical: he perpetuates their line. Equally significant, though, is the baby's bond with Madge's son. The boy's name, Tom (*HE* 297), echoes Tom Howard, who would have kept the house in the Howard family, had he lived to procreate. Young Tom has no Howard blood, but the rhythmic logic of Fosterian narrative makes him a Howard anyway – through the symbolism of his name, his physical proximity to Howards End, his work on Howard land, even his aunt Miss Avery's counterfactual marriage to Tom Howard. The boy's link to Howards End is finally formalised by his friendship and (as Forsterian antecedents suggest) future homoerotic bond to Helen's son. A 'wonderful nursemaid', Tom takes the baby 'to play with hay', stakes his legitimate claim on Howards End through the promise of a 'lifelong' friendship (*HE* 333). Ultimately, then, the house will revert to both Leonard's son and to young Tom. Howards End's heir, or rather heirs, are like Jacky's 'hair, or rather hairs', combining the reversionary genealogical stream going 'down her back' and the future-oriented stream 'created for a higher destiny' (*HE* 48).

So the house returns to the yeoman stock characterised by Miss Avery's 'unostentatious nobility' and by Ruth's 'instinctive wisdom . . . to which we give the clumsy name of aristocracy' (*HE* 267, 19). It is 'not an aristocracy of power, based on rank and influence' (*TC* 70) but, as Forster advocates in 'What I Believe', 'an aristocracy of the sensitive, the considerate and the plucky . . . found in all nations and classes' (*TC* 70). Rather than division, but also against the greyness of too homogeneous a unity, this aristocracy 'represent[s] the true human tradition, the one permanent victory of our queer race over cruelty and chaos' (*TC* 70). It takes all kinds to make a Forsterian aristocrat, and in *Howards End* the characters who finally inherit the house are products of mixed blood and mixed inheritances. This mix is not a union or synthesis but a weave – a 'rainbow bridge' (*HE* 183) – whose beauty inheres in the combined effect of multi-coloured, distinct threads.

Even optimistic readers of *Howards End* must acknowledge that its happy ending is happier for some than for others. Its happiness is also under threat: the 'permanent' idyll of Howards End, though 'coloured' by Helen and Margaret's 'memories', is endangered by the 'creeping' entropy of London's 'red rust', itself 'only part' of a global tendency towards sameness (*HE* 337). As Margaret puts it, 'life's going to be melted down, all over the world' (*HE* 337). Places like Howards End, she admits, are merely 'survivals, and the melting-pot was being prepared for them. Logically, they had no right to be alive' (*HE* 337). Still, Margaret dares to put her 'hope . . . in the weakness of logic' (*HE* 337). It is a hope Forster delivers, thematically and structurally, throughout the novel. Margaret can therefore allow herself to comfort Helen by citing the possibility of a historical return, a reversion whose unlikelihood is mitigated by the reality of Mendelian throwbacks:

> This craze for motion has only set in during the last hundred years. It may be followed by a civilization that won't be a movement, because it will rest on the earth. All the signs are against it now, but I can't help hoping, and very early in the morning in the garden I feel that our house is the future as well as the past. (*HE* 337)

A scientific vision may not seem especially suitable to those who hang their hopes on 'the weakness of logic' (*HE* 337). 'Science', Forster wrote in a letter to Lorna Wood in 1919, 'will get deeper into the facts of life, and the *fact* of life will always elude it, like the retreating rainbow' (1983: 301). Be that as it may, Forster seems to have recognised the power of new scientific ideas – the power to defy conventional logic. By favouring 'the rainbow bridge' (*HE* 183) over the 'universal gray' (*HE* 125), *Howards End* suggests that although science 'will never explain the ultimate constitution' (Forster 1983: 301), it may help us see our own constitution anew. As Clarke Nuttall writes in an early attempt to bring Mendelism to 'the general public', the 'larger value' of the 'new era in the study of heredity' is its 'suggestiveness; . . . it stimulates the imagination with its possibilities; it opens up a fresh point of view from which to make observations . . .' (1908: 529).

After reading Eddington's *Nature of the Physical World* in 1928, Forster marvelled that 'our spasmotic instincts and confusions about time have a value which "Astronomer Royal" time hasn't, that one thing – the quantum – appears to have absolute existence in the physical world' (1985: 46). These facts have no direct link with genetics and genealogy in *Howards End*, yet conceptually the 'quantum' is a subatomic counterpart of Mendel's atomistic gene, and the relativities of post-Einsteinian time mirror the independent trajectories of Mendelian traits from generation to generation. In any case, Helen is wrong to think that her plans for herself and her baby 'won't be changed by a slight contretemps' (*HE* 291); the contretemps is actually what ensures their 'futures' (*HE* 291). *Contre-temps*, against-time, aptly captures the novel's reversionary impulse.[10] A term from music, prosody and dance, contretemps is peculiarly well suited for the poetics of reversionary modernist fiction, in which, as Woolf proclaims, 'the accent falls a little differently' (*EVW* iv.162). Margaret and Leonard certainly live slightly off-beat. Each is somehow out of time, out of the main genealogical current: Margaret is intentionally childless, Leonard a case of 'degeneracy' (*HE* 249); measured by contemporary norms they both 'cannot develop as they are supposed to develop' (*HE* 335). Mendelian logic defies these norms by allowing both to benefit – indirectly, but undeniably – because her nephew, his son, will 'throw back to a nobler stock' (*HE* 320).

Notes

1. Leonard Bast plays a similar mediating role between the diverging Wilcox and Schlegel families, but contrarily to Carpenter's model it is the reproductive function which bridges opposing sensibilities, both of them coded as non-reproductive and non-biological – the Schlegels are linked with culture and idealism, the Wilcoxes with tradition and 'the sneaking belief that bodily passion is bad' (*HE* 183).
2. The motifs circulating along and across genealogical lines include the resemblance to rabbits which links the Wilcoxes (*HE* 1–2, 3, 271) to Tibby (*HE* 8, 297) and to Leonard (*HE* 44), as well as to the clerks working at the Wilcoxes' West African Rubber Company (*HE* 193); the affliction of hay fever which links the Wilcoxes to Tibby (*HE* 269–70); and the rhythmic association with hay and grass which connects Ruth Wilcox to Margaret, Helen, Leonard, Miss Avery, Madge's husband, young Tom and Helen's baby (*HE* 2, 19, 71, 96, 245, 270, 297, 327, 331, 333, 340). There are also bonds of special friendships between Ruth and Margaret, between Margaret and Helen, and between young Tom and Helen's son.
3. 'Reversion' is defined in inheritance law as 'The return of an estate to the original owner, or his or her heirs, after the expiry of a grant or death of the grantee' (*OED* n^{1b}).
4. The best account of *Howards End*'s engagement with *Bildung* (though the term is never used) is David Deutsch's (2010) study of music, cultural development and liberal humanism in the novel. Peter Firchow quotes Forster's manuscript note that Margaret and Helen's father Ernst was 'a distant relation of the great critic' (presumably August or Friedrich von Schlegel), stressing the influence of German Romanticism on *Howards End* and the 'background of Father Schlegel and his children' as 'the biological and spiritual descendants of Romantic, idealist Germany' (1981: 57–8).
5. It is Leonard's quasi-atavistic contact with the land rather than his theories which prompts Margaret to call him 'a real man' (*HE* 144). The novel makes it clear his decline is not genetic but precipitated by his poverty and 'the terrible necessity of

being cultured' identified by Trilling as 'the new obligation that democracy has brought' (1962: 111).

6. Forster would return to the oscillation between Wilcox-style progress and Schlegel-style reversionary stillness in 'What I Believe'. Initially opposing Social Darwinism, with its efficiency and force to the calm needed for 'civilization', he finally admits that 'all society rests upon force' (*TC* 68). True development, however, depends on times of calm: 'all the great creative actions, all the decent human relations, occur during the intervals when force has not managed to come to the front' (*TC* 68). Overlooking these 'periods of quiet that are essential to true growth' (*HE* 77) is one of Margaret's failures, though one she ultimately redresses.
7. Forster's rivers are also symbolic routes to the world of fantasy where, as Miracky (2003) observes, there is room for homoerotic camaraderie, friendship, spiritual unions (*HE* 46, 151). Looking up the river from Oniton, Margaret thinks 'Fairy-land must lie above the bend' (*HE* 221). She is right: the 'murmurs of the river that descended all the night from Wales' (*HE* 236) link Margaret and Helen symbolically and structurally; its 'murmurings' (*HE* 240) fill the air when they are most divided, one of them betraying Leonard with a hypocritical letter, the other bedding him through misguided pity; the sound of the water anticipates the reconciliation occasioned by Helen's pregnancy, at Howards End.
8. Entropy threatens not only the fortunes of Howards End's legatee Charles Wilcox, but also the gradual extinction of the Howards, who lose the house because 'things went on until there were no men' (*HE* 271). This extinction mirrors the 'decline of the [British] birth-rate' which so worries Mr Cunningham (*HE* 45).
9. Forsterian 'rhythm' (*AN* 112) is one means of dissociating modernist narrative from story's 'time-sequence' and plot's 'causality' (*AN* 20, 60). Crucially, rhythm can forge atemporal or anti-chronological relations because it operates by 'radiat[ing] in several directions' (*AN* 114).
10. The 'contretemps' (*HE* 291) recalls the easily overlooked character of Tibby Schlegel, who, 'profoundly versed in counterpoint' (*HE* 29), is *Howards End*'s quiet spokesman for the homoerotic underplot.

4

'TAMPERING WITH THE EXPECTED SEQUENCE': HETEROCHRONY AND SEX CHANGE IN *ORLANDO*

> Something that everyone disapproved of, something that linked the present to that early continuous development, before school, war and a thousand tiny barriers had divided her spirit into a dozen diverse strands.
>
> – Bryher, *Two Selves* (2000: 266)

When, in the middle of Virginia Woolf's *Orlando*, the protagonist awakens to find 'he was a woman' (*O* 137), the narrator does not linger on causes and explanations. Remarkably casual in the face of the transformation, she offers merely the 'simple fact' that 'Orlando was a man till the age of thirty; when he became a woman and has remained so ever since' (*O* 139). There is then little to add, other than to normalise the metamorphosis further: 'the change seemed to have been accomplished painlessly and completely and in such a way that Orlando herself showed no surprise at it' (*O* 139). Woolf's narrator admits 'many people' will think 'such a change in sex is against nature', but she refuses to sensationalise or explicate the event, leaving it to 'other pens [to] treat of sex and sexuality' (*O* 139). As to the identity of these 'other pens', she offers only a hint, albeit an intriguing one: 'Let biologists and psychologists determine' (*O* 139).

Apparently dismissing science, she may also be inviting us to take her at her word. On information pointedly omitted by the narrator, 'biologists' might have something to say. Jean-Jacques Mayoux thought as much, noting in a review of *Orlando* that 'this change of sex' and the fact that 'sexes intermix' reflect 'the very opinions of contemporary biology' (1930: 119). Mayoux says nothing else on the topic, but he is right. Beginning in the 1910s with Richard Goldschmidt's moth-breeding experiments, the study of sex determination would become by the early 1920s one of 'the most active lines of work' in genetics and sexual physiology (Gates 1921: 571). It would radically reimagine sex as fluid and variable, and though its findings were based mainly on insects and frogs, they inevitably implicated humans. 'The fact of intersexuality' in animals very different from us, argues Julian Huxley, 'shows us that we may have to revise not only our moral judgments but our legal practice with regard to various abnormalities of sex in human beings' (1922c: 241). It also suggests an intriguing link between biology and *Orlando*'s depictions of sex and sexuality. What, then, might the 'biologists' determine in the curious case of Orlando? More generally, how might a *Bildungsroman* exploit the modernist biology of sex in order to dispense with recapitulatory models of sexual development, thereby enabling wholesale re-visions of character and the relations between life and history, between mind and body, and of course between gender and sex? Taking these biological models into consideration, this chapter presents *Orlando* as a far more innovative response to the problematics of female *Bildung* than most critics acknowledge. Founding a *Bildungsroman* on alternatives to the recapitulatory models of sexual development inherent in contemporary psychoanalysis and sexology, Woolf imagines *Bildung* outside the traditional binaries of sex/gender, body/mind, nature/culture and woman/man.

Biology is thus critical to *Orlando*'s feminism. If such a statement seems counterintuitive, it is only because feminist theory has, as Stacy Alaimo points out, too often dismissed biology for 'serv[ing] the armory of racist, sexist, and heterosexist norms' (2010: 6). This reaction is understandable but unfortunate, for it paints with a single brush a science expansive enough to contribute productively to feminist thought: 'the notion of biology as destiny, which has long haunted feminism, depends on a particular – if not peculiar – notion of biology that can certainly be displaced by other models' (Alaimo 2010: 6). In the context of the early twentieth century, the kind of biology rejected by Alaimo – deterministic, hierarchical, complicit with the exclusions of patriarchy, imperialism and sexual morality – is epitomised by recapitulation theory, while her 'other models' would correspond to the alternatives of modernist biology.

Orlando is coy about biology. The other novels examined in this book flag their complex biological engagements, often quite literally; lacking such explicit allusions, *Orlando*'s biological engagements are more circumstantial and tenuous. This is not, however, to call it insignificant. Woolf was a keen naturalist, knowledgeable about plants, birds and especially butterflies and moths, and her appreciation of Darwin and T. H. Huxley is well documented

(Alt 2010: 38). She was also attentive to contemporary biology, citing Julian Huxley in *Three Guineas* (1998: 412n48) and dabbling in 1931 into *The Science of Life* (Alt 2010: 38), in which she may have read passages on 'sex reversal' and 'intersexes' (Wells et al. 1937: 568, 569–75). These examples postdate the publication of *Orlando*, but Woolf also offers hints of an earlier interest in modernist biology. She mentions Mendelism in *Night and Day* and in *Mrs Dalloway*, for example. She knew J. B. S. Haldane by 1924 and Julian Huxley probably even earlier,[1] and may have heard about cutting-edge biology from them or from their specialised or popular writings.[2] She may also have heard about contemporary problems in biology from Huxley's and Haldane's literary siblings, Aldous Huxley and Naomi Mitchison. In 1915 Mitchison, a possible model for Olivia in *A Room of One's Own*, co-wrote an article with her brother which appeared in the *Journal of Genetics*; the article 'was known to Woolf' and 'resonates', observes Aaron Jaffe, with her interest in the 'link between education and experiment, communication and biology' (2016: 493).

The best reason to read *Orlando* biologically lies, paradoxically, in those aspects which seem most unnatural and thus remote from biological possibility: extreme longevity and sex change. Few character developments seem less scientific than Orlando's change from male to female, and most interpretations of *Orlando* celebrate it as a critique of or escape from biological determinism. Melanie Micir pits the novel's fantastical aspects against common-sense but ideologically suspect 'somatic and social facts', identifying its 'combination of reality and fantasy' as a solution to 'the major problem with biography' – 'its inviolable progression of the body through time' (2012: 12). Because they are so strange, Orlando's lifespan and sex change tend to lead interpretation away from science towards allegory and symbolism. Karen Kaivola, for example, argues that Woolf 'playfully posits a vision of identity that transcends the physical sex of the body' (1999: 235), while Jill Channing proposes that, 'paradoxically and magically, Orlando is able to embody a plethora of sexualities' which 'Woolf would not have been able to overtly express' in realistic ways (2005: 11). In the specific context of the *Bildungsroman*, Helena Feder considers the sex change a case of 'fantastic wish-fulfillment' which 'defies human logic and the "laws of nature"' in order to elude the 'specter of biology' (2014: 90, 75). Intuitive as they are, such readings overlook a simple question posed by Pamela Caughie in a loosely related context: if Woolf's goal is to free biography from the constraints of biological existence, 'is a sex change necessary for that?' (Caughie 2013: 518). By way of answer, I would caution against too quickly reading the sex change as a rejection of biology, not least because the transformation happens *to* the body and affects biological sex rather than cultural gender and sexuality. Woolf's experiment in *Orlando* is radical not because it denies biological sex but because it so thoroughly reimagines how biological sex – reconceived as a dynamic and fluid aspect of development – participates in self-formation.

Without dismissing figural, imminent-critical or psychoanalytic interpretations of Orlando's strange life history, I propose a more significant role for the novel's bodily aspects and their illuminating links with contemporary genetics. The sex change is not, or not only, an allegory for transsexuality or lesbianism, not merely an oblique stand-in for a transgression which, if named, would invite censure and censorship. The sex change is also, literally, the bodily transformation of a man into a woman. The question of why Woolf would stage such an event is central to her exploration of sex and gender in the process of *Bildung*. Because the body is central to that process, *Orlando*'s depiction of development is more engaged with biology than Feder recognises when she concludes that 'the specter of biology haunting biography, feminism, and history (the body, the more-than-human world), like the many selves floating inside Orlando, becomes something joyfully, materially mysterious rather than a threat to be conquered' (2014: 96). Neither a foil nor vaguely 'something joyfully, materially mysterious', modernist biology and its reconceptions of the developing body help define the nature and politics of *Orlando*'s unnatural narrative.

Orlando and the Double Bind of Female *Bildung*

Sex was an important consideration for the early theorists of *Bildung*. Essential biological differences between the sexes, they believed, limited full developmental potentiality to men; 'by equating women with nature', writes Todd Kontje, these theorists 'denied women any chance of participating in the process of *Bildung*' (1993: 7). For this reason the female *Bildungsroman* has always offered a vexed picture of development as a conflict between the ideal of individual autonomy and the familial relationality which defines traditional female roles. The result, argues Susan Fraiman (1994), is a persistent focus on *Bildung* not only as a given trajectory and goal, but as an ill-fitting imposition to be treated ironically and dismantled in search of other narrative possibilities. Almost by definition, then, the female *Bildungsroman* tends to foreground techniques akin to those I call modernist reversions. As Ruth Parkin-Gounelas observes, '"progress"' in Victorian female *Bildungsromane* 'seemed not linear but circular, from one domestic sphere to another, and maturity more often meant a return to, rather than a casting off of, fundamental childhood concerns' (1991: 19). In this context, Orlando's sex change from male to female is a modernist reformulation of the problem, a reversionary disruption of the recapitulatory progressivism which equated maleness with maturity.

In structure and style, *Orlando* seems less innovative than Woolf's more celebrated novels of development. *Orlando* might consequently seem less critical, less modernist than *Jacob's Room*, *Mrs Dalloway*, *To the Lighthouse* and *The Waves*. These novels retain some 'narrative patterns' of the *Bildung* plot but only 'to disrupt them or reveal their insignificance' (Abel 1983: 161); *Orlando*, meanwhile, limns closer to the structure of the classical *Bildungsroman*. The contrast is superficial, however. *Orlando*'s plot may be more legible, but it is innovative and strange in ways which exceed simple formalism. Formal devices and patterns are not limited to one ideology, and even canonical plot structures mean differently depending on who writes them and who inhabits them (Felski 1995: 149). The most traditional use of the *Bildung* plot can be disruptive if the protagonist's identity deviates somehow from expectations. Merely casting a woman as the hero of a *Bildungsroman* would thus challenge the conventions by which the form delivers its content. Woolf takes the challenge much further than casting a female protagonist, of course. Uncoupling, by means of the sex change, the parallel between sexual and socio-artistic development, she thereby simultaneously dismantles the parallel between the female body, conceived as more primitive and immature than the male, and women's limited capacity for aesthetic and social formation. Thus *Orlando* rehabilitates the ideal of *Bildung* by releasing it from the plot of female formation exemplified by *Jane Eyre*, *The Mill on the Floss* and even *The Voyage Out*, novels in which sex (and the gendered identities founded on the sexed body) limits the possibility and extent of self-realisation. This equation depends on a fixed correlation between bodily form and psycho-social development which uses the female body as an insurmountable impediment to mental, moral and social development. The view was so thoroughly naturalised that Geddes and Thomson simply have to 'insist upon the biological considerations underlying the relation of the sexes' (1889: 267) to confirm what was, as they point out, obvious to most biologists (1889: 37). Women's inferiority was determined aeons ago, they argue, before making an infamous proclamation: 'what was decided among the prehistoric Protozoa cannot be annulled by Act of Parliament' (Geddes and Thomson 1889: 267). In short, 'the development of woman is early arrested by procreative functions' (Geddes and Thomson 1889: 37). Given this context, Woolf's decision to locate Orlando's dramatic transformation in the body can be read in two ways, neither likely to please Geddes and Thomson. The first is simply to adapt Geddes and Thomson's logic to the new data provided by the novel: Orlando's change into a woman, followed by social and artistic success, would thus suggest that the superior sex is in fact women. The second and more radical reading is that that establishing superiority on such grounds is untenable or, as Stephen Jay Gould writes of ranking races and sexes on developmental scales, 'fundamentally unjustified' (1996: 150). Undoubtedly Woolf would have favoured the second reading. By incorporating Orlando's development, then, Woolf paradoxically releases the narrative of female *Bildung* from the myth of anatomy as destiny.

Orlando's plotting is therefore much less conventional than its apparently linear narrative makes it seem. The equation of linearity and normativity is itself facile, as Brian Richardson has rightly insisted. Many counter-ideological narratives are chronological, notes Richardson, citing *Orlando* as a pre-eminent exemplar. The argument bears repeating. It is often unclear, however, how critics including Richardson understand narrative linearity. Richardson writes that 'even *Orlando*'s differential chronologies, in which the protagonist ages at a different rate from those around her/him, are linear' (2000: 686) – 'linear' because the novel's many individual or historical plots are all chronological. Yet chronology, the one-to-one correspondence of story order and discourse order, is only one of many features of narrative linearity. Linearity is not a single device but a syndrome of formal features – including chronology but also gradual change, unbroken succession, more or less consistent pacing and the illusion of causal coherence – whose combined effect is to naturalise plots. With its sex change and inexplicable shifts in mode and tempo, as well as its frequent metafictional intrusions, *Orlando* is clearly non-linear. Its individual and historical plots may be chronological, but two or more chronologies do not produce a linear plot unless they are also isometric, or parallel. *Orlando*'s timelines proceed, as Richardson puts it, at 'different rate[s]' (2000: 686). Taken together, 'differential chronologies' (Richardson 2000: 686) are by definition relativistic and non-linear, even if each timeline is linear on its own.[3]

The non-linearity of *Orlando*'s narrative is especially visible in its parody of periodisation,[4] 'a key organising feature of Victorian historical discourse' (de Gay 2006: 139). In this respect, Woolf's parodic energies are also implicitly directed against recapitulation theory, in which the order and progressive succession of historical stages are necessarily identified and morally coded. Instead of representing history as a continuous linear movement from sixteenth to twentieth century, Woolf depicts the Renaissance, Enlightenment and 'present moment' (*O* 298) as a discontinuous series linked by aesthetic and other social affinities. History is a pendulum rather than a progression, and because Orlando is comically susceptible to 'the spirit of the age' (*O* 236), her development as a character and artist is likewise fitful and recursive. Woolf's novel thus questions the related notions of development as sublative progress and of 'history as a discourse that kills off the past' (de Gay 2006: 142). Orlando's history is not a one-dimensional line from past to present but a multidimensional space, and the novel therefore represents memory 'spatially rather than temporally, so that [the past] still exists to be viewed from the present' (de Gay 2006: 142). Neither inert and fossilised nor superseded and obsolete, the past is a 'raging torrent beneath' Orlando 'as she crossed the narrow plank of the present' (*O* 299). At 'the oncome of middle age' in the 1920s, Orlando senses that 'time has passed over me', suggesting a sense of having fallen out of step with history (*O* 304). If so she is not wrong, but another implication asserts itself: time past has washed over her like a wave, mixing with time present. In either case, the novel's various temporal scales are not isometric. In the resulting mix 'nothing is any longer one thing' (*O* 305). The realities of 1928 are also, for Orlando, reversions. Her immediate impressions, 'when I step out of doors – as I do now' (*O* 305), reflect her current surroundings but also revive the 'little herbs', 'goat bells' and 'mountains' of her youth (*O* 305). This living past makes of her an amalgam rather than a culmination of her history, a multiplicity composed of 'these selves of which we are built up, one on top of another, as plates are piled on a waiter's hand . . .; for everybody can multiply from his own experience the different terms which his different selves have made with him' (*O* 307–8). In no way does such a life history recapitulate an ideal, original order.

I will return to the relation between Orlando's 'different selves' and the novel's structure. First, it is necessary to stress how the novel's deceptive linearity relates to its content, an issue overlooked in Richardson's discussion of linearity but crucial to the specifics of Orlando's sex change from man to woman. Non-linearity is never exclusively an issue of form; it is, rather, a deliberate or unwitting mismatch of form and content. When a female protagonist bears children before (or without) marrying, for example, the thematic event is also implicated inextricably in narrative structure; mistiming motherhood relative to marriage, the protagonist shuffles the expected story and violates the conventions of the genre (whether *Bildungsroman*, family novel, or marriage plot).

The sex change is *Orlando*'s most glaring transgression, but Orlando's extreme longevity also wreaks havoc with the *Bildung* plot as a particularly integrated nexus of content and form. Her extended lifespan releases her from having to settle for either one of the two compromised endings awaiting protagonists of classical female *Bildungsromane*: dying young or 'becom[ing] vessels of descent . . .: child-bearing' (Beer 1996: 14). Only by perishing can Rachel Vinrace in *The Voyage Out* escape a developmental plot whose *telos* is marriage and procreation. Woolf, in her discussion of modern women's fiction in *A Room of One's Own*, lavishes great praise on the (fictitious) novel *Life's Adventure* because its protagonist Olivia manages to elude Rachel's awful sacrifice. Olivia enjoys motherhood and marriage at home alongside a satisfying professional life in a biological laboratory with her friend and colleague Chloe (*ROO* 110). For Olivia, reproduction is neither 'the beginning of death' (*PA* 230) nor the end of development. Longevity grants the same advantage to Orlando, offering her a richness and diversity of experience which would not fit into 'the sixty-eight or seventy-two years' of a normal life (*O* 305). Her ontogeny stretches out so long that she matures enough to publish her life's work, 'The Oak Tree', without forgoing love, marriage or motherhood.[5] Orlando's procreative act occurs late enough in her life not to interfere with her *Bildung*; she bears her son without sacrificing any personal experience to the genealogical imperative. She has world enough and time to be a profligate youth, diplomat, exile among gypsies, socialite and successful poet; she exuberantly exploits the many ways of being which a long life allows her. I will return later in the chapter to the formal consequences of this experiential diversity. It is worth stressing one final point about the son's arrival, however, which is its irrelevance, its complete lack of impact on the plot of Orlando's development. From the perspective of her artistic, romantic or quotidian life, the birth is a non-event.

Troubling sexual categories, *Orlando* brings female *Bildung* into conflict with traditional conceptions of sex, gender and sexuality, but also, more complexly, with the more recent models and politics of sexology. In the early twentieth century, some sexologists aggressively pathologised non-normative sexualities, while others concealed a progressive agenda under a façade of scientific objectivity. There is a well-recognised relation between sexology and literary modernism, as Richard Brown, Barbara Fassler and others have shown, and indeed Paul Peppis has grouped some literary and sexological texts under the umbrella 'sexological modernism' (2014: 103). Anticipating the now better-known Alfred Kinsey, British sexologists Havelock Ellis, J. Arthur Symonds and Edward Carpenter participated in a broader modernist reaction against moral and legal parochialism. Unsurprisingly, this project implicates *Bildung*, since sexual life was by the turn of the twentieth century viewed as a central site of identity formation as well as psychophysical development. The relation between *Bildung* and sexuality is pertinent to any form of ostensibly deviant sexuality – including female sexuality – but it is particularly stark in the case of male homosexuality. As Peppis contends, the understated polemic of Ellis's *Sexual Inversion* (co-authored with an uncredited Symonds) is couched explicitly within 'the Enlightenment philosophical and literary paradigm of *Bildung*, adapting its ideals of individual development, education and social integration to the project of homosexual apology and sex reform while rejecting *Bildung*'s common connection to heterosexual romance and marriage' (2014: 103). This ambivalence towards the *Bildung* tradition is analogous, though not identical, to the complicated situation which Fraiman and others detect in the female *Bildungsroman*.

Despite the undeniably transgressive open-mindedness of some of its practitioners, however, sexology was unable to produce radical critiques of sexual and gender categories. Its critical power was limited by the contradictions Peppis identifies in both *Sexual Inversion* and Forster's *Maurice*. Both texts, Peppis argues, 'normalize homosexuals and homosexuality, delivering them from the margins of pathology', yet both also 'resist the implications of their own arguments, unwilling or unable to pursue their critiques of the Victorian sex system as far as they might, as far as some modernist literary texts later will' (2014: 102). Such limitations notwithstanding, Peppis is right to defend

Sexual Inversion and *Maurice* 'as significant works of sexological modernism' (2014: 103). As for the more radical critiques Peppis attributes to Joyce, Barnes, Stein and Loy, though, these do not represent a more thoroughgoing 'sexological modernism'; they were possible only by dispensing with the 'sexological' altogether.

The limitations of sexological thinking are evident in *Bildungsromane* informed or influenced by that science, including Radclyffe Hall's *The Well of Loneliness* and Bryher's *Development* and *Two Selves*.[6] The protagonists in these novels clearly manifest symptoms of sexual inversion as theorised by sexologists – as a mismatch between female body and male psyche. Like Hall's heroine Stephen Gordon, Bryher's Nancy experiences what we would now call gender dysphoria. This condition, she imagines, could be resolved through a sex change which would grant her a boy's body to match her 'boy's heart' (Bryher 2000: 156). A sex change would align Nancy's sexuality and gender not only with her anatomy but also with her traditionally male aspirations to be a poet, sailor, archaeologist and palaeontologist. By relying on sexologists such as Ellis and Symonds for their understanding of sexual development, Bryher as well as Hall end up replicating notions of sexual development which, according to Jeffrey Weeks, 'fit into existing concepts. In so doing they failed to develop a radical critique of sexual oppression' (1977: 50). I do not mean to dispute the transgressive and critical powers of novels such as those by Hall and Bryher; nor would I say they fail to challenge prejudices which found scientific support in the biogenetic law. Yet because sexology and the narratives it inspires retain pre-existing categories and hierarchies, their transgressions are better suited to challenging moral and legal attitudes than to radically reconfiguring sex, gender and sexuality.

In *Orlando*, by contrast, Woolf presents a very different perspective on *Bildung* and sexual identity, a difference foregrounded when the protagonist undergoes the sex change Bryher's Nancy so desired but, crucially, in the opposite direction. What is most significant about the transformation is not its effect in propelling or impeding Orlando's self-formation but, rather, its lack of consequence for her gender and sexuality. After the sex change, indeed, the narrator pointedly notes that 'in every other respect, Orlando remained precisely as he had been' (*O* 138). This inconsequentiality is remarkable because a sex change should, it would seem, change everything. Orlando's self-consistency is thus perhaps the most radical aspect of her reversionary sex change, just as Gregor Samsa's transformation is stranger for leaving his human mind intact (intact and, indeed, endowed with aesthetic sensibilities he lacked as a human). Far from solving the problem of a 'feminine soul enclosed in a male body' (Carpenter 1918: 19), Orlando's new female body has no stabilising or unifying effect on her rebelliously polyvalent identity and sexuality. In no way does Woolf present the sex change as the discovery of Orlando's 'real self'

(O 314), as such a transformation would have for Nancy or Stephen Gordon. Few notions are more suspect in *Orlando*, indeed, than the 'real self' – an ideal whose embodiment in the novel is, fittingly, a 'wild goose' (O 313).

A key difference between 'sexological modernism' (Peppis 2014: 103) and the more transgressive sexual modernism of *Orlando* lies in their differing relationships with recapitulation theory. Recapitulation formed the theoretical bedrock of early twentieth-century sexology, just as it did in its close relative, psychoanalysis. Carrying this theoretical burden, even the most progressive sexologist could not avoid seeing homosexuality and even femaleness as development gone wrong or left incomplete. Implicit in such claims is the idea that normal sexual development in the individual recapitulates the evolution of sexuality from the undifferentiated asexuality of unicellular organisms, through the hermaphroditism of snails, earthworms and some fish, to the fully differentiated sexes of humans and other so-called higher animals (Darwin 1981: i.207–8). Goethe's model of plant metamorphosis thus considers reproduction by 'two genders' to be the top rung of nature's 'spiritual ladder' (1988: 76). The more differentiated the two sexes, then, the more advanced the species; the more differentiated the individual, the greater its development. For sexologists, then, imperfect differentiation in any form – including hermaphroditism, androgyny, gender dysphoria and homosexuality – is an arrest in development which leaves the individual stuck at an immature stage. 'At conception', writes Havelock Ellis, a person has

> about 50 per cent. of male germs and about 50 per cent. of female germs, and . . ., as development proceeds, either the male or the female germs assume the upper hand, until in the maturely developed individual only a few aborted germs of the opposite sex are left. In the homosexual, however, . . . the process has not proceeded normally. (H. Ellis 1906: 184)

'Inversion', Ellis adds, is the result of 'twisted' development (1906: 184), when female and male elements fail to become fully segregated. Though males and females contribute equally to procreation, however, most sexologists assumed that femaleness was less differentiated, less evolved and less mature, than maleness. Thus the 'tendency for sexual inverts to approach the feminine type' (H. Ellis 1906: 167) is homologous and not merely analogous with the 'tendency for inverted persons to be somewhat arrested in development, approaching the child type' (H. Ellis 1906: 172). Given the recapitulatory basis of sexological models of development, the homosexual is analogous with the child and the woman – all incomplete versions of male, heterosexual maturity.

As Ellis's parallels between 'invert', 'child' and 'feminine type' suggest, sexological models of development provide crucial context for Woolf's novel not only as an exploration of same-sex desire and love but also, and perhaps more profoundly, as a study of female development. In Peppis's study, sexology informs narrative experimentation from Edwardian through to high-modernist literature. There are indeed some similarities between efforts by sexologists 'to make *Bildung* . . . available to English homosexuals' (Peppis 2014: 104) and Woolf's attempt to make the *Bildungsroman* possible for a female artist. Yet those similarities are overstated by Peppis when he draws a direct connection between the 'early modernism' of 'new woman' and 'homosexual' novels like *Maurice* (2014: 145) and what he calls 'queer modernism' (2014: 124). This literary genealogy smooths over differences more profound than mere historical and aesthetic 'distance' (Peppis 2014: 107) between the 'sexological modernism' of Ellis and Forster and the 'intimati[ons]' of 'postmodernism and queer theory' in works 'like Stein's *Tender Buttons*, Woolf's *Orlando*, or Barnes's *Nightwood*' (Peppis 2014: 124). In *Orlando*, as in the other high-modernist works, the challenge posed to traditional thinking, and the narrative forms deployed to explore and enact that challenge, go far beyond normalising purportedly aberrant sexualities.

Recapitulation theory's hold of late nineteenth- and early twentieth-century thought hung to a great extent from the lynchpin of women's childlike primitiveness. In the popular late-Victorian textbook *The Evolution of Sex*, Patrick Geddes and J. Arthur Thomson cite as unarguable the fact that 'from the earliest ages philosophers have contended that woman is but an undeveloped man' (1889: 37). The same argument is allowed into *Orlando*, with evident sarcasm, when Lord Chesterfield whispers conspiratorially to his son that 'women are children of larger growth' (*O* 213). In this view, femaleness and femininity were synonymous with incomplete development or degeneracy (Gould 1996: 145). Thus recapitulation theory found its practical standard in the women, a ubiquitous population whose ostensibly self-evident passivity, childlike emotionality and timidity could be transferred onto other, perhaps lesser familiar groups. In anti-Irish rhetoric, notes Joseph Valente, 'Irish simianization' and 'feminization' were contrasted with '(Anglo-Saxon) manliness' (2000: 102). Non-whites were routinely described as feminine, as were criminals, neurotics, artists, 'the proletarian and the petit-bourgeois masses' (Kane 1999: 88) and of course homosexuals (Rohy 2009: 10). For Theodor Eimer, the evolutionary function of females is conservatism, providing necessary but ultimately counterproductive checks to the progressive evolution propelled by males. The evolutionary 'law of male preponderance', argues Eimer, states that 'when new characters appear, the males . . . acquire them first', while 'females on the contrary remain always at a more juvenile stage' (1890: 28). In the terminology of Modernist Studies, recapitulationists saw females as keepers of an outdated but necessary tradition, defenders of an order established in the past by a male avant-garde now engaged in more original pursuits. The same logic is patent in G. Stanley Hall's astonishing musings on sex and suicide:

> Woman's body and soul is phyletically older and more primitive, while man is more modern, variable, and less conservative. Women are always more inclined to preserve old customs and ways of thinking. Women prefer passive methods; to give themselves up to the power of elemental forces, as gravity, when they throw themselves from heights or take poison, in which methods of suicide they surpass man. (Hall 1904: ii.194)

Silly as it may seem, Hall's conjecture shows how well recapitulation theory helped legitimate an old tradition which opposes active, creative men to passive women. The bias is directly relevant to Woolf's portrait of Orlando as a woman writer. The fact that 'the growing animal tends to recapitulate, during its development, the changes through which its ancestors have passed' was, to William Keith Brooks, the reason why artistic greatness is the domain of men, whose 'originating and progressive power . . . is shown in its highest forms by the ability to pursue original trains of abstract thought, to reach the great generalizations of science, and to give rise to the new creations of poetry and art' (1883: 253–4, 259).

Obviously Woolf resented such sexist appeals to biology, as her comment about 'Italian and German dictators' in *Three Guineas* attests (1998: 412n48). But like Forster in 'Racial Exercise', the target of her critique is not biology itself but pseudo-science and outdated science. Tellingly, the same note in *Three Guineas* cites Julian Huxley as a modern authority, qualified to discredit the pseudo-science behind Nazi race policy (1998: 412–13n48). More broadly, Woolf's fictional and nonfictional explorations of sex and gender counter aspects of sexology which remained steeped in nineteenth-century thought. As Karen Kaivola argues, 'Woolf's representations of androgyny in the 1920s' (1999: 247) respond directly to the treatment of sexual difference in nineteenth-century science, especially its view of 'mixed forms . . . as degenerate throwbacks in the healthy evolutionary progress of the white race' (Kaivola 1999: 247). This model, inherent as we have seen in even the most open-minded sexological work of the period, is the target of *Orlando*'s devastating critique, the seriousness of which is, for many readers, undetectable within the novel's whimsy and fantasy.

In the context of the *Bildung* tradition and sexological science, then, Woolf's intervention depends not as much on the sex change itself as on its specific direction. Had Orlando turned from woman to man and artist, the plot would have been odd but not at odds with traditional gender roles or with recapitulatory models of sexual development. A metamorphosis from male to female, by contrast, is a reversion of the 'natural' order of sexual differentiation in both developmental and evolutionary senses. In the *Bildung* tradition and in recapitulation theory alike, the prototypically male protagonist should grow *manlier* as he matures, and full maleness should occur only at and as the end of development. Orlando achieves this male end prematurely, halfway through the novel, when he is promoted to the socially and nationally important position of English diplomat in Turkey. All further developments – artistic, social and romantic – occur after Orlando has stepped back, as it were, into female immaturity. This anatomical reversion is accompanied by and may be said to enable Orlando's artistic progress: as a boy and youth earlier in life, Orlando was rough, impetuous and lustful and his poems were sentimental and imitative. Given that Orlando's artistic success comes only once she is a woman, a recapitulationist like William Keith Brooks would protest that Woolf's story perverts the natural trajectory from 'conservative' female immaturity to 'originating' male maturity (1883: 253). Arranging the sex change from male to female without altering the linkage between maturity and artistic realisation, Woolf thus jettisons the recapitulatory framework of *Bildung* and sexology.

Stated so baldly, Woolf's use of the sex change may seem critically simplistic – even petty. I would argue, however, that Orlando's transformation is more than a mere reaction to a tradition which has excluded or sidelined female characters and discounted the possibility of female self-cultivation. Narrating Orlando's reversionary progress from man to woman, Woolf stages a feminist intervention equivalent to her thought experiment about Shakespeare's sister in *A Room of One's Own* (*ROO* 60–6). The contrast between William and Judith Shakespeare offers a damning exposition of how the sexed body limits social, political and artistic potential. The contrast between Orlando's younger male and older female selves does the same, though by different means. Woolf takes care to mention that Judith is as 'extraordinarily gifted' as William, suggesting that the siblings differ in achievement only because her sex bars her from schooling (*ROO* 60–1). *Orlando* makes the same point from a different, rather more fantastical angle: if Orlando manages to succeed as a female artist, it is because her peculiar life history allowed her to reap the benefits of a male childhood. Otherwise she would have missed the formal education she received as a boy – a 'wild boy' who also enjoyed the same informal education as William, 'who poached rabbits, perhaps shot a deer, and had, rather sooner than he should have done, to marry a woman in the neighbourhood' (*ROO* 60). Judith's disadvantages are predominantly cultural, but they originate in the biological fact of her sex at birth. It is to stress this fact that Woolf prevents Orlando's sex change from altering any other aspect of her character.

The reversionary sex change from female to male is therefore much more than an ironic reversal of the gendered masterplot of development. If the classical *Bildung* plot puts female protagonists in a narrative bind, offering them only 'models for "growing down" rather than "growing up"' (Pratt 1981: 14), *Orlando* dissolves the binary oppositions which give 'up' and 'down' meaning and value. Abandoning the up and down arrows of progressive and retrogressive development, Woolf shuffles the traditional hierarchies of sexual difference. As both Pamela Caughie and Adam Parkes point out, *Orlando*'s feminist intervention is deconstructive, dissolving rather than using existing structures to imagine new relations between gender, sex and sexuality. The novel abandons 'all normative sex and gender codes, destabilizing the very grounds on which sexological as well as legal conventions were founded' (Parkes 1994: 436). In doing so, it propels *Orlando* beyond reaction against or reform of the female *Bildung* tradition, and into a distinctly high-modernist exploration of sex and gender, as well as body and mind. Woolf's novel shies from treating these categories as stable binaries or dialectic oppositions destined to a final synthesis, presenting them instead as interpenetrating aspects of an ever-changing mosaic self. In this it is remarkably consistent with the models of sexual development taking hold in contemporary biology.

The Modernist Biology of Sex Determination

Earlier I suggested that Orlando's longevity enables a proliferation of life histories to coexist within a single lifetime. Her experiential richness and diversity is also concurrent: at any given moment Orlando inhabits several simultaneous developmental plots. On one hand, she is 'growing up, which is not necessarily growing better' (*O* 282). She grows up as a *Künstlerroman* would demand, moving, like the elevator she rides towards the end of the novel, 'smoothly upwards' (*O* 300) to artistic realisation in the publication of her award-winning poem, 'The Oak Tree'. On the other hand, she grows in fits and false starts; like Rasselas, she successively tests and discards ways of living. On the third hand (we are dealing with unusual development, after all), Orlando grows backwards – according to contemporary norms, that is – from maleness to femaleness. Finally, as the narrator observes, 'through all these changes she had remained . . . fundamentally the same' (*O* 237). If there seems to be a contradiction between these disparate developmental trajectories, it is only because *Orlando* rejects the unified self in favour of a 'great variety of selves' (*O* 309). Imported into the *Bildungsroman*, the notion of multiple selves in a single body 'br[eaks] the sequence – the expected order' (*ROO* 119) – of individual life history as conceived not only by classical conceptions of *Bildung* but also, as we have seen, by recapitulation theory. Indeed, *Orlando* overlaps most with contemporary biology in its insistence that a body can develop as a weave of different temporalities.

Woolf's model of time and selfhood also closely resembles that of philosopher Jules de Gaultier, proposed in *La Fiction universelle*. Living things are by definition always changing, argues Gaultier, so the only way to retain self-identity is to invent it: 'for something whose essence it is to become at every moment other than it was, the need to remain oneself can be realised only by means of fiction' (1903: 16). This act of invention latches onto those qualities and traits which change slowest, our least mutable parts; other parts change too quickly to serve the fiction of self-sameness. We are thus a fabric of different temporalities: 'some of the parts that make up every living thing – slower to modify themselves, repeating themselves as other changes animate the remainder – help to hold together the more ephemeral, ever-flowing elements with which they successively form relations' (Gaultier 1903: 16). This view of identity clarifies *Orlando*'s statement that 'there are (at a venture) seventy-six different times all ticking in the mind at once' (*O* 308). For some people, observes Woolf's narrator, these various times are harmonised because these 'most successful practitioners of the art of life . . . somehow contrive to synchronise the sixty or seventy different times which beat simultaneously in every normal human system' (*O* 305). Gaultier would say these people are fully convinced by their self-fictionalisation. But such synchrony is beyond other people, who like Orlando 'are hundreds of years old though they call themselves thirty-six' (*O* 305).

These accounts of multitemporal development by Woolf and Gaultier are psychological rather than biological, mental rather than corporeal. In a much-quoted passage, clearly influenced by Bergson and probably by Einstein,[7] *Orlando* promotes psychological and spiritual life over mere bodily existence:

> Time . . . though it makes animals and vegetables bloom and fade with amazing punctuality, has no such simple effect upon the mind of man. The mind of man, moreover, works with equal strangeness upon the body of time. An hour, once it lodges in the queer element of the human spirit, may be stretched to fifty or a hundred times its clock length; on the other hand, an hour may be accurately represented on the timepiece of the mind by one second. (*O* 98)

Despite 'this extraordinary discrepancy between time on the clock and time in the mind' (*O* 98), however, *Orlando* as a biographical narrative also necessarily, if silently, implicates the biology of growth and development.

Age may be in the mind, but of course it is also very much in the body, as suggested by Woolf's Bakhtinian phrase, 'the body of time' (*O* 98). It is the body's unalienable materiality, writes Caroline Walker Bynum, which ensures the crucial link between the self's 'is' and 'was', so that 'the body carries the story' (2005: 177–8). In this sense, *Orlando*'s narrative 'deviation and acceleration' and 'deceleration' (Rosen 2006: 29) inevitably reflect Orlando's body as well as her consciousness. The persistent substance of Orlando's body is what allows Woolf to stretch *Bildung* over the historical span of the family novel – what Conrad Aiken praised in his contemporary review as 'the really first-rate idea of embodying . . . racial evolution in one undying person' (qtd in Majumdar 1997: 235). The resulting genre-blending reveals the novel as a *Bildungsroman* in which ontogeny, rather than paralleling phylogeny, has absorbed it into a single if mutable body. On logical grounds alone, it follows that 'the slippage of time between chronology and age in Orlando's story' (Rosen 2006: 29) manifests itself at least partly in the flesh. The narrator often reminds us of her body, noting 'shapely legs' and 'healthy body' (*O* 14, 102), and more significantly speaks of self-continuity as the state of being 'still flesh and blood' (*O* 204). During the car trip which leaves Orlando 'disassembled' and lays bare the novel's multiple temporalities, it is indeed 'the body and mind' which 'were like scraps of torn paper tumbling from a sack', some 'more slowly' than others, some 'turning over by themselves in the air', as if motionless (*O* 307). It is from such a 'disassembl[age]' of the self in time that Orlando awakens to find himself a woman. Gaultier would say that Orlando's identity is formed from her slower-changing traits, that her female traits, already evident during her male youth, are more stable or durable, remaining in place while the initially more visible male traits vanish in the constant flux of becoming. *Orlando* endorses such a reading by representing the sex change as a reconfiguration of existing parts rather than a radical transformation.

It may yet be hard to grasp how a body could incarnate multiple, non-linear temporalities. This difficulty follows from a latent organicism in our sense of the body as a singular, integrated whole. When the body is thus conceived, it must inevitably stand apart from the mind whose memorial and intellectual faculties can range backwards and forwards in time, voluntarily or not. As we saw in Chapter 1, however, modernist biology was revealing an adult body which does not in fact gather all parts into a single form, subsuming all previous movements into a totalising developmental time. Each organ has its own end and its own developmental schedule. Development is *heterochronic*, composed of different timelines in much the same manner as Gaultier's model of fictional identity formation. Adulthood is thus not the stage when each of the ends becomes harmonised but, more simply, the stage when reproduction becomes possible. At that point in a life history, some organs may remain relatively undeveloped – a condition known as *neoteny*, the retention of juvenile traits into adulthood (on which I say much more in Chapter 5). Heterochrony would seem at best tangentially relevant to *Orlando*, except that one of its effects, much discussed in the decade preceding the novel's publication, was the production of what William Bateson calls 'intersexes, gynandromorphs, and other sex-monstrosities' (1921: 720).

Heterochrony and Sex Determination

The biology of sex was radically rewritten by experimental studies in Mendelian genetics and heterochronic development. Mendelism, which views the organism as 'an aggregate of unit-characters' (Punnett 1907: 74), locates sex in organs and cells, among which it can vary. In the insects which make up the bulk of contemporary sex-determination research, an individual might carry male genes and female genes, which might work in combination or separately. Sex in these organisms is thus not an absolute and discrete condition. This finding rebuffed common sense as well as previous scientific assumptions, which sees sex as a self-evident, discrete and binary category. Rare cases of hermaphroditism notwithstanding, individuals were obviously either male or female, whatever their gender expression and sexual preference. It is against these assumptions that Richard Goldschmidt concludes his essay on 'Intersexuality and the Endocrine Aspect of Sex', noting

> that every individual is able to develop into one sex or the other or any stage between; further that every individual contains all the elements necessary for the development of either sex and its attributes; [and] further that these elements or substances must have a certain quantitative relation to each other. (Goldschmidt 1917: 439)

I should clarify here that Goldschmidt refers to certain insects, and that his claims do not pertain to humans or other animals which have completely different genetic bases for sex. In any case, if the notion of 'quantitative' rather than qualitative sexual differences seems paradoxical, it is only because 'we take the fact of the existence of the two sexes for granted' (Goldschmidt 1917: 433). As Julian Huxley comments, received ideas about sexual difference are the product of 'the historical fact that sex-difference was recognised before the nature of sexual fusion was understood or even discovered, and that, consequently, the word sex etymologically implies a difference' which does not reflect genetic or cellular facts (1922d: 188). The assumption was challenged by new models of sex determination which saw sexual anatomy as the changeable manifestation of dynamic developmental processes, not as the true expression of some underlying and absolute essence.

Sex would therefore become a major area of interest for biologists exploring the implications of a broader revolution in the study of genetics and development – the fact, reported by Huxley and Ford in 'Mendelian Genes and Rates of Development' (1925), that some genes regulate the timing of developmental processes. If a gene controls the onset, cessation and speed of growth in one part of the body, while other genes control growth in other parts, the organism as a whole is an assemblage of many relative temporalities: 'the time of action of a number of genes could be accelerated or retarded simultaneously' (Haldane 1932: 20). The relativity of developmental trajectories, or *heterochrony*, makes of developing organisms not integrated wholes but, rather, 'mosaics' comprised of 'the expression of small differences in the velocity of differentiation' (Goldschmidt 1918: 37). Heterochronic development is nicely summarised by D'Arcy Thompson, who states that 'every part of . . . a growing organism'

> has its own specific rate of growth, referred to a particular direction. It is the ratio between the rates of growth in various directions by which we must account for the external forms of all, save certain very minute, organisms. This ratio between rates of growth in various directions . . . may sometimes be a very constant one, in which case the organism, while growing in bulk, suffers little or no perceptible change in form; but such equilibrium seldom endures . . ., and when the ratio tends to alter, then we have the phenomenon of morphological 'development', or steady and persistent change of form. (D. Thompson 1917: 54)

This discovery had major implications for developmental biology because it dispensed with the assumption that linear, coordinated development between various parts of the organism is the norm or ideal. As Stephen Jay Gould explains, 'the concept of "mosaic evolution" . . . refuted the notion of harmonious development by affirming that individual organs could have independent phyletic histories' (*OP* 234). The resulting model of organic change amounts to a pluralisation of development time into developmental times. Contrasting the linearity (isometry) of simple growth with the non-linearity (allometry) of development, Thompson's model is wonderfully evocative of the disharmonic 'compact of all the selves we have it in us to be' (*O* 310) which influences how Orlando develops. Her self-dissociation is thus fittingly revealed by her sudden shift in velocity when she speeds away in her motorcar: 'the process of motoring fast out of London so much resembles the chopping up small of body and mind' (*O* 307), notes the narrator, representing Orlando as a mosaic of young and old parts, 'a person entirely disassembled' and thus one who is prone to 'astonishing changes' (*O* 308).

Heterochrony, biologists had recently discovered, was responsible for 'astonishing changes' much like Orlando's. In fruit flies, reports Julian Huxley, uneven development produces 'sex-mosaics', 'curious individuals . . . in which some part of the body – usually a half or a quarter – is male in character, while the rest is female. These are known as *gynandromorphs*' (1922c: 238). In such cases, developmental unevenness is literally mechanical: 'a lagging of one of the X-chromosomes after one of the early cell-divisions of a female embryo' leaves part of the body male (J. Huxley 1922d: 197). In other more discussed cases, uneven development is temporal, as Goldschmidt found in his hybridising experiments with gypsy moths (*Lymantria dispar*). Hybrid moths, Goldschmidt found, are not 'sex-mosaics in space, but in time' (J. Huxley 1922d: 197), undergoing over the course of their development an anatomical and sometimes functional change in sex ranging 'from very slight to complete sex-reversal' (*EE* 22). Unlike humans, gypsy moths carry both male- and female-determining genes; normally, the genes determining one sex or the other act more quickly and powerfully, and so they determine the moth's sex throughout its life. In hybrid moths, the regulation of these genes is uncoordinated, and the initially faster and dominant male gene, say, is eventually overtaken by the female. Had Orlando been a gypsy moth, with her mixed peasant and 'noble' parentage (O 14), a 'mixture of brown earth and blue blood' (O 28), she might have explained her own sex change along such lines.[8]

Orlando's Embodied Feminism

Tempting as it is to read *Orlando* in light of these discoveries, the evidence is scant. Woolf may well have known about the remarkable genetics of gypsy moths, being enamoured with Lepidoptera and acquainted with Huxley and Haldane, but the likelihood cannot support claims that biology influenced or even inspired her portrait of Orlando. Still, even without such an influence, the novel and contemporary biology exhibit a remarkable and illuminating confluence in their respective deconstructions of common-sense notions of the body, gender and sexuality. The biology can therefore clarify the nature and implications of Woolf's experiment with the novel of development. Most important in this respect is the fact that modernist biology revealed a body just as amenable to departures from chronology, that not only the mind can travel back and forth in time. This insight dissolves the division between Orlando's mind and body, and thus challenges an assumption all too common in narratological studies of modernist fiction – that the mind and narrative *discourse* are infinitely flexible and free from the body's materiality in the inexorably chronological *story*. In so doing, it removes an intransigent obstacle to recognising the nature and radicalness of *Orlando*'s experiment with the plot of sexual development and gender identity.

Through the subtle but unmistakable incorporation of her narrative, Woolf explodes a veritable suite of traditional dualisms. As long as Orlando's many 'different selves' (O 308) are purely of the mind and spirit – as long as their multiplicity excludes the body – the *Bildungsroman* can uphold a battery of other divisions: culture and nature, male and female, gender and sex, and even discourse and story. Woolf refuses, however, to exclude bodily development from her model of 'different times all ticking in the mind at once' (O 308). The extent of *Orlando*'s feminist critique is thus inaccessible to readers who view biology merely as an empirical backdrop, a drab reality against which Woolf erects a '(compensatory) fantasy' (V. Smith 2006: 60). This view, though intuitive, does not do justice to either biology or to the seemingly unnatural events which befall Orlando; it certainly fails to recognise the extent to which biology and the fantastical metamorphosis are interwoven. Rightly claiming that *Orlando* 'moves beyond the male literary canon . . . while challenging Freud's claim that anatomy is destiny in the figure of Orlando himself', Helena Feder then unfortunately interprets 'anatomy' as if it were synonymous with 'biological determinism' as well as with 'patriarchal history' (2014: 78). If we think

Orlando's sex change occurs outside or beyond nature, then it cannot really challenge the ostensibly natural laws on which patriarchy claims to base its nature/culture binary. Unless we seriously consider Orlando's transformation as a literal bodily transformation, the novel can only be said to operate 'within and not against the predominant dualisms' (Alaimo 2010: 5). To recognise the body's role is thus to recover the scope and radicalness of *Orlando*'s critique, a deconstruction of sex/gender and nature/culture which anticipates feminist studies of science and culture.

Charting development both cultural and bodily, then, *Orlando* seeks the rehabilitation of the flesh since advocated by feminists concerned with women's embodied experience. These theorists propose that biology – heredity, physiology, anatomy – should no longer be considered the fixed opposite of an endlessly malleable culture. Nancy Tuana, for example, has insisted on the 'intra-active' nature of biology and culture, two inextricable parts divided 'through the false dichotomy of sex/gender' (1996: 57), while Lauren Goodlad identifies 'embodiment and particularity' (2005: 216) as the leverage feminist and queer studies might use to counter the universalising and consequently exclusionary tendencies of liberal humanism. Stacy Alaimo suggests that 'perhaps the only way to truly oust the twin ghosts of biology and nature is, paradoxically, to endow them with flesh, to allow them to materialize more fully, and to attend to the precise materializations' (2010: 6). Only by seeing the body in the flesh, as it were, can feminism cast off the sex/gender division which forces it to operate within the 'gendered dualisms – nature/culture, body/mind, object/subject, resource/agency, and others – that have been cultivated to denigrate and silence certain groups' (Alaimo 2010: 5). Rather than denying scientific accounts of the body, feminism might attend more carefully, if not uncritically, to what biology tells us about ourselves. The notion of biology as essence and determinism might then give way to a dynamism and mutability which might serve Lynda Birke's feminist argument for 'thinking about the biological body as changing and changeable, as *transformable*' (1999: 45). One of the ways to effect this change is to redress the fact that 'human development – the processes of becoming human as we enter the world, or of becoming adult as we grow' – has been 'missing from feminist insistence on "lived bodies" or social constructionism' (Birke 1999: 45, 46).[9]

The body's recalcitrance is one of the ways in which *Orlando*, like *A Portrait of the Artist*, refuses to chart development as a progressive movement from brute body to verbal mind, from primitive bodily nature to mature spiritual culture. This refusal, as we have seen, manifests itself literally in Orlando's bodily reversion from male to female. But the novel features other significant reminders and remainders of the natural and the bodily, including two whose recurrence throughout the novel makes them telling markers of Orlando's development. One, 'the wild goose' (*O* 313), is a mere symbol in bird's clothing, representing the phantom of 'a single self, a real self' (*O* 314). The other, the oak tree at Knole, is a real live tree. As part of the natural world, it plays a central role in *Orlando*'s self-conscious deconstruction of the *Bildungsroman* as a narrative form founded, as Helena Feder claims, on the nature/culture binary (2014: 18–19).

At first glance, the oak tree might seem to enforce rather than dissolve this binary and, by extension, the related oppositions of body/mind, female/male and sex/gender. The tree would appear to be an objective correlative of the natural, factual and chronological world in which Orlando's body exists alongside those 'animals and vegetables [which] bloom and fade with amazing punctuality' (*O* 98). It would thus serve as the antithesis to the artistic, fictional and multitemporal life of 'the mind of man' (*O* 98), whose own correlative would be Orlando's poem, 'The Oak Tree'. The oak tree and 'The Oak Tree' thus seem to represent separate aspects of her person and different kinds of temporality. A living organism growing alongside Orlando, centuries old and yet 'still in the prime of life' (*O* 324), the tree seems to model development in obeisance to the arrow of time. Ever taller and stronger, it grows ever upwards. As England's national tree, the oak carries connotations of the history and power of the nation and the genealogy of its old families. Thus the 'solid' oak offers much needed support to young, sentimental Orlando – 'something which he could attach his floating heart to' (*O* 19). Centuries later, 'the bones of the tree running out like ribs from a spine this way and that beneath her' (*O* 324) still serve to ground Orlando in the real. As 'something hard' (*O* 324), the oak recalls the 'granite' which Woolf associates with prose and fact, in seeming opposition to the ethereality of the 'rainbow' of poetry and imagination (*O* 77). The regularity of the tree's biological lifecycle, 'put[ting] forth its leaves and shak[ing] them to the ground a dozen times' (*O* 100), similarly contrasts with the process of poetic composition, a chaotic 'succession' of themes and metaphors which 'jostle' for expression (*O* 100), displacing each other repeatedly so that nothing can be 'settled' (*O* 100). A patchwork of revisions, the poem does not grow progressively over time, as does the tree; in keeping with 'the cardinal labour of composition, which is excision' (*O* 71), it shrinks 'as if in the process of writing the poem would be completely unwritten' (*O* 113), and like Orlando's body its 'style' alters 'amazingly', shedding 'floridity' and 'abundance' for something 'less thorned and intricate' (*O* 113). The poem grows sparser and shorter, against the expectations of increasing complexity characteristic of linear development. Yet it also grows better. In short, the poem appears to represent Orlando's mind, that 'perfect rag-bag of odds and ends', while the 'solid' tree in concert with Orlando's animal body supply the clock, so that the 'assortment' of her mind can yet be 'stitched together by a single thread' (*O* 78). It is tempting, then, to associate the tree simply to biology, body, clock time and story, and the poem to culture, mind, *durée* and discourse. *Orlando* dissolves such oppositions, however.

While the tree suggests progressive development with its growth in height, Woolf also stresses its expansion in more complex dimensions, not only 'bigger, sturdier' but also 'more knotted' (O 323), spreading its 'frilled leaves' in all directions (O 324), mimicking the fractal temporalities of Orlando's woolgathering and the narrator's digressions. Meanwhile the ostensibly airy poem insists on its materiality, its text inseparable from its physical medium, a 'roll of paper, sea-stained, blood-stained, travel-stained' (O 236). The poem is not the just the paper on which it is written, yet it is nothing without the manuscript which Orlando

> carried . . . about with her for so many years now . . . that many of the pages were stained, some were torn, while the straits she had been in for writing paper when with the gipsies, had forced her to overscore the margins and cross the lines till the manuscript looked like a piece of darning most conscientiously carried out. (O 236)

Only because of its physical form does 'The Oak Tree' survive the centuries – pressed, significantly, against Orlando's body 'in the bosom of her dress' (O 280).

The poem's physicality reflects the inextricability of mind and body in Orlando's identity and development. Her cumulative experience is fittingly described as 'those scored parchments which thirty years among men and women had rolled tight in his heart and brain' (O 100). The implication is that the protagonist *is* the text. But if Orlando is 'The Oak Tree', she is also the tree which motivated the poem's genesis and repeatedly spurs its ongoing composition. Appearing together throughout Orlando's development, the tree and poem meet most tellingly during the early meeting with Elizabeth I, who 'read him like a page' (O 25) and adopted him as 'the oak tree on which she leant' (O 26). These two sides of Orlando are not distinct or distinguishable. Despite associative differences between them, Woolf stresses their affinities, dissolving the neat identifications of male with mind and culture, female with body and nature. These associations are subverted by the facts of oak tree reproduction and the compositional history of 'The Oak Tree'. Symbolically, the oak tree may be phallic and linked to the nation's history, while the poem may be sentimental and written on soft foolscap. A more literal reading would counter that oak trees are hermaphroditic, and that the poem, a collaboration between Orlando's young and older selves, has thus had both male and female authors. Orlando is not a poetic mind and a wooden body but a blend 'of clay and diamonds, of rainbow and granite' (O 77), the natural and cultural elements 'stuffed' together (*O* 77). Just like the 'new biography' Woolf advocates, Orlando and *Orlando* are 'that queer amalgamation of dream and reality, that perpetual marriage of granite and rainbow' (*EVW* iv.476); at the same time they also personify Woolf's ideal of 'modern fiction' as 'that queer conglomeration of incongruous things' (*EVW* iv.436).

As a work of art, then, 'The Oak Tree' contributes to Woolf's 'treatise against patriarchal history and biological determinism' (Feder 2014: 78), but not, as Feder argues, as in opposition to 'anatomy' (2014: 78). It is in conjunction with the biological tree that the poem challenges the structural and thematic constraints of the female *Bildungsroman*. Deftly blending memory with nature, Woolf avoids associating the 'single thread' of time only to biology (*O* 78) and the elasticity of time only to the realm of mind or spirit. She thereby muddies the binaries on which the classical *Bildung* plot erected its ranking from crude bodily immaturity to refined masculine adulthood. The resulting novel – an early case of *fiction théorique* (theory-fiction) – is both a specimen of and an investigation into the methods and aims of the modernist, reversionary *Bildungsroman*. The links between these methods and aims and the biology of sex in the 1920s remain no more than suggestive, but they are tantalising. Echoing *Orlando*'s narrator, who leaves explaining the sex change to 'biologists and psychologists' (*O* 139), Woolf writes in *A Room of One's Own* that while 'sex and its nature might well attract doctors and biologists' (*ROO* 34), the topic's fascination among male writers is 'difficult of explanation', their only claim to insight being the fact 'that they are not women' (*ROO* 34). If *Orlando* is Woolf's corrective response to this situation, it would seem biology hangs over her project even if it does not directly motivate its form and content.

For obvious reasons, I have focused on the metamorphosis which changes Orlando's body from male to female, the most compelling connection to the biology of intersexes and sex reversal. But given that her body ages so slowly, the novel also reflects contemporary biological concerns with decelerated development. Orlando is indeed a poster child for the modernist trope of arrested or deferred development, confronting the *Bildung* tradition with a protagonist whose reversions eschew the putative certainties and fixities of maturity. The narrator twice mentions that Orlando is 'like a child' (*O* 156, 263). Although Woolf hints that this youthfulness is a product of the mind's timelessness, it also unequivocally manifests in the body. After 358 years Orlando does not merely feel she is 'thirty-six': she also 'scarcely looked a day older' (*O* 302). Her ability to bear children in her third century is also, of course, a marker of biological youth. Retaining youthful features long after they would be expected to have disappeared, Orlando is a case of neoteny – a topic examined in Chapter 5.

Rather than impeding *Bildung*, Orlando's extended youth enables it, allowing her repeatedly to change lifestyles and poetic style – in short, to change herself. Able to renew the potentialities of youth, Orlando eschews the irreversible, cumulative model of development she herself endorses as she walks 'among the tombs where the bones of her ancestors lay' (*O* 174), thinking 'I am growing up' (*O* 175). Surveying 'the progress of her own self along her own past' (*O* 176), she realises that her experience, embodied in 'twenty-six volumes' of poetry (*O* 176), is neither progressive nor teleological. Instead, the 'change was incessant, and change perhaps would never cease' (*O* 176). Though *Bildung* has always been concerned with the process of formation as well as with finished form, modernist *Bildungsromane* strongly privilege such a continual 'process of fabrication' (*O* 175). In lieu of *telos*, *Orlando*'s developmental vision includes reversionary dynamics which, together with other temporalities, produce the portrait of the artist as a vessel of inexhaustible potentiality. The novel's end leaves Orlando not completed but, rather, poised for further change. She is not at the end but in the midst of 'life' (*O* 324), a Woolfian word which is, like Orlando, 'ineluctably mutable' (DiBattista and Wittman 2014: xii). Unending mutability is incompatible with historical linearity and thus, as we shall see in the following chapters on Huxley and Beckett, one of modernism's developmental ideals. By reconstituting the ending as a constant middle, as Frank Kermode might say, Woolf's novel leaves Orlando and *Orlando* in the thick of life.

To rewrite the female *Bildungsroman* in this way, with 'no plot, no comedy, no tragedy, no love interest or catastrophe in the accepted style' (*EVW* iv.160), is clearly part of Woolf's reason for 'tampering with the expected sequence' (*ROO* 106). In this context, Orlando's reversionary metamorphosis upends the 'sequence' of sexual development, a 'sentence' which has placed the ending and the emphasis on mature maleness. Key to Woolf's feminist intervention, then, is the narrator's observation that 'when we write of a woman, everything is out of place – culminations and perorations; the accent never falls where it does with a man' (*O* 312). Rather than submit to a pre-existing narrative, Woolf alters 'accent' and trajectory, recreating the *Bildung* plot in the image of a protagonist newly invested in a woman's body – 'the book', as she writes in *A Room of One's Own*, 'has somehow to be adapted to the body' (*ROO* 101). *Orlando*'s form reflects its content, an ideal of fictional construction Woolf compares, in her preface to *Mrs Dalloway*, to a snail 'secret[ing] a house for itself' (*EVW* iv.550). In this sense, Woolf's feminism is coextensive with her modernism. In her comments about new 'accent[s]' and newly placed 'culminations' of women's fiction, *Orlando*'s narrator unmistakably echoes Woolf's vision of 'giving things their natural order, as a woman would, if she wrote like a woman' (*ROO* 119). She also echoes Woolf's hopes for 'modern fiction' in general, in which 'the accent falls differently from of old; the moment of importance came not here but there' (*EVW* iv.160).

NOTES

1. Woolf met Haldane in 1924, if not before, when she presented what would become 'Mr Bennett and Mrs Brown' to the Cambridge Heretics. She likely met Julian Huxley along with his brother Aldous when the Huxleys were frequenting Bloomsbury gatherings in the mid-1910s, but the only documented meeting between her and Julian was in 1935 (Hovanec 2013: 257n36).
2. Unsurprisingly, scientific findings about intersexes and sex change were reported in non-scientific forums. In *The New Age*, for example, A. E. R. proclaims a new model of sexual difference based on 'a new humanism [as] the only scientific basis for modern society' (1921: 35). Disputing the recapitulatory model of sex, A. E. R. adds that

   > man is not a differentiation from the female any more than woman is a differentiation from the male; both alike have in varying proportions the qualities of both sexes, and the existence of the 'inter-sex,' which sometimes presents all the ordinary female sex characteristics, and yet possesses male sex glands, indicates that neither feminism nor hominism is worth a moment's consideration. (A. E. R. 1921: 35)

3. Woolf is quick to dispel any parallel between Orlando's life and other temporal markers. Early in the novel 'his age – he was not yet seventeen' (*O* 16) – is neatly coupled with 'the spirit of the age' (*O* 236), for 'the sixteenth century had still some years of its course to run' (*O* 16). But the age–Age isometry of sixteen years and sixteenth century is fleeting: by the nineteenth century Orlando is 'a year or two past thirty' (*O* 244) and by 1928 she is 'thirty-six' (*O* 302).
4. Like 'Oxen of the Sun', *Orlando* apparently progresses through a historical sequence of prose styles, a feature recognised by contemporary critics such as J. C. Squire, Conrad Aiken and Raymond Mortimer (qtd in Majumdar 1997: 228, 235, 241), and discussed by Beth Boehm (1992) and Max Saunders (2010). In one of the best accounts of *Orlando* as a *Bildungsroman*, Amy Elkins (2010) compares the approved Hogarth edition to the special Gaige edition of the novel, noting that the latter more blatantly subverts the parallelism between individual life and national history.
5. *Orlando* contrasts procreation and poetic creation, as Aimee Armande Wilson argues when she stresses the Victorian birth of Orlando's 'involuntarily conceived son' as the unfortunate counterpart to the more timely birth of 'The Oak Tree' in the twentieth century (2016: 86). The opposition between the 'child of her body' and the 'child of her mind' (Wilson 2016: 91) is deceptive, however, just as it is in *A Portrait of the Artist*, when Stephen Dedalus diverts reproductive language into spiritual art, or in *A Passage to India*, when Fielding claims he had 'rather leave a thought behind [him] than a child' (Forster 1978: 110). After all, Stephen fails to exorcise the body from his art, and Fielding ultimately welcomes his imminent fatherhood.
6. Forster's *Maurice* also relies on sexological sources, probably Ellis's *Sexual Inversion* and definitely Carpenter's *The Intermediate Sex*. I am persuaded, however, by

Peppis's argument that Forster's novel transcends the normative pull of sexological accounts, a resistance manifested in the sudden generic shift at the end of the narrative. Rather than find a way to accommodate his homosexuality to his society, Maurice and his lover Alec disappear into 'the greenwood' (Peppis 2014: 123) – out of the *Bildungsroman*, into romance.

7. Of the many critics to link time in *Orlando* with Einstein, including Parsons (2007: 113) and O'Sullivan (2014: 41), Julia Briggs most insightfully connects Orlando's persistent youth to a specific implication of relativity theory – that a fast-travelling observer ages more slowly than her surroundings (2005: 199). On Woolf and Einstein more generally, see Whitworth (2001).
8. Another intriguing connection: the sex change described above resulted from crosses of 'European ♀ x Japanese ♂' (Bateson 1921: 719), while that of Orlando is likewise orientalised (it takes place in Turkey; see K. Lawrence [1992]). That these experiments were conducted on gypsy moths might also inform the fact that the sex change occurs at a time when Orlando 'must have been in secret communication' (O 141) with 'the gipsy tribe to which Orlando had allied herself' (O 140). Lepidoptera were dear enough to Woolf for her to call Vita Sackville-West 'an Emperor moth' (1977: iii.243). *Orlando*'s intersection of race and hermaphroditism has been examined by Celia Caputi Daileader (2013). More critically, Urmila Seshagiri examines the novel's Orientalism (2010: 176–91), remarking that Orlando, by rejecting the exoticism and primitivism of Turkey and the gypsies, ultimately 'achieves the racial and national integration that concludes a nineteenth-century bildungsroman' (2010: 179).
9. Birke's view resembles several feminist readings of *Orlando* which acknowledge the relevance of the protagonist's changing body; see Nancy Cervetti (1996), Pamela Caughie (2013), Erin Douglas (2009), Melanie Micir (2012) and Brenda Helt, who stresses Orlando's 'living corporeally as both a man and a woman' (2010: 145).

5

ANACHRONY, NEOTENY AND THE 'EDUCATION OF AN AMPHIBIAN' IN *EYELESS IN GAZA*

> My novelist must be an amateur zoologist. Or, better still, a professional zoologist who is writing a novel in his spare time. His approach will be strictly biological.
>
> – Aldous Huxley, *Point Counter Point* (1928: 320)

In his innocuously titled essay 'The Theory of Recapitulation: A Critical Restatement of the Biogenetic Law' (1922), Walter Garstang delivers a devastating attack on the biogenetic law. Reserving particular scorn for Haeckel's dictum that 'Phylogenesis is the mechanical clause of Ontogenesis', Garstang presents ontogeny as a creative process rather than a mere effect of history, giving the individual a leading role in the evolutionary process. 'Ontogeny', he continues, 'is not an animated cinema show of ancestral portraits; but zygotes may be likened to conjurers playing the old tricks for the most part, and occasionally opening a surprise packet' (Garstang 1922: 81, 100). Few passages better support my claim that the narratives emerging in early twentieth-century biology look distinctly modernist. There are, indeed, intriguing similarities between Garstang's rejection of linear recapitulation and Woolf's dismissal of plot as a 'series of gig lamps symmetrically arranged' (*EVW* iv.160), or Forster's hopes for novels which bring 'not rounding off but opening out' (*AN* 116). Yet Garstang's metaphor has undeveloped potentialities of its own. He sees film merely as a succession of images, each displacing its predecessor and running through the same steps in the same order; he seems not to recognise that film might exemplify the new, non-linear dynamics he found in evolutionary embryology.

Many of Garstang's contemporaries were more receptive to film as a medium able to explore hitherto unthinkable narrative possibilities. Among them was Aldous Huxley, who notes in 'Where Are the Movies Moving?' (1926) that the techniques of film editing allow 'the maker of films' to break new ground where the writer deals with words, which are 'traditional and hereditary things, impregnated by centuries of use with definite meanings and association' (1926a: 184). These inherited limitations certainly include plot structures, including the *Bildung* plot he mocks in *Crome Yellow* (1921) and avoids in ten of his eleven novels. Film is by contrast unencumbered by convention, and the ease with which it breaks sequences and associations represents one of 'the most pregnant potentialities of the cinema'; unlike the written word, writes Huxley, film 'may be developed into something entirely novel' (1926a: 184).[1] It is fitting, then, that his only *Bildungsroman* breaks radically from the ordered succession of stages leading from childhood to youth to maturity. This novel, *Eyeless in Gaza* (1936), abandons the genre's native chronology in favour of techniques which, like those of film, 'dissociate long-united ideas' and 'bring together ideas which have never previously been joined' (1926a: 184).

Two years before the publication of *Eyeless in Gaza*, Huxley complained to Mary Hutchinson about his struggles to find an appropriate temporality for representing development. 'I am looking for a device to present two epochs of a life simultaneously', he writes, 'for when one considers life one is equally struck by both facts – that one has remained the same and become totally different' (2007b: 292). This perspective recalls *Point Counter Point*'s attempt 'to show a piece of life from many different points of view . . ., in many different ways simultaneously' (2007b: 185), but whereas the earlier novel confronts the panorama of modern 'life' (society), *Eyeless in Gaza*, as a *Bildungsroman*, strives to unify the diversity of '*a* life'. Seeing the self's diversity as partly an artefact of linear time, Huxley structures his *Bildungsroman* by replacing *Point Counter Point*'s multi-perspectivism with its temporal equivalent: anachrony. Typically modernist for refusing 'the explanatory power of linear narrative' (Abbott 2010b: 6), his anachrony is also unusual for being mimetic, though not, as in Wordsworth or Proust, mimetic of memory's fluidity; instead, it mimics a model of growth Huxley adapted from contemporary biological research, much of it by his brother Julian, on frogs and salamanders.[2]

For both Huxleys, personal multiplicity was what Aldous called a kind of 'amphibiousness', a consequence of being 'indigenous to half a dozen incompatible worlds' (1956: 9–10). Both also saw in the amphibian's metamorphosis from aquatic larva to land- and water-dwelling adult what R. S. Deese describes as 'a living symbol of our potential to transform ourselves, both as individuals and as a species' (2014: 183). As Aldous writes in 'Education of an Amphibian', however, we usually fail to harmonise our 'double lives', whereas 'the tadpole knows precisely when to get rid of its tail and gills, and become a frog' (1956: 9). The potential for change is too often wasted on humans, who age without maturing, and Aldous's fiction teems with 'asymmetrical tadpoles', grown-up infants 'full of batrachian grapplings in the dark' (*PCP* 83, 173). The best amphibian mascot for the Huxleys was therefore not the frog but the axolotl. This Peter Pan of salamanders 'fails to metamorphose, and attains full size and sexual maturity while keeping its larval characters', including gills for a fully aquatic lifestyle (J. Huxley 1920a: 435).[3] Five years before Aldous published *Eyeless in Gaza*, Julian wondered at the 'arrest of personality' which causes 'half our young men [to] arrive at manhood, as Mexican axolotls do at their maturity, while still in the tadpole stage?' (1968: 20). Axolotls play a similar role in Aldous's satires: *Antic Hay*'s ridicule of the Bright Young People concludes in a lab stocked with 'black axolotls' (1923: 326), while *Point Counter Point*'s infantile Lord Edward studies 'the sexual activities of axolotls' (*PCP* 187).

More enigmatic is the axolotl's appearance in *Eyeless in Gaza*, where it symbolises not immaturity but the unrealised potential to achieve complete maturity. In the novel's final pages, protagonist Anthony Beavis muses: 'sheep's thyroid transforms the axolotl from a gilled larva into an air-breathing salamander, the cretinous dwarf into a well-grown and intelligent human being' (*EG* 612). It is a clear allusion to Julian's 1920 experiment demonstrating how axolotls fed sheep's thyroid become normal, terrestrial adult salamanders (J. Huxley 1920a: 435). Axolotls have lost the ability to produce their own thyroid, the hormone involved in amphibian metamorphosis, yet they remain receptive to its effects: all it takes is a thyroid supplement 'to "pull the trigger" of metamorphosis' (de Beer 1951: 167). This discovery explains Anthony's cryptic musings: proclaiming induced metamorphosis as *Eyeless in Gaza*'s privileged mode of development, this passage is a crucial indicator of the amphibian trope which the novel otherwise deploys formally, through anachrony. If thyroid supplements induce metamorphosis (developmental completion) in a stunted salamander, Huxley's experimental shuffling of chronology serves to induce the 'transformation of [Anthony's] raw material into the finished product' (*EG* 361).

Eyeless in Gaza is one of the most visible instances of the modernist 'aspiration toward Bildung in new and startling formats', the experimental renegotiation and reconception of development designed to rehabilitate *Bildung* as the 'aesthetico-spiritual' ideal devised by the Weimar classicists (Castle 2006: 29, 63). In Huxley's novel, the experiment involves a typically modernist subversion of 'both the ideology of linear progress and the allegorical bonding of a nation to a life' (Richard Murphy 2013: 78). Exploiting the correlation between the *Bildung* plot and models of biological development, Huxley manages to sever the former's problematic reliance on linearity by remodelling its narrative based on new, non-linear theories of embryological and evolutionary change. As it rejects the 'ideology of linear progress', that is, his novel's anachrony also serves the more constructive role of performing a version of the temporally dysregulated development by which the axolotl remains juvenile in form even as an adult, making the animal available for induced metamorphosis.

Huxley's quarrel with linear growth reveals a paradox at the heart of *Bildung* in its narrative form. *Bildung* was theorised by Goethe, Humboldt, Schiller and others as harmonious diversity, a multidirectional process which has been likened to the images in a kaleidoscope. But narration is a linear, sequential process, so narrating *Bildung*, in literature as in personal experience, appears doomed to failure. In social life too, *Bildung* is an impossible ideal, impossible because even those with leisure to explore all their interests lack the time necessary to develop every potentiality to the fullest. Time constrains our choices, driving us ever further from full development, inevitably towards greater specialisation. This was a paradox which preoccupied many thinkers other than the Weimar classicists and Huxley. The criminologist and ardent recapitulationist Cesare Lombroso notes that 'all progress is based upon regress, . . . that every new organ or degree of perfection acquired by an animal is formed at the expense of other organs in which progress has provoked a partial or total atrophy' (1898: 377). For Lombroso, whose theory of criminal types draws on recapitulatory accounts of degeneration and atavism, increasing individuation is inevitably accompanied by a concomitant loss of adaptability. This 'most paradoxical' situation (Lombroso 1898: 377), which bears comparing with Goethe's confused treatment of the role of irregular metamorphosis in relation to plant development (1988: 63), reveals one of the central incoherencies of *Bildung* conceived as a strictly progressive process. In short, full development of one faculty can be achieved only at the expense of others, while *Bildung* ideally requires the development of all faculties. This ideal, which motivates Huxley's desire for 'general, all-round progress' (*EM* 263), accords perfectly with Weimar conceptions of *Bildung*. 'The true end of man', Humboldt asserts in *The Limits of State Action* (1792), 'is the highest and most harmonious development [*Bildung*] of his powers to a complete and consistent whole', an end incompatible with narrow specialisation (1969: 16). Specialisation, however, is the fate reserved for 'us moderns', as Schiller writes in *The Aesthetic Education of Man* (1794): a mere 'fragment', modern 'man . . . never develops the harmony of his being, and instead of putting the stamp of humanity upon his own nature, he becomes nothing more than the imprint of his occupation or of his specialized knowledge' (1967: 33). In 1931 Huxley would find these conditions unchanged, writing that 'if society continues to develop on its present lines, specialization is bound to increase', and individuals will be reduced to 'cogs in an industrial machine', bereft of 'a full, harmonious life' (1931: 146–7).

A mainstay of Huxley's oeuvre from 'The Farcical History of Richard Greenow' (1920) to *Island* (1962), specialisation, or 'being lop-sided', afflicts most of his characters, very few of whom can hope to find the 'harmony and completeness' necessary for 'civilization' (*PCP* 144). Reduced by their specialised education and stultifying jobs to 'live as idiots and machines all the time' (*PCP* 417), they are unable 'to develop to the full' (A. Huxley 1927: 90). What his characters lack is 'a principle of integration . . . that will co-ordinate the scattered fragments, the island universes of specialized or merely professional knowledge, . . . that will help, perhaps, to transform them from mere spectators of the human scene into intelligent participants' (*EM* 198–9). It is in light of this integration that we must read *Eyeless in Gaza*, for this is the 'proper correlation' which permits 'progress, not only as a citizen, a machine-minder and machine-user, but also as a human being' (*EG* 328, 329).

In addition to rejecting the 'ideology of linear progress', his novel's anachrony serves the more constructive role of performing a version of the temporally dysregulated development which causes the axolotl to remain juvenile even as an adult, and thus avails the animal of the potential for induced metamorphosis. These aspects of axolotl biology provide a model for Anthony's own *Bildung* plot, but they also find significant structural analogues in William James's psychology and philosophy of religious experience as well as in contemporary hypotheses about the possibility of rapid and radical evolutionary change. By incorporating theories from biology, psychology and spiritualism into its form, *Eyeless in Gaza* participates in a cultural project Huxley shared with several contemporary writers, activists and scientists, including his brother, who believed science does not disprove 'mystical experience' but, rather, provides solid ground for understanding it by 'laying a foundation for the proper spiritual training and development of human mind' (A. Huxley 1926a: 301–2). Specifically, Aldous draws on the theories of Garstang, the ardent enemy of recapitulation quoted at the beginning of this chapter. As early as 1898, Garstang proposed that evolutionary novelty might be produced not by terminal addition, as recapitulation theory would have it, but by the opposite process of delayed maturation. Alistair C. Hardy, Garstang's son-in-law and Julian Huxley's collaborator, would later explain this hypothesis in 'Escape from Specialization', offering at the same time what might be the objective of Aldous Huxley's experiment with anachronic *Bildung*:

> Times out of number specialization has indeed led to an evolutionary *cul-de-sac* and even to racial extinction; occasionally, however, a very unusual process has intervened and enabled one line or another to escape from such an ending and pass on to quite another road: perhaps to progress and [adaptive] radiation. How can it be done? Can evolution be put into reverse so that the race retreats backwards away from specialization

> down the pathway up which it came? Not exactly, but something very like it. Garstang has shown us the key with which such animals may sometimes escape from the maze. (Hardy 1958: 123)

Garstang's 'key', as Hardy then explains, is developmental delay, or 'paedomorphosis', a process which produces an adult retaining the juvenile or even embryonic features of its ancestors. This condition, known as 'neoteny' (Hardy 1958: 123), is most famously exemplified by the axolotl. Hardy, like Garstang and Gavin de Beer before him, makes far-reaching claims for the 'conception of paedomorphosis linked with that of neoteny': 'some of the most successful advances in evolutionary progress have been due to this factor and . . . some of the major groups in the animal kingdom might never have been evolved without it' (Hardy 1958: 123). This picture of evolutionary flourishing through the process of growing young corresponds neatly to my thesis – that it is in reversion that modernists including Huxley sought a new *Bildung* plot.

Yoking the modernist interest in sudden, metamorphic change (Stephen's epiphanies, Orlando's sex change, Gregor Samsa's transformation) with contemporary paradigm shifts in biology, Huxley imagines a form of *Bildung* capable of meeting or preventing the ever-greater threats of 'fascism', 'communism' and 'nationalism' (*EG* 523), which fragment and isolate rather than unite us. Whereas David Daiches calls *Eyeless in Gaza*'s anachrony an uncritical imitation of modernist forms (1939: 209), my biological reading interprets it instead as a unique take on the more general modernist desire to find or create coherence in the chaotic modern world by combining heterogeneous and disparate aspects of reality. In other words, departures from linearity and its association with specialisation bring Huxley's novel back to the Weimar classicists' ideal of *Bildung* as 'the idea of a harmonious form of cultivation (*Bildungsharmonie*) – unifying divided talents and actions' (Martini 1991: 5). More schematic than Joyce, Eliot or Woolf in the pursuit of the world's complex fullness, Huxley's *Bildungsroman* is therefore engaged in a kindred project of responding to modernity's impulse towards specialisation, dissolving boundaries and levelling the hierarchies between the various realms of human experience.

Time and Discontinuity in *Eyeless in Gaza*

Chronology is native to the *Bildungsroman*, as we saw in the Introduction, and *Eyeless in Gaza* is so clearly a *Bildungsroman* that early reviewers could see its device only as a gimmick (Watt 1975: 245–82). To Daiches it was 'wholly unnecessary, having no functional purpose' beyond obscuring 'the straightforward history of the development of the hero' (1939: 209–10). Anachrony is almost antithetical to the *Bildung* plot. Even otherwise innovative modernist *Bildungsromane* texts (*Sons and Lovers*, *Jacob's Room*) tend to be conservative in this respect. Of modernist novels such as *Lord Jim* 'we cannot speak of the

Bildungsroman genre, only of Bildung effects', as Gregory Castle describes *Mrs Dalloway* (2006: 231). Proust's *Recherche*, an obvious influence on *Eyeless*, is wildly non-chronological, but its anachronies are naturalised as the actions of memory, whereas Huxley's jarring shifts, blatantly labelled with a date stamp, resist naturalisation. These shifts appear random, and the consciousness responsible for marking the dates is mysterious, suggesting the work of a Joycean Arranger whose agency transcends that of both hero and narrator.

Huxley's use of anachrony is puzzling because it seems haphazard, as shown in Figure 5.1, which plots the order of the novel's chapters (discourse order) against the order of events in the story. A chronological narrative would graph simply as a straight line rising from the Cartesian origin towards the top right-hand corner; in such a novel, say *Great Expectations*, the relation between story order and discourse order is linear (see Figure 1.1, Chapter 1). By contrast, the same relation in *Eyeless in Gaza* is non-linear and apparently chaotic: from any given chapter it would seem impossible to guess when the next chapter will be set.

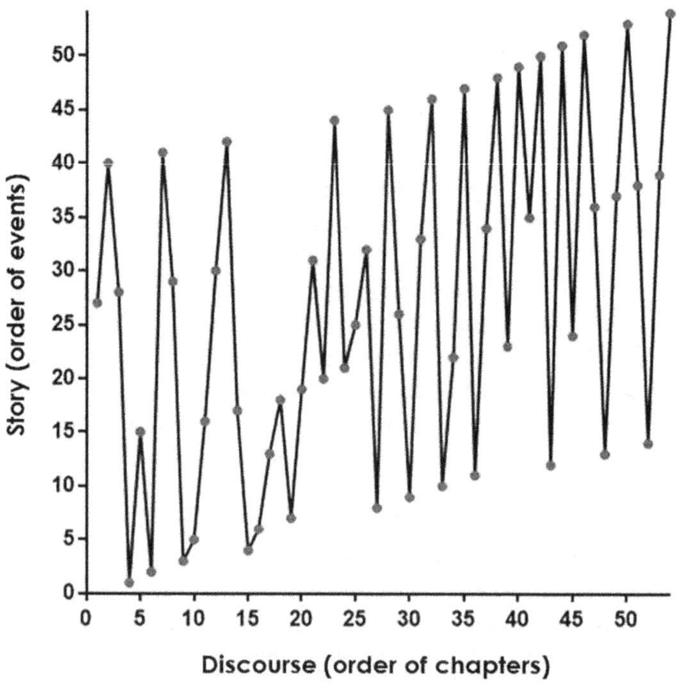

Figure 5.1 Graph plotting the order of chapters in *Eyeless in Gaza* in relation to the order of events in the story. Apart from a slight overall tendency upwards, the novel's temporal structure is non-linear and apparently without order.

A different perspective, however, finds a distinct pattern hidden in the seeming confusion of Figure 5.1. Instead of a single, chaotic developmental line, Figure 5.2 reveals four separate developmental lines, each corresponding to a discrete period of Anthony's life. Following the narrative along the graph's *x*-axis, we find four parallel and chronological developmental plots, though each plot is repeatedly interrupted by the insertion of episodes from the other three plots. The result is as close as a linear narrative can come to showing 'two epochs of a life simultaneously so as to show their relations with one another' (A. Huxley 2007b: 292).

Masking rather than denying the role of temporal sequence in development, anachrony foregrounds counterpoint as an alternative ordering principle. Bridges are created between various aspects of Anthony, whose various

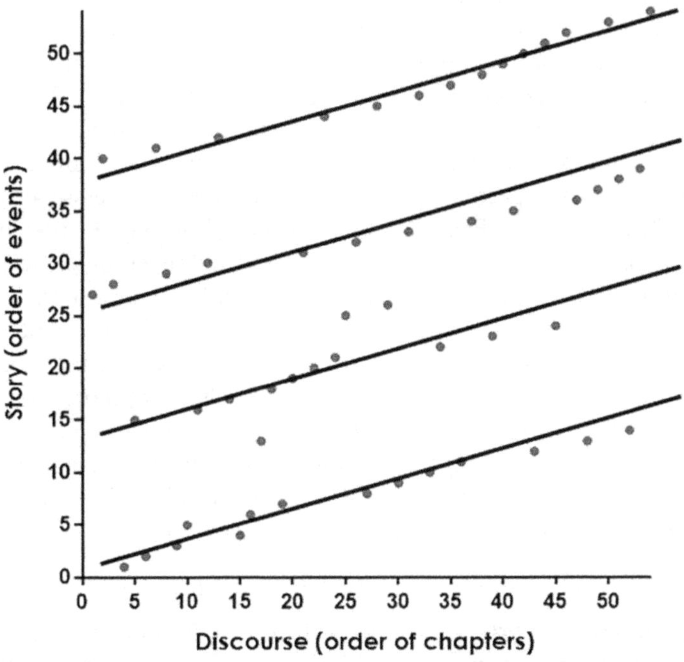

Figure 5.2 The same plot as Figure 5.1, but highlighting the pattern obscured by the single line connecting all grey dots in order. The distribution of the dots clearly suggests four separate lines, corresponding to the four periods of Anthony Beavis's life: childhood, 1902–4; youth, 1912–14; adulthood, 1926–8; and middle age, 1931–5. There are thus two simultaneous forms of temporal continuity: at the level of story, the 'natural' order and causal chains of Anthony's life remain; at the level of discourse, however, this order is altered, suggesting the possibility of non-temporal forms of causality.

selves at different ages coexist. Instead of temporal and causal determinism, this arrangement suggests growth through leitmotifs, thematic affinities and contrasts, ironic juxtapositions and verbal echoes. At the end of Chapter 30 (7 Jul. 1914), for instance, Anthony's father makes a lame 'philological joke', calling his pencil 'my teeny weeny' and embarrassing young Anthony because 'it was the first time . . . his father had ever, in his presence, made any allusion to the physiology of sex' (*EG* 408). Chapter 31 (6 Sept. 1933) opens with the inevitable counterpoint of sex: 'Death' (*EG* 409). Nineteen years separate these contiguous moments, whose relation is non-causal in the story, but productive in the discourse of a kind of textual causation which links Anthony's middle-age morbidity to his youthful specialism in sexual indulgence. As Robert Caserio has characterised this strange logic, 'it would seem as if memory, and the long-buried past, have a *causative* effect on Beavis's ascent out of the realm of ego, personality, and will, and into the realm of spirit' (1999: 134). Certainly, the temporal arrangement of the novel is not 'random' (*EG* 25).

Critics perplexed or irritated by Huxley's novel sensed a dissonance between form and content. It is because she recognises the novel as a *Bildungsroman* that Phyllis Bentley sees the formal experiment as a gimmick which not only distracts from but even interferes with the theme. Huxley's 'jumbling method', she argues, 'does not permit the slow development of personality' (qtd in Vitoux 1972: 212–13). As Pierre Vitoux responds, however, Bentley has missed the point. What concerns Huxley is not 'the slow development of personality' but, rather, 'a crisis, psychological and moral, leading to a conversion; his vision is not evolutionary but climactic or mutative' (Vitoux 1972: 213). The form of *Eyeless in Gaza*, in other words, is not a perverse attempt to complicate or obscure the familiar mechanics of the classical *Bildung* plot; nor is its order as 'alogical' as Caserio concludes (1999: 134). It is, rather, an effort to find the form appropriate to a new understanding of how *Bildung* might be achieved. To see *how* this non-random anachrony functions in Huxley's modernist take on *Bildung*, we must turn to the biology of the axolotl.

Neoteny and Developmental Flexibility

Vitoux's criticism of Bentley is correct, on the whole. But his own account of Huxley's method is also compromised because he stakes too much on the contrast between evolution and mutation. Just as non-chronology conflicts with nineteenth-century notions of development, so does mutation conflict with the gradual incrementalism of Victorian evolutionism. By the 1930s, however, the conflict was largely mitigated by the successful synthesis of Mendelian genetics and evolution by natural selection. Advances in experimental embryology, with which Huxley was familiar, did even more to accommodate sudden and dramatic change into Darwinian theory. As Huxley observes in *Ends and Means*, evolution proceeds not only by gradual 'natural selection' but also by abrupt 'hybridization, retardation of growth and foetalization' (*EM* 261). The latter two processes are especially relevant to his view of *Bildung* because they result in neoteny. Suggestive of infantilism, neoteny (or foetalisation) might suggest a form of regression; indeed, recapitulationists explained it as degeneration or stalled development (*OP* 132). But biologists in Huxley's immediate circle, including his brother, believed retaining juvenile or larval features in adulthood was the key to the evolutionary 'escap[e] from the blind alleys of specialization, into a new period of plasticity and adaptive radiation' (J. Huxley, qtd in Montagu 1989: 254).

Anthony is neotenous. Nicknamed 'Benger . . . because [he] looked so babyish', he also resembles 'the infant Samuel' (*EG* 5, 362). For the most part, though, the concept of neoteny is latent rather than plainly evident in *Eyeless in Gaza*; as a positive force for humanity it receives more explicit treatments in the novel's predecessor *Brave New World* (1932) and successor *After Many a Summer* (1939). In *Brave New World*, the Director of Hatcheries defends the production of 'below par' individuals (2007a: 11) because full development is wasted on menial workers. What is redundant in low-caste 'Epsilons' is 'that fruit of delayed development, the human intelligence' (2007a: 11). The Director acknowledges a problem, however: 'though the Epsilon mind was mature at ten, the Epsilon body was not fit to work till eighteen . . . If the physical development could be speeded up till it was as quick, say, as a cow's, what an enormous saving to the community!' (2007a: 11). Getting more technical, the Director muses about 'the abnormal endocrine co-ordination which made men grow so slowly . . . Could the effects of this germinal mutation be undone? Could the individual Epsilon embryo be made to revert . . . to the normality of dogs and cows?' (2007a: 12). The same abnormality of human development process is described in *After Many a Summer*: 'There's a kind of glandular equilibrium . . . Then a mutation comes along and knocks it sideways. You get a new equilibrium that happens to retard the development rate' (*AS* 102). In the later novel, however, this deceleration is praised as the source of positive youthful qualities in humans, rather than deplored as an inefficient waste. A human is a foetal ape just as 'a dog's a wolf that hasn't fully developed. It's more like the foetus of a wolf than an adult wolf . . . It's a mild, tractable animal because it has never grown up into savagery' (*AS* 102). The implication in both novels is that our most human qualities stem from 'abnormal' deviations from ancestral 'normality'. The society in *Brave New World* is dystopic, then, because it straightens the non-linear dynamics of *Bildung*, reversing the 'humanizing principle of pedomorphism' (Drennan, qtd in Montagu 1955: 22).

As we saw in Chapter 1 and again in the case of Orlando's sex change, the developmental process behind the condition of neoteny is heterochrony, 'the displacement in time of the appearance of a particular feature relative to the time that the same feature appeared in an ancestral form' (McNamara 1997: 19).

Neoteny occurs when bodily maturation decelerates relative to sexual maturation, resulting in a reproductive adult with a juvenile morphology. An axolotl never grows out of what is, in its salamander relatives, the larval stage. By the same logic, as the anatomist Louis Bolk observed as early as 1918, humans are also paedomorphic or neotenous, never growing out of what is, in our ape relatives, the juvenile or even foetal stage. Bolk put it plainly, in an especially potent challenge to human vanity: 'man, in his bodily development, is a primate foetus that has become sexually mature' (qtd in *OP* 361). Aldous knew Bolk's theory long before he explicitly quoted his theory of the human as 'a foetal ape' (*AS* 311). In *Jesting Pilate* (1926), he muses that 'we are like angels when we are children . . . In youth and earliest maturity we are human; the angel dies when we are men . . . As middle-age advances, we become less and less human, increasingly simian' (1926b: 98). Citing the developmental homology between foetal ape and adult human, Huxley also highlights one of its bizarre implications: ageing without true development is regression, not maturation. This is the fate of most of Huxley's 'parodies of grown men' (*EG* 558). Yet in *Jesting Pilate* Huxley also anticipates Anthony's conversion. If most people 'gr[o]w back in the process of growing up' (*AS* 103) and 'remain ape-like to the end', a few may 'become for a second time something more than human' (1926b: 98). Neoteny allows maturation rather than mere ageing, and, as 'one of the mechanisms of evolutionary development' (*AS* 102), provides a way to put 'evolution . . . into reverse so that the race retreats backwards away from specialization' (Hardy 1958: 123).

Anthony's neoteny is not good in itself. It is both peril and potential: on its own it is merely another form of immaturity, but as a state of potentiality it avails him of metamorphic self-development. *Eyeless in Gaza* makes a point of stressing Anthony's (eventual) conscious choice of change over perpetual adolescence, whose threat hangs over the whole narrative. The alternative fate awaiting Anthony explains why he is linked not only to the axolotl but to another neotenous cave-dwelling salamander, which likewise enjoyed much scientific attention in the nineteenth and early twentieth centuries: *Proteus anguinus*, the olm or 'human fish', so called because of its fish-like appearance and pink skin (Voituron et al. 2011: 105). Despite their superficial resemblance to axolotls, olms are 'permanently neotenic' (Huxley and Hogben 1922: 38), and for reasons then unknown, 'no amount of thyroid treatment will induce metamorphosis' (J. Huxley 1923a: 7). Suggesting what Julian Huxley calls 'the resistance of the larval tissues to metamorphosis' (1922a: 357), the 'human fish' is an apt model for Anthony's extended reluctance to self-improve and a hint at the alternative fate which might have awaited him. The fact that 'the strange Proteus' is 'blind, with tiny, sightless eyes' (Wells et al. 1937: 915) resonates with Aldous Huxley's connection of Anthony with *Samson Agonistes*, a text likewise concerned with literal and moral blindness and of course the source of the title *Eyeless in Gaza*. The most intriguing connection between Anthony and the olm occurs during a party with Anthony's university friends, a scene Anthony drunkenly perceives as a quasi-mystical vision of 'an illuminated aquarium':

> the aquarium was not only without, it was also, mysteriously, within him. Looking through the glass at those sea flowers and submarine gems, he was himself a fish – but a fish of genius, a fish that was also a god. ICHTHUS – *Iesos Christos theou huios soter*. His divine fish-soul hung there, poised in its alien element, gazing, gazing through huge eyes that perceived everything, understood everything, but having no part in what it saw. (*EG* 133)

Given the olm's common name of 'human fish', there is something intriguing about eyeless Anthony believing himself a 'fish [which] had found a tongue' (*EG* 135). The passage above clearly hints at Anthony's potential for change as well as his risk of failure. He is antisocial, aloof in his 'detached and irresponsible sensuality' and his 'detached irony' (*EG* 24, 616); yet his detachment also anticipates his eventual elevation above the jolly cynicism he shares with his companions. The identification with Christ is hubristic, to say the least, but it indicates his potential for 'heightened consciousness' (*EG* 328) and the better, 'potentially more than human' self he might become (*EM* 197).

In this moment, fittingly imagined in an aquarium where Julian Huxley might have housed his salamander, Anthony is both potential olm, fated to permanent neoteny, and potential axolotl, open to change. He eventually opts for the latter, but a vision of what might have been is available in the protagonist of Huxley's novel *Time Must Have a Stop* (1944), Sebastian Barnack, whose sensuality, intellect and cynicism echo those of Anthony before his conversion. If Anthony chooses the axolotl route, Sebastian opts for the other of the 'two roads' (1944: 254) and discovers that

> now he was what an old man ought not to be; and so, by straining to remain unmodified, had transformed himself into a gruesome anomaly. And, of course, in an age that had invented Peter Pan and raised the monstrosity of arrested development to the rank of an ideal, he wasn't in any way exceptional. (A. Huxley 1944: 304)

There were, the young Sebastian had learned from a pious friend, 'two roads' by which to 'escape from the unutterable wearisomeness, the silly and degrading horror of being merely yourself, of being only human': 'Apotheosis and deification' (1944: 254). How Huxley defines these terms is highly informative in the context of the fate of Sebastian, the merely human fish, and that of

Anthony, the potential Christ-fish. In the case of 'apotheosis', Sebastian reflects, 'the personality [is] exalted and intensified to the point where the person comes to be mere man or woman and becomes god-like' (1944: 253); but as the Biblical echo suggests, this is an illusory divinity:

> Under triumphal arches, along an avenue of statuary and fountains, you marched in pomp towards an ultimate frustration – dead end of your own selfhood. And the dead end was solid marble, of course, and adorned with the colossal monuments of your power, magnanimity and wisdom, but no less of a wall than the most grotesquely hideous of the vices down there in your old, all too human prison. Whereas the other road . . . (A. Huxley 1944: 254–5)

The other road, 'deification', is 'personality annihilated in charity, in union, so that at last the man or woman can say, "Not I, but God in me"' (1944: 253).

Apart from its role as the axolotl's foil, however, the contemporary history of biological experiments on olms may have something else to contribute to our understanding of Anthony's bizarre developmental trajectory. Though olms cannot be induced to metamorphose, they were known to be capable of changes which parallel Anthony's growth from eyelessness to 'insight' (*EG* 616). As the staunch Lamarckian (and ardent recapitulationist) Ernest MacBride reports in 1932, the Austrian biologist Paul Kammerer had apparently disproved the Darwinian hypothesis

> that the blindness of cave-animals was due to their having by chance inherited eye defects: for in 1923 he produced in my laboratory large specimens of the blind cave-newt *Proteus anguinus* with fully developed eyes, evolved by exposing the animals at the proper stage of growth to the action of red light. (MacBride 1932: 901)[4]

This experiment was designed to show – and was interpreted as demonstrating – the Lamarckian hypothesis that the olm is blind not because of chance mutations but rather because the caves it inhabits offer no opportunity to see, in other words that 'the cause of blindness is not congenital defect, but lack of stimulus to growth, for Proteus can . . . under proper conditions, produce a perfectly normal eye' (MacBride 1925: 818). Though Aldous Huxley, like his brother, held that 'the evidence of Lamarckism is extremely inadequate' (*EM* 260) and therefore doubted that use or disuse could affect how an organ would be transmitted to future generations, he was fully and reasonably convinced that the same mechanism does have effect on an individual's development. A disciple of F. M. Alexander's method, Aldous believed an individual's physical state was constrained but not fully determined by habit, which could be broken with 'creative conscious control' (*EM* 222). With 'improved physical co-ordination', he argued, an individual could achieve 'a general heightening of consciousness on all levels' (*EM* 222). It is therefore when Anthony accepts that 'use conditions function' (*EG* 85) – what Kammerer thought he had shown in the case of the olm's blindness – that he becomes receptive to change. Behaviour is largely reflex conditioned by habit, and, as Anthony comes to believe, 'if reflexes can be conditioned, then, obviously, they can be re-conditioned' (*EG* 84). Thus, as Anthony realises, 'old age . . . [is] largely a bad habit . . . Behave like an old man and your body will function like an old man's, you'll think and feel as an old man' (*EG* 85). By consciously acting mature instead of ever-infantile or prematurely aged, Anthony avails himself of metamorphosis.

By prolonging immaturity, neoteny defers the regression 'into savagery' which comes with mere ageing (*AS* 102) and the ossification of habit which comes with a long life of repetitive action. It may also, as Julian Huxley's research on induced metamorphosis suggests, allow the individual a certain accumulation of experience without which metamorphosis can be dangerous: in the 'young larvae' of frogs, for example, 'any large or moderate dose of thyroid causes disharmonic metamorphosis, with limbs not nearly large enough for adult life' (1925a: 374). As Lloyd Morgan puts it in *Habit and Instinct*, a 'period of youthful plasticity' divides 'the earlier stereotyped congenital response' of the infant from 'the later stereotyped acquired response' of the adult (1896: 158). For psychologists and biologists of the period, this plastic period was late childhood and adolescence. In any case, a protracted youth extends 'the plastic years of childhood' (A. Huxley 1927: 232) or, as William James called the period of greatest receptivity to conversion, 'the moulting-time of adolescence' (1985: 199). In a 1916 letter to Lady Ottoline Morrell, Huxley had referred to such a reservoir of latent potentiality in a comic key: 'I am reading Havelock Ellis on sex and discover . . . that I have within me the seeds of every known sexual aberration! – happily undeveloped!' (2007b: 37). 'Happily undeveloped' may well sum up Anthony's situation as neoteny safeguards his 'actualizable potentialities' until he is ready, in his infantile middle age, to 'modify himself' (*EG* 513, 522).

Bildung as Broken Habit

In dismissing *Eyeless in Gaza*'s anachrony as a gimmick, early reviewers (understandably) failed to see that it enables events from late in Anthony's story to find gainful employment, as it were, early in the discourse of his life. These critics unwittingly agree with the pre-conversion Anthony, a flawed character who tells himself he 'is simply a succession of states' in order to absolve himself of ethical responsibility – because then 'good and evil can be predicated only of states, not of individuals, who in fact don't exist, except as the places where the states occur' (*EG* 144–5). After his moral cowardice precipitates his friend

Brian's suicide in 1914, Anthony conveniently defines individuals as 'formless collections' (*EG* 147) of states, each isolated from the others, because this definition gets 'rid of responsibility and the need for consistency' (*EG* 365) and allows him, paradoxically, to remain 'unchangeably himself' (*EG* 24). 'What right had the man of 1914 to commit the man of 1926?' (*EG* 151), he asks, trying to exorcise his guilt for Brian's death. These are rationalisations which the text (as well as Anthony after his conversion) plainly refutes. In his self-serving view, a betrayal leading to Brian's suicide is no worse than a betrayal following the suicide (as it is presented in the text). This view only seems to explain the novel's anachrony, especially when Anthony imagines memory as

> a lunatic [who] shuffled a pack of snapshots and dealt them out at random . . . There was no chronology. The idiot remembered no distinction between before and after . . . At the time of the event certain participles happened to be in a favourable position. Click! The event found itself caught, indelibly recorded. For no *reason* whatever. (*EG* 23–4)

Tempting as they are to read as a key to the novel's form, these reflections are misleading. The narration is so tightly focalised through a character we know to be wrong that it could be called unreliable. The unreliability is in the timing (in the story): these reflections are from a character whose conversion will invalidate the nihilism of his younger self. And even he suspects a hidden logic beneath the randomness. He tells himself memories arise 'for no reason' but then wonders if perhaps 'the reason were not before the event, but after it, in what had been the future' (*EG* 24) – the Bergsonian notion of events retrospectively creating their own possibility.

In *Point Counter Point*, the novelist Philip Quarles imagines a novel about an asymmetrically developed character who, like himself and like Anthony, 'has always taken pains to encourage his own intellectualist tendencies at the expense of all the others. He avoids personal relationships as much as he can, he observes without participating' (*PCP* 473). The resemblance to Anthony increases when Quarles describes his character's relation to time and habit:

> he has always been careful not to distinguish one day . . .; not to review the past and anticipate the future . . ., not to revisit scenes from his childhood . . . He seems to himself to be achieving freedom . . . But in reality, as he gradually discovers, he has only narrowed and desiccated his life. (*PCP* 473–4)

The character 'desires, in theory, to change. But it's difficult to break life-long habits' (*PCP* 474). Fittingly, then, Anthony's conversion is framed as a breaking of the habit of being 'unchangeably himself' (*EG* 24). It is significant, then, that

Anthony's self-isolating 'habit of avoiding personal relations' manifests itself in the act of counting (*EG* 15, 19). As William James defines it in *The Principles of Psychology*, habit is a similarly mindless succession: 'a series of movements repeated in a certain order', writes James, 'tend to unroll themselves with peculiar ease in that order for ever afterward. Number one awakens number two, and that awakens number three, and so on' (2007: i.504). When Anthony caresses his lover Helen, he maintains a self-protective aloofness by counting

> one, two, three, four – each movement of his hand . . . The gesture was magical, would transport him, if repeated sufficiently often, beyond the past and the future, beyond right and wrong, into the discrete, the self-sufficient, the atomic present . . . Thirty-two, thirty-three, thirty-four, thirty-five. (*EG* 25)

The sequence recapitulates Anthony's whole life at this moment, 'the thirty-five years of his conscious life', before being interrupted by the beginning of a new chapter, set twenty-five years earlier, when Anthony counts billboards – 'thirty-one . . . thirty-two' (*EG* 23, 26) – in order to distract himself from the pain of his mother's death. This new sequence is obviously related to the sequence in the previous chapter, but the relation is neither one of anticipation (it is shown after) nor one of continuation (it jumps back from thirty-five to thirty-one). If the classical *Bildungsroman*'s linear correlation of story order and discourse order is perilously aligned to the 'peculiar ease' of habitual repetition, Huxley's re-vision of *Bildung*'s contrapuntal temporality breaks the linear sequence.

'To create a personality', Huxley writes almost a decade before *Eyeless in Gaza*, 'one must devise an ideal framework in which the naturally discontinuous materials can be harmoniously fitted. Temporal gaps separate the elements of a personality from one another; the framework should span these gulfs of time' (1927: 235). The device Huxley uses to 'compose' his hero's personality is anachrony, through which

> time-divided elements [and] discontinuous states may reveal themselves as a part of a whole, developing in time. The most perfect personality is that in which the natural discords are harmonized by some principle of unity, in which the discontinuous psychological elements are fitted into a framework of purposive ideals strong enough to bridge the gaps between them. (A. Huxley 1927: 235, 243–4)

This 'principle of unity' counters 'the principle of continuity' (1927: 250), suggesting that although the whole 'develop[s] in time', development is inadequately represented as a function of time.[5] Against continuity, Huxley foresees the role he would later assign to anachrony: 'the man who would co-ordinate his personality must devise a technique for association-making' (1927: 249–50). By shuffling discourse order, *Eyeless in Gaza* levels the walls between distinct phases of Anthony's life. Though his conversion occurs late in both story and discourse (7 Feb. 1934: Chapter 52), he first appears as a convert early in the discourse (4 & 5 Apr. 1934: Chapter 2). This mature Anthony contrasts with both the cynic of 1933 (Chapters 1 and 3) and the sensitive boy of 1902 (Chapter 4). Yet together the contrasting stages 'reveal themselves as part of a whole' (1927: 243–4).

The anachronous arrangement of chapters gives a synoptic view of Anthony's life. Rather than charting his growth from one age to the next, the narrative skips from age to age. As a result Anthony is never limited for very long to one age or one set of qualities. Instead, his lifelong self-diversity is continually foregrounded and related to Anthony's desire 'to develop all [his] potentialities' (*EG* 121), a notion recalling Humboldt's definition of the *Bildung* ideal. *Eyeless in Gaza*'s anachrony may therefore seem to model a psychological or mental freedom from time's arrow, in contradistinction with the linearity intuitively associated with biological development. Stuck in time, the successiveness of biological change would therefore seem insufficiently hospitable to the complex temporalities required for *Bildung*. But Huxley's novel does not reject biology at all: instead it replaces one kind of biological time with another, one more reflective of contemporary science – and modernist aesthetics. As the biogenetic law fell out of favour, embryologists and developmental geneticists were replacing its parallel (and therefore effectively synchronous) temporalities with heterochronic models which allowed ontogenetic events to vary in length, schedule and order relative to phylogenetic ones. To apply such non-linear models into a *Bildungsroman* is to reimagine *Bildung* as both product and process.

Huxley continually treats education, development and specialisation in relation to the biological sciences in which he was so well-versed. In his novelistic treatment of *Bildung*, as in his essays on education and psychology, he assumes 'mind and body are closely interdependent: they come to maturity more or less simultaneously' (1927: 16). The young mind and body, he continues, are 'undifferentiated and unindividualized', and 'a young child looks and thinks like other children of the same age and not like his parents', who have had the time to develop in body and acquire culture; at the early stages of the 'fertilized ova' or the 'very similar infants' there is no evidence of the profound differences which will later distinguish 'Shakespeare and Stratford's village idiot' (1927: 16–17). Differentiation is not specialisation, however; Huxley would say that the 'village idiot' is indeed both more undifferentiated and more specialised, that his failure to develop and harmonise a wide range of his potentialities has limited him to a single, machine-like role in his society. To be mature, for Huxley, is to transform and integrate the latent possibilities of infancy, and so radical is this transformation that 'to study human psychology exclusively in babies is like studying the anatomy of frogs exclusively in tadpoles' (1927: 17). This analogy, which effects a rapprochement between human mind ('human psychology') and animal body ('anatomy of frogs'), exemplifies Huxley's tendency to ground his views on education in biology. In *Ends and Means*, a nonfiction counterpart to *Eyeless in Gaza*, he argues that among all species 'man alone has kept himself free from specialization' and has therefore 'been able to go on progressing in the direction of greater awareness, greater intelligence' (*EM* 264). This is the same trajectory he values for individual humans in the social sphere: 'The qualities which have led to biological progress are the qualities which make it possible for individual beings to escape from their separateness – intelligence and the tendency to co-operate' (*EM* 301). By contrast, specialisation and its associated ills suggest bodily atrophy, degenerative disease and species extinction; they are also linked directly by Huxley to the modern notion of linear time, 'our tyrant' (1936b: 122).

Nevertheless, much of *Eyeless in Gaza*'s developmental vision depends on the ending, when discourse order merges with story order, suggesting some loyalty to the classical *telos* of mature fulfilment.[6] Anthony ends up accepting 'what was in store for him' in a state of 'serene lucidity . . . Whatever it might be, he knew now that all would be well' (*EG* 620). This optimism may well be ironised by the text, but Huxley evidently agrees with Anthony's mature belief that 'complete knowledge (with the whole mind) of the complete truth' – a synoptic survey of life – is the 'indispensable preliminary condition of any remedial action, any serious attempt at the construction of a genuinely human being' (*EG* 522). If Anthony ever is 'complete', it is in the final restoration of chronology, a fact which undermines Krishnamoorthy Aithal's claim that anachrony alone 'enacts his final transcendence from the temporal prison of the self' (1984: 49). Anachrony is the 'preliminary condition' for the 'remedial action', not the remediation itself.

Clandestine Evolution: Escape from Specialisation

Enlisting neoteny by heterochronic development as a generative process for Anthony's development, Huxley subtly extricates *Bildung* from the inimical narrative grammar of recapitulation. The best argument against the universality of recapitulation, argues de Beer, is the changeability and plasticity of immature stages: 'the inability of the theory of recapitulation to accord an evolutionary significance to embryonic and larval variations' (1938: 1). If novelty can arise not only at the end of ontogeny but at any earlier stage, the mechanism responsible for the conservation of the phylogenetic sequence is lost. By prolonging larval or immature plasticity into adulthood, furthermore, neoteny effectively reverses the direction of recapitulation (as we saw in Chapter 1, recapitulation pulls and compresses juvenile stages towards the beginning of ontogeny, thereby making room for the addition of novel traits at the end). By making Anthony's relatively old person modifiable by 're-conditioning', Huxley echoes Julian Huxley's cautions against seeing the adult form as a finished product. In a 1925 article with E. B. Ford, Julian had concluded that the various parts of an organism continue to develop, each along its own lines, by means of a 'definite relation between Mendelian factors [genes] and the rates of a process which is continuous throughout most of an organism's life' (1925: 863). Closer in time and theme to the project of *Eyeless in Gaza*, Julian writes with Gavin de Beer in *Elements of Experimental Embryology* that 'development is not merely an affair of early stages' (1934: ix). Development also includes 'the form-changes accompanying growth; senescence and natural death itself', 'the processes of amphibian metamorphosis or of human puberty' and, significantly, 'regeneration' (J. Huxley and de Beer 1934: ix). Because so much education occurs after childhood, anachrony permits the child to learn, as it were, from the adult version of itself.[7]

Anachrony performs this work by mimicking a phenomenon de Beer termed 'clandestine evolution' (*EE* 30), which depends on neoteny. The mechanics of clandestine evolution are complicated, but they bear structural affinities to James's attempts to explain religious experience empirically. A discussion of these attempts (which are, moreover, central to Huxley's project) should help introduce the specifics of their biological counterpart. Exploring the modernist recoil from gradualism in life narratives, H. Porter Abbott notes that, after Darwin, religious conversion stood as the 'last remaining outpost' of non-gradual change 'at the ontogenetic level. And as the stubborn remnant of *supernatural* causation it demanded urgent scientific attention, which it got in the form of a sustained effort to "naturalize" this unnatural event' (2010b: 5; original emphasis). Deeply committed to this effort, Huxley revered William James for striving 'to keep religion in connection with the rest of science' (James 1985: 513) by developing psychological explanations for the mysterious phenomena of genius and mystical insight. In Huxley's cherished *Varieties of Religious Experience*, James elegantly resolves the unity–diversity paradox by psychologising religious experience, without yet invalidating 'the theologian's contention that the religious man is moved by an external power' (1985: 512). His resolution depends on dividing the psyche into distinct but interacting parts:

> It is one of the peculiarities of invasions from the subconscious region to take on objective appearances, and to suggest to the Subject an external control. In the religious life the control is felt as 'higher'; but since on our hypothesis it is primarily the higher faculties of our own hidden mind which are controlling, the sense of union with the power beyond us is a sense of something, not merely apparently, but literally true. (James 1985: 512–13)

In this naturalistic mysticism is a hint at how anachrony can participate in the linear process of *Bildung*. In the divided psyche, the conscious and unconscious interact dynamically; like a boat on rough seas, consciousness is continually flooded, with unpredictable results, by unconscious thoughts. This dynamic, which James first described in 'Great Men and Their Environment', is not supernatural but 'darwinian' (1960: 247). A genius's mind innovates by shaping materials 'originally produced in the shape of random images, fancies, accidental out-births of spontaneous variation in the functional activity of the excessively instable human brain' (James 1960: 247). If habit takes the form of stepwise progression (as in Anthony's defensive counting), transformative thought is random anachrony:

> Instead of thoughts of concrete things patiently following one another in a beaten track of habitual suggestion, we have the most abrupt cross-cuts and transitions from one idea to another, the most rarefied abstractions and discriminations, the most unheard-of combinations of elements, the subtlest association of analogy. (James 1960: 248)

In Huxley's search for 'harmony between conscious self, personal not-self, and vegetative soul' (1956: 18), James's unification of the mystical and the psychological finds its necessary bodily complement in the new biology. In James's random associations 'many of the performances of genius . . . have their origin' (1985: 512), just as radically new animal morphologies emerge from the heterochronic rearrangement of the mosaic organism.

James's 'cross-cuts' mirror the dissociations of heterochrony, and their results (creative genius, divine inspiration) mirror the evolutionary novelties de Beer attributed to clandestine evolution.[8] In neoteny, the individual becomes reproductively mature before its body has passed through all the stages of its ancestors' life history: barring induced metamorphosis, axolotls never reach the terrestrial stages of salamander adulthood. They have 'lopped the dry land phase off the end of the ancestral life cycle' (Dawkins 2004: 326). Because even the fertilised egg of an animal contains all the genetic material to make an adult, such truncations of the later stages of ancestral ontogeny can open new developmental and evolutionary avenues. Thus, explains de Beer,

> a species undergoing paedomorphosis will find itself in possession of a number of genes whose functions were to control characters which no longer appear, since the old adult characters will be lost in neoteny . . . It is, therefore, possible to imagine that these 'unemployed' genes are available for new variation. (De Beer 1940: 82)

Hypothetically, the genes formerly responsible for the adult salamander's lungs could be put to radically new uses in the neotenous axolotl which, being aquatic, does not need lungs. Several biologists believed such repurposing of formerly adult features could trigger an 'unexpected abrupt modification', sending the species' evolution 'in a new direction altogether' (*EE* 31).

In a series of articles published between 1894 and 1928, Garstang promoted a controversial but influential account of how neoteny led to the emergence of vertebrates from some rather unpromising invertebrate ancestors. Rather than springing from the most advanced adult proto-vertebrate, the first vertebrates according to Garstang arose from heterochronic disruptions of development in a marine species which, like today's sea squirts and corals, have a free-swimming larva and a sedentary adult which is essentially 'a bag filled with sea water, plus a gut and reproductive organs, anchored to a rock' (Dawkins 2004: 377). Though the animal has the same genetic constitution all its life, then, its larval and adult manifestations are profoundly different. The larva has a tail for swimming and the sophisticated sensory and mental faculties required for an active life; thus in larval life 'the nervous system is now at the height of its development' (Garstang and Garstang 1928: 14). When it metamorphoses into an adult, whose sessile lifestyle obviates the need for an elaborate sensory and mental capacity, it undergoes 'degeneration of the tail and larval nervous system' (Garstang and Garstang 1928: 14). The traits differentiating larva from adult are, however, latent in the adult, and all it takes to express them in adults of the next generation is a minor alteration in the schedule of trait expression. In Garstang's hypothesis, then, our vertebrate lineage began when heterochrony delayed the development of certain larval traits, preventing them from undergoing metamorphic change and therefore allowing them to persist in the adult. This new adult form was suddenly extremely adaptable: able to seek mates and food actively and to occupy new habitats, its lineage would have undergone an evolutionary flowering, or adaptive radiation. In his lively retelling of Garstang's hypothesis and clandestine evolution, Dawkins writes that 'we vertebrates . . . are descended from sea squirt *larvae* – larvae that never grew up: or rather larvae whose reproductive organs grew up but who never turned into sea squirt adults' (2004: 379–80). Such a strange transformation, Dawkins muses, might have inspired a novel from 'a second Aldous Huxley' (2004: 380).

Neoteny likewise contributes to the amazing adaptability of humans, combining adult qualities derived from long-term experience with conserved juvenile qualities. Recapitulation, meanwhile, leads to 'small groups of animals, which become more and more specialized and incapable of evolving further' (*EE* 91). There is an obvious parallel between this critique of recapitulation and the modernist critique of *Bildung* plots which lead inexorably to 'finished adults' (Esty 2012: 53). Sounding not unlike Yeats or Eliot, de Beer endows neoteny with the promise of renewal, in individuals, in species and even in the universe. As 'the cause of the retention of plasticity' (that is, 'the potentiality of evolving further'), neoteny can reverse evolutionary entropy: 'We do not know how energy is built up again in the physical universe although it must happen somehow; but the analogous process in the domain of organic evolution would seem to be paedomorphosis' (*EE* 91, 95).

De Beer's dubious certainty that evolutionary rejuvenation 'must' have a cosmological homologue signals a faith in correspondences much in evidence in Huxley's view of *Bildung* as the bridging of separate faculties. It is in search of such correspondences that Huxley randomises the chapters of *Eyeless*. In other words, the novel's anachrony is the formal manifestation of a thematic pressure: the need for Anthony to change himself. More than a good metaphor, metamorphosis is for Huxley the basis of a new narrative – a new *narratology* even – of human development. Formal devices always mean more than our interpretations of them might suggest; nevertheless, *Eyeless in Gaza*'s anachrony does clearly mimic both induced metamorphosis and clandestine evolution. Anachrony puts effects before their causes (and so, in the discourse, allows effects to *cause* their causes), just as heterochrony shuffles the developmental schedules of various organs, resulting in new associations among them and, thus, in new morphologies. The 'proper correlation' of Anthony's faculties requires rearranging the habitual linear plot; no wonder his conversion persuades him to rethink the 'shape' of his own book, *The Elements of Sociology*: 'it would be silly not to put my materials into shape. Into a new shape, of course' (*EG* 328, 15).

Ontogeny to Phylogeny: The Politics of Huxley's *Bildung*

The title of Anthony's book is apt because Huxley's novel is ultimately concerned not only with the individual's conversion but also with his ability to spur social change. The same goal animates Julian Huxley's concern with the evolutionary repercussions of developmental change and James's belief that great individuals reshape their world through acts of genius. Though Jerome Meckier calls *Eyeless in Gaza* a satire of the *Bildungsroman* (1969: 144), its use of biology suggests an earnest attempt to reimagine the genre's central concern with social integration. In the end, chronology restored, Anthony advances 'step by step towards the experience of being no longer wholly separate, but unified at the depths with other lives, with the rest of being' (*EG* 618). This social unification differs markedly from submission demanded of the protagonist in the classical *Bildungsroman*, whose youthful hero may be eccentric but can mature only by acquiescing to the social order. Anthony inverts this trajectory: rather than conform to society, he pledges to forge it into his image. Maturity for Anthony, as it does for Stephen at the end of *Portrait*, means being ready to change the world around him.

As Huxley writes in *Ends and Means*, individuals are 'capable not only of achieving personal enlightenment, but also of helping whole societies to deal with their major problems' (*EM* 323). For Anthony this means growing up in order to help other 'individual men, women, and children' become 'full-grown human beings' (*EG* 452–3). Anthony subscribes to F. H. Alexander's technique for re-conditioning reflexes and habits, the constraining and mindless sets of actions which limit development not only in the individual but also in society. As William James famously proclaims, habit, society's 'most precious conservative agent', prevents 'different social strata from mixing' because it 'dooms us all to fight out the battle of life upon the lines of our nurture or our early choices . . . because there is no other for which we are fitted, and it is too late to begin again' (2007: i.121). Tempering James's pessimism, *Eyeless in Gaza* explores the possibility that it is not too late for *Bildung* or for true progress in society.

With this enlightened view Anthony finally comes to meditate on 'identical patterns, and identical patternings of patterns . . ., the thought of life incessantly moving among the patterns, selecting and rejecting for its own purposes. Life building up simpler into more complex patterns – identically complex through vast ranges of animate being' (*EG* 612). The theme of this abstract passage is development, the emergence of complexity from simplicity, as well as the unity or universality of patterns which underlie all mutability. From these abstractions Anthony's thoughts about patterns turn towards the biological:

> The sperm enters the egg, the cell divides and divides, to become at last this man, that rat or horse. A cow's pituitary will make frogs breed out of season. Urine of a pregnant woman bring[s] the mouse on heat. Sheep's thyroid transforms the axolotl from a gilled larva into an air-breathing salamander, the cretinous dwarf into a well-grown and intelligent human. (*EG* 612)

Highlighting the transformative power of hormones, Anthony gives voice to the analogy embodied in the novel's form – the link between the human potential for harmonious self-realisation and the axolotl's potential for induced metamorphosis. In a sense, then, *Eyeless in Gaza* is a study in 'the correlation found between regeneration rate and susceptibility to hormones' (J. Huxley and de Beer 1934: 370). In *Mechanism, Life and Personality*, J. B. S. Haldane stresses the accidental aspects which can make or break development, referring to 'the known fact that some organic defect – for instance, in his thyroid gland – may make him an idiot' (1913: 134). It is tempting in light of this passage to wonder if Huxley's 'cretinous dwarf', an 'idiot [who] remembered no distinction between before and after' (*EG* 23), might not become 'a well-grown and intelligent human' by the intervention of what might be called narrative thyroid. Our axolotl has metamorphosed.

This correlation between individual 'axolotl' and individual 'dwarf' also entails another, related analogy between individual regeneration and group progress, as well as between individual body and cosmic harmony. The action of hormones in the development of an axolotl (or mouse, or frog) also implies their action across individuals – what Aubrey Schneider calls, in an essay citing Julian's axolotl research, 'the universal action of thyroid' (1939: 431). Hormones are physiologically efficacious in their native bodies, but they act also when transposed into other bodies, even across species – hence Anthony's insight that 'between one form of animal life and another, patterns are interchangeable' (*EG* 612–13). The implication is that there is more to Anthony's self-realisation than 'choos[ing] one set of patterned atoms to represent his personality rather than another' (*EG* 147–8); he must also merge the personal pattern with larger, 'super-personal' patterns (*EM* 325).[9] In a related discussion in *After Many a Summer*, Huxley has his spokesman Bill Propter define the 'good' as the harmony between two levels, cosmic and individual: 'On the lower level, good exists as the proper functioning of the organism in accordance with the laws of its own being', a psychological but also bodily state which includes 'correct body posture' (*AS* 120, 121), and 'on the higher level, it exists in the form of a knowledge of the world without desire . . ., as the transcendence of personality, the extension of consciousness beyond the limits imposed by the ego' (*AS* 120).

If Anthony ever achieves maturity, it is when he recognises super-personality as a means of harmonising the 'good on the . . . two levels' mentioned by Propter (*AS* 120), as the solution to the paradox of 'unity even in diversity' (*EG* 612). This is surely what Huxley has in mind when he praises William James's notion of the 'continuum of cosmic consciousness' (James, qtd in A. Huxley 2002: 58). Such a consciousness helps explain chapters from which Anthony is absent, as well as the otherwise inexplicable date stamps. Like Woolf's *The Waves*, *Eyeless in Gaza* embeds its characters within a larger textual consciousness, wherein they achieve 'union with what is above personality' (*EM* 73). Only after his conversion does Anthony realise that the self's unity lies 'outside the boundaries' of personality (*EG* 143). 'Most human beings', he writes, fail to achieve their developmental potential because they 'do not know how to travel upwards from personality into a region of super-personality' (*EM* 71–2). This might be read as a mystical statement of belief in some transcendental mind, but *Eyeless in Gaza* offers a more mundane, and naturalistic, commitment to social life. This is certainly how Haldane, a clear influence on Huxley, understands the development of personality in relation to 'the still wide life that the race itself is living': 'our personal existence', he writes, 'implies in its very nature participation in a wider personal life . . . In losing his individual personality in the wider personal life he realises his true personality' (1913: 127–8). Social connection is, along with individual freedom, 'an essential condition' of true *Bildung*, at least as Wilhelm von Humboldt saw it (Sorkin 1983: 58–60). In any case, the idea of a 'super-personality' clarifies *Eyeless in Gaza*'s ambivalent relation to Proust, who, Huxley thought, insightfully modelled the human mind but failed to apply those insights to social improvement (1927: 247). Huxley exploits Proustian memory within chapters, but the temporal shifts between chapters transcend the boundaries of the self.

Anthony's 'travel upwards' enables him to elevate others, most notably Helen, the first person he allows himself to love (*EG* 154). Helen enjoys so much narrative attention – featuring her own network of chapters, motifs and associations – that *Eyeless in Gaza* can scarcely be read in terms of Anthony's *Bildung* alone. One of her functions is to contrast with Anthony (he becomes a pacifist, she a bloodthirsty communist), but she also participates in his growth. At the very beginning it is Helen who triggers the cascade of Anthony's Proustian memories which, like a fugue's exposition, introduce key motifs which will resonate throughout the novel; the narrativisation of Anthony's *Bildung* is thus performed as a social rather than merely individual process. His life-changing trip to Mexico is spurred by a chance meeting with Helen; his conversion is prefigured in his spontaneous empathy for her; and his final choice to face physical danger and deliver a pacifist lecture follows a debate with her. This influence is reciprocal: the formative events in Helen's life involve Anthony. In the end, her belief in political violence wavers and she seems ready for Anthony's pacifism (*EG* 608). Though the novel ends before she can choose either option, her new receptivity to his ideals signals a major change of heart. The novel's structure reflects Anthony's growth in mutual interaction with Helen's.

Grasping that 'between one form of animal life and another, patterns are interchangeable' (*EG* 612–13), Anthony has not merely grasped a basic fact of endocrinology. The miraculous effect of thyroid, he learns, is a molecular counterpart to the emotions humans share: 'the mental pattern of love can be transferred from one mind to another and still retain its virtue, just as the physical pattern of a hormone can be transferred, with all its effectiveness, from one body to another' (*EG* 613). Huxley bridges the apparent differences between physiological process and emotional attachment, biological transmission and cultural communication, biosphere and noosphere. Not mere analogies, these are homologies. The hormone and 'the mental pattern of love' *seem* distinct, one perceptible to our senses, the other only to intuition and emotions, yet they are actually aspects of one reality. Anthony's conversion occurs when he accepts that his personality is neither atomically dissociated in time nor separate from other personalities but, rather, embedded with them in the super-personal, just 'as a hand is committed to the arm' (*EG* 611). This is the way to bridge his development with social and evolutionary progress: 'Love and understanding', argues Huxley,

> are valuable even on the biological level. Hatred, unawareness, stupidity, and all that makes for increase in separateness are the qualities that, as a matter of historical fact, have led either to the extinction of a species, or to its becoming a living fossil, incapable of making further biological progress. (*EM* 301–2)

In retrospect, such views may appear unaccountably sanguine. Time has not looked kindly on *Eyeless in Gaza*, whose political naïvety seems downright silly in the wake of World War II. But if this *Bildungsroman* fails to articulate what Iris Murdoch calls 'a satisfactory Liberal theory of personality, a theory of man as free and separate and related to a rich and complicated world' (1961: 18), its formal incorporation of biology still constitutes an important and undervalued part of the story of modernism's efforts to safeguard *Bildung* from modernity. Julian Huxley writes of human development: 'that moulding of matter by spirit is, under one aspect, Science; under another, Art; under still another, Religion. Let us be careful not to allow the moulding forces to counteract each other when they might be made to co-operate' (1923c: 302). Forty years later, the same warning echoes in Aldous's *Literature and Science* in a passage which sheds retrospective light on the experiment of *Eyeless in Gaza*:

> Words are few and can only be arranged in certain conventionally fixed ways . . . That the purified language of science, or even the richer purified language of literature should ever be adequate to the givenness of the world and of our experience is in the very nature of things, impossible. Cheerfully accepting the fact, let us advance together, men of letters and men of science, further and further into the ever-expanding regions of the unknown. (A. Huxley 1963: 99)

Only 'together' can science and literature transcend the 'fixed', sequential nature of language and, by extension, plot. In its attempt to model this combined effort *Eyeless in Gaza* represents an important record of modernist art aligning itself, in its reaction against modernity, with what I would call modernist science. Its dizzying adaptation of the new biology makes it one of the century's fascinating attempts to make *Bildung* possible in the modern world.

For all its idiosyncrasy, Huxley's exploitation of neoteny and clandestine evolution echoes through the works of a remarkably diverse range of public intellectuals, most notably John Dewey, Konrad Lorenz and Timothy Leary. (The trend continues: a Google Books search for 'human neoteny' yields an abundance of more or less creditable titles in psychology, pedagogy, theology, self-help and more.) Closer to Huxley, Gerald Heard would argue in 1941 that humanity's survival rests on a 'sporadic outcrop of men who manage to retain, with full mental stature, the radical originality and freshness of a vigorous child' (1941: 160). This view rests in equal parts on James's model of individual genius and on de Beer's clandestine evolution: 'radical, creative hypotheses do not result from specialized accumulation of data' but 'spring from minds which . . . combine absorption with detachment, interest with wonder. It is this combination which produces the mental explosion, the intellectual ignition, after which the idea is found precipitated' (Heard 1941: 160). In *Growing Young*, Ashley Montagu declares that neoteny's 'ramifications for the future of each of us and of humanity in general are so staggering that an understanding of it should be a part of everyone's equipment' (1989: 1), and that education should strive to 'cultivate the child's neotenous traits' (1989: 223). In the same intellectual tradition is the late twentieth-century reconciliation of evolutionary and developmental biology, catalysed largely by Stephen Jay Gould's *Ontogeny and Phylogeny* (1977), a book documenting the often ugly legacy of recapitulation theory and exploring alternative models provided by heterochrony (McNamara and McKinney 2002: 17).

Nor was Huxley alone in treating these ideas in literature. Especially intriguing is the 'Verse Commentary' to W. H. Auden's sonnet sequence 'In Time of War' (1938). Initially a student of biology, Auden credits humans for having developed our potentialities so much that our 'boneless worm-like ancestors would be amazed / At the upright position, the breasts, the four-chambered heart, / The clandestine evolution in the mother's shadow' (1977: 13–15). More recently, Margaret Drabble's *The Sea Lady* relates the possibility of later-life *Bildung* to the 'evolutionary miracle' of neoteny and 'the "little thyroid gland that makes us wise or stupid"' (2008: 57). Zia Haider Rahman's *In the Light of What We Know*, meanwhile, details the life history of the 'axolotl' as an allegory of the mixed blessings of postcolonial *Bildung*. A man raised by his own bootstraps from the backwaters of Bangladesh into the top spheres of global finance and then international human-rights law is thus like a juvenile salamander 'induced into metamorphosis', so that 'it can never go back to what it was' (Rahman 2014: 283). Such literary engagements with neoteny and progress suggest that biology, despite the persistent myth of the Two Cultures rift, remains for modernism (and beyond) a potent source of imaginative possibility, innovation with narrative forms and new ways of understanding our experience.

Notes

1. These sentiments are prefigured in a letter Huxley wrote eight years earlier to his wife Maria Nys Huxley. Against the stale conventions of nineteenth-century realism, he writes,

> I believe the cinema method is rather a good one to give a series of short scenes, each of which would be a slice of life, with very little explanation in between. But I really can't make up my mind; one can only discover the best methods by experiment, and I will have to write a great deal more till I begin to theorize. (A. Huxley 2007b: 79)

If anything Huxley wrote approaches the condition of the cinema, with unexplained gaps between 'slices of [a] life', it is *Eyeless in Gaza*.

2. On Julian Huxley's scientific coterie and its relation to Aldous Huxley, see Clayton (2016).
3. Amphibian metamorphosis and the effects of thyroid occupied Julian Huxley throughout the 1920s. His short note in a 1920 issue of *Nature* was followed by detailed studies of amphibian endocrinology, including two articles on 'Ductless Glands and Development' (1922a, 1923a) and two on 'Experiments on Amphibian Metamorphosis' (1922b, 1925b).
4. Like MacBride, Kammerer supported Lamarckian inheritance long after it had been dismissed by most biologists. He was something of a star biologist among the public in Europe, Britain and the US. His bitter feud with William Bateson and eventual fall from grace are described in Arthur Koestler's wonderful *The Case of the Midwife Toad* (1971). In *The Science of Life*, Wells, J. Huxley and Wells offer a Darwinian explanation for the olm experiment (without mentioning Kammerer) (1937: 915).
5. The influence of André Gide's *Les Faux-monnayeurs* is clear in Huxley's essay, as it is throughout *Point Counter Point* (as Philippe Birgy [1997] has shown) and in the temporal structure of *Eyeless in Gaza*. Gide's narrator

   > can admire, in some rare cases, what is called 'the spirit of continuity'; but usually this aspect of being is obtained only by a vain stubbornness and at the expense of the natural. The more generous the individual and the more abundant his potentialities, the more disposed he is to change, the less willing to allow his future to be determined by his past. (Gide 1975: 324)

6. Jerry Wasserman's ingenious study of *Eyeless in Gaza* (1980) as a retelling of Kierkegaard's *Either/Or* comes to the opposite conclusion, arguing that the patterns of Anthony's behaviour to date militate against his future success.
7. In contrast with James's and Huxley's non-linear developmental dynamics, particularly as these play out during the chrysalis-like period of adolescence, G. Stanley Hall viewed the role of adolescence in overall development within the linear, progressive framework of recapitulation:

   > for those prophetic souls interested in the future of our race and desirous of advancing it, the field of adolescence is the quarry in which they must seek to find both goal and means. If such a higher stage is ever added to our race, it will not be by increments at any later plateau of adult life, but it will come by increased development of the adolescent stage, which is the bud of promise for the race. (Hall 1904: i.50)

8. De Beer's analogy has been used in other contexts, including Stephen Gould's account of 'regulatory DNA', which controls the rate, timing and regulation of cellular mechanisms, and which can jump from chromosome to chromosome, with 'profound immediate effects' on development: 'Inserted into a new chromosome, . . . [i]t may, for example, bring together the products of two genes that had never been in proximity.

This new combination may benefit the organism' (1984: 171). This description helps clarify not only de Beer's explanation but also William James's theory of genius and the motivation for Huxley's use of anachrony.

9. Huxley's vision of the personality immersed within a larger super-personality might seem to contradict the anti-fascist and anti-totalitarian thrust of his theories of development and self-formation, but the mystical communion he desires is explicitly not rooted in national, racial, or any other kind of membership. It is an emergent rather than inherent unity of purpose which produces the good society, the consequence of rational and ethical *means* rather than the assertion of power and suppression of dissent in the interest of a desired or expected end. This model of community is evidently at odds with the teleologies of fascism and Leninism, as is its fundamental rejection of justifying violence or the assertion of power over others. Huxley's promotion of means over ends is also, of course, completely consistent with his fidelity to the late eighteenth-century notion of *Bildung*, of a development whose end is formation rather than mere form.

6

BEGINNING AGAIN: DARWIN'S CATERPILLAR FROM GEORGE ELIOT TO BECKETT

> Man, in the course of his individual evolution, passes through a series of transformations no less astonishing and remarkable than the well-known metamorphoses of the butterfly.
>
> – Ernst Haeckel, *The Evolution of Man* (1883: 3)

Freighted with mythic and religious resonances, butterfly metamorphosis is probably the most important biological counterpart of the *Bildungsroman*. The two developmental narratives chart the individual's progress from earthbound body (the caterpillar-child with its corporeal appetites) through introspective mind (the chrysalis-adolescent) to beautiful spirit (the imago-adult). In the myth of Psyche, whose name means *soul* and *butterfly*, metamorphosis is a transformation from mortal to goddess.[1] This allegory adapted easily to Christianity, representing the release of the immortal soul from the mortal body, or else the awakening of being born again. It was a favoured image of Symbolist and *fin-de-siècle* poets. Thomas Mann made it a 'central issue' in his recuperation of *Bildung* (Vuillet 2012: 99). The trope persists in the secular ideal of maturity as self-realisation and autonomy in pedagogy, psychoanalysis and human rights.

The spiritual dimension of the butterfly allegory is a frequent target of modernist irony. Joyce, as we have seen, undercuts Stephen's vision of 'spiritual progress' (*PA* 148) as a metamorphic renewal, 'as if his very body were divested with ease of some outer skin or peel' (*PA* 149). Musil mocks his protagonist Törless's similarly sanguine outlook on his own education as a mere 'game; something to help through this larval stage [*Larvenexistenz*] of school life. It had no connection with his true nature, which would only emerge later, at some as yet remote and undecided time in the future' (2013: 47). The spiritual allegory is travestied in the reversionary transformations of Orlando and Gregor Samsa. Deflations of the butterfly allegory culminate in Henry Green's *Blindness*, whose division into three parts entitled 'Caterpillar', 'Chrysalis' and 'Butterfly' suggests the successful *Bildung* of would-be writer John Haye. Undermining the promise of the three subtitles, however, is the persistent ironic deflation of John's aspirations. Determined to write a novel, John makes a final announcement – 'I am going to settle down to writing now' (Green 2008: 505) – as ambiguous as that of Stephen Dedalus. Seemingly triumphant in the end, John is in fact stating an intention he has already repeatedly expressed without writing anything. Procrastinating to the end, he remains more chrysalis than imago, not flying but 'boxed up' (Green 2008: 499), 'muffled' (Green 2008: 500), 'helpless' and 'enveloped' (Green 2008: 501).

John's development, however, does not necessarily end in failure. The novel leaves him, rather, in an indefinite state of 'failing', a condition preferable to success because the *Bildung* ideal cannot be reached and still be truly *Bildung* (Castle 2015: 487).[2] John's repeated deferrals keep him in a state of flux and potentiality, living each day as if it were his first. The penultimate chapter of 'Butterfly' is called 'Finishing' (Green 2008: 465), suggesting irrevocability and closure. But this gloomy implication is reversed by the title of the final chapter: 'Beginning again' (Green 2008: 493).

Beginning again is a characteristically modernist device, a formal and ideological intervention which, as Edward Said argues in *Beginnings: Intention and Method*, challenges inherited and common-sense notions of origins, causality and mimesis (1975: 66). These challenges are particularly visible in modernist narratives of personal and historical change. Repeated beginnings are a stylistic and thematic hallmark of Gertrude Stein's prose. *Ulysses* begins twice at eight in the morning. *Lord Jim* and *Nostromo* reiterate beginnings – the former thematically, in Jim's attempts to 'begin with a clean slate' (Conrad 1976: 142), the latter formally, in the loops which repeatedly lead the deposed dictator Ribiera and his decrepit mule into Sulaco. Flann O'Brien's *At Swim-Two-Birds* begins with 'three openings entirely dissimilar' (2001: 9). *Zeno's Conscience* is 'a history of [Zeno's] smoking habit' (Svevo 2001: 7), a therapeutic narrative whose telling promises to make him 'whole' (2001: 7); unfortunately, Zeno admits, 'I can't seem to begin, so I must seek help from my cigarettes' (2001: 7). His narrative is therefore a succession of last cigarettes, each one a new beginning. In Edwin Muir's *The Marionette*, Hans inhabits a fantasy which arrests his growth, keeping him 'unchanged' and forcing him 'to begin perpetually again' (1987: 79). Graham Greene's *The End of the Affair* begins by suggesting that any moment might be a beginning: 'A story has no beginning or end: arbitrarily one chooses that moment of experience from which to look back or from which to look ahead' (2000: 7). So much depends on that choice – generically, ideologically, aesthetically. Begin a *Bildungsroman* too soon, or end it too late, and it is a family novel like *The Rainbow*. Begin too late, as in *The Return of the Soldier*, and it loses its kinship with the genre altogether.

Most modernist *Bildungsromane* present beginning again as a state of flux, poised between failure and potential. These reiterations go far beyond those repetitions which give unity and continuity to modern conceptions of selfhood – the repetitive acts of remembering (Locke), habit (Samuel Butler), transference (Freud) and performance (Judith Butler). Too much repeating produces disruptive narrative turbulence and epistemic uncertainty – for many modernists a positive outcome. Repetition, argues J. Hillis Miller, challenges 'the straightforward historical movement suggested by Aristotle's comments on beginning, middle, and end' with an alternative movement of 'constant reversal' (1982: 35), which 'affirms now one possibility, now another, now all three at once, . . . since each possibility contains the others and calls them up' (1982: 230). Miller does not mention the *Bildungsroman*, but the genre's historical relation to chronology makes it an especially potent target for the condition of 'constant reversal', a reversionary dynamic which repeatedly interrupts only to restart the developmental clock.

This chapter explores beginning again as a means of interrupting the recapitulatory *Bildung* plot, focusing on the literary afterlife of a developmentally confused caterpillar described in *The Origin of Species*. Darwin's caterpillar appears in several Victorian novels, frustrating the expected developmental arc or suggesting alternative trajectories before incorporating itself, nearly invisibly, in the novels of a modernist for whom beginning again was particularly dear. Samuel Beckett is a fitting endpoint for a study of the modernist *Bildungsroman*. His major fictions coincide with a period of humanist crisis, occasioned by the Second World War and the Holocaust, mixed with guarded optimism about the possibility of *Bildung* as a universal human right (Slaughter 2009: 1–45).

Until recently, pairing Beckett and *Bildungsroman* would have seemed incongruous. *The Unnamable*, after all, *begins* by summarily dispatching setting, character and time, the fundamental aspects of the genre: 'Where now? Who now? When now?' (*UN* 331). Yet, though Beckett's novels are not *Bildungsromane*, they constantly call on the biographical mode by means of plot fragments, allusions, negative patterns and wanderings mistaken for quests. In *Dream of Fair to Middling Women*, the narrator alludes to the *Bildung* tradition, and perhaps to the opening of *A Portrait of the Artist*:

> we were once upon a time inclined to fancy our self as the Cézanne, shall we say, of the printed page, very strong on architectonics. We live and learn, we draw breath from our heels now, like a pure man, and honour our Father, our Mother, and Goethe. (Beckett 1993: 178–9)

In this sarcastic remark, writes Patrick Bixby, the narrator situates 'his narrative and, indeed, Beckett's entire oeuvre in a parodic relationship with Schiller's educational ideal of the "pure man" and Goethe's narrativization of the same' (2009: 27). Jed Esty similarly writes of Beckett's invitation to readers 'to recognize the residual signs of a soul-nation allegory, then to delight in their comic devastation' (2012: 204); Paul Sheehan calls the so-called Trilogy 'a *Bildungsroman* evisceration' (2004: 182) which replaces organic development with 'a series of switches, shuttling back and forth between human and inhuman, narrative and antinarrative' (2004: 184).

The target of Beckett's irony, it bears mentioning, is not development *per se* but its privileged status in realist fiction. Railing against 'Balzac, for example, and the divine Jane [Austen]' (Beckett 1993: 119), the narrator of *Dream of Fair to Middling Women* deplores 'the procédé that . . . consists of dealing with the vicissitudes, or absence of vicissitudes, of character . . . as though that were the whole story' (Beckett 1993: 119). What offends him is not character and development but the idea that these are 'the whole story'. Beckett's complaint thus echoes Woolf's exasperated question, 'Is life like this?' (*EVW* iv.160). As Leland de la Durantaye points out, 'Beckett rejects realism not because it aspires to reflect the world around it, but because it so abjectly fails at the task' (2016: 25), leaving out too much of the world. Beckett's theoretical and stylistic debts to Gide, Sartre and Sade, investigated by John Bolin (2013), suggest that he was striving to conceive character and selfhood anew, not necessarily reduce then to mere language games.

Biographical plots remain, fragmented but recognisable, in Beckett's novels from *Murphy* (1938) to *How It Is* (1961). Their dynamics are insistently reversionary. *Murphy* contrasts the Irish condition with the ideals of *Bildung* and progressive evolution: Miss Counihan, 'an Irish girl . . . quite exceptionally anthropoid' (*MU* 69), exhibits a morphological arrest in development equivalent to the ignorance of 'analphabets, especially those of Irish education' (*MU* 115). In an Irish version of Defoe's 'True-Born Englishman', Beckett includes information on 'the effects of insularity, notably the retarded development of Irish flora and fauna' (Van Hulle 2014b: 31). In the entry on 'Larval Existence' in *The Grove Companion to Samuel Beckett*, Ackerley and Gontarski describe Murphy's attempt to 'regain the lost coenaesthesis of the embryonic stage' and note that '*Comment c'est* determines the phylogeny of "l'homme la[r]vaire" crawling through the mud in a denial of metamorphosis' (2004: 309). It is indeed in an anecdote Darwin tells about interrupted metamorphosis that Beckett found his reversionary master-trope. By repeating fragments of the biographical plot instead of letting it unfold fully, Beckett lets development run amok, formless yet undeniably vital. There may be no escape from the world of shit, he writes in *Molloy*, but constant movement rewards you at least with 'a change of muck' (*MO* 43), and 'it's good to have a change of muck, to move from one heap to another a little further on, from time to time, fluttering you might say, like a butterfly, as if you were ephemeral' (*MO* 43).

Darwin's Caterpillar from Victorian Pathology to Modernist Promise

In the chapter on 'Instinct' in *The Origin of Species*, Darwin discusses the link between habitual repetition and ordered sequences (a topic also discussed in Chapter 5). Darwin notes that when we are interrupted in the middle of a song, we often forget where we were and need to start again from the beginning in order to complete the song. He then summarises an experiment conducted by the naturalist Pierre Huber on the larva of the apple leaf miner (*Lyonetia clerkella*), a caterpillar which 'makes a very complicated hammock' (chrysalis) (*OS* 208). When Huber

> took a caterpillar which had completed its hammock up to, say, the sixth stage of construction, and put it into a hammock completed up only to the third stage, the caterpillar simply re-performed the fourth, fifth, and sixth stages of construction. If, however, a caterpillar were taken out of a hammock made up, for instance, to the third stage, and were put into one finished up to the sixth stage, so that much of its work was already done for it, far from feeling the benefit of this, it was much embarrassed, and, in order to complete its hammock, seemed forced to start from the third stage, where it had left off, and thus tried to complete the already finished work. (*OS* 208)

In theory, if the experiment continued indefinitely, the caterpillar would persist in deferring its metamorphosis indefinitely and would thus remain juvenile. One way to make sense of Darwin's caterpillar is to view its repetitions as a vicious cycle, a pathological diversion from the line of true development. The result is a breakdown of what Pierre Brunel calls the 'palingenetic myth' [*le mythe palingénésique*] of metamorphosis (1974: 166), the symbolic reversal of death by means of rebirth or resurrection as an 'attempt at a resolution to a fundamental contradiction in our existence' (Brunel 1974: 167). If so, the embarrassment of Darwin's caterpillar is acute indeed, for it repeatedly fails to complete and redeem its development; its repetitive looping offers an especially vivid picture of the doubts latent in Victorian progressivism.

Alternatively, Darwin's caterpillar offers a completely new model of development. As George Levine has shown, the gradualistic model of change inherent in Darwinism was so engrained in Victorian thought that it 'helped determine the way novels were written', making 'continuity and connection' (1988b: 224) synonymous with narrative itself. Victorian fiction, however, adopted a mere fraction of Darwinism's potential contributions to narrative, dismissing its 'incoherence', 'deep irrationality' and 'series of disruptions' (Levine 1988b: 227). As Levine argues elsewhere, there was another Darwin, less amenable to Victorian realism's 'uniformitarian and scrupulously sequential' plots (1988a: 263) – 'a Darwin more disruptive, perhaps, than even the greatest of literary followers can suggest, a Darwin who, if fully absorbed by his contemporary novelists, might well have led to other kinds of narratives' (1988a: 22). Such is the Darwin of the caterpillar anecdote, in which novelists both Victorian and modern recognised a new kind of developmental plot. The caterpillar's iterative reversions to the larval stage anticipate a feature of the twentieth-century *Bildungsroman* identified by Susan Gohlman: the need protagonists have to interrupt their own development, 'reject[ing] everything they had learned and painstakingly creat[ing] a new or revised set of values' (1990: ix).

The earliest literary use of Darwin's caterpillar is probably in *Silas Marner*, written shortly after George Eliot read *The Origin*.[3] Though rarely called a *Bildungsroman*, *Silas Marner* is profoundly concerned with Silas's development, which stalls after his expulsion from Lantern Yard and becomes pathologically cyclical as his love of gold drives him ever more deeply into his weaving and out of society. Silas's work is already suggestive of kinship with a caterpillar continually spinning its hammock; the relation is bolstered by references to his 'insect-like existence' (*SM* 13), his eyes 'like an insect's' (*SM* 47) and his 'metamorphosis' (*SM* 5). Eliot's reference to a 'web' has encouraged some readers to compare Silas to a spider, but his life of habit is far more suggestive of a silk-spinning caterpillar. Silas's repetitive routines, writes Eliot, 'helped, along with the weaving, to reduce his life to the unquestioning activity of a spinning insect' (*SM* 12). Setting aside the fact that spiders are not insects, the description just quoted does not suggest a spider spinning a web for capturing prey; despite his age, Silas lives a larval existence, caught in a vicious cycle of repetition like Darwin's caterpillar. Silas recalls Darwin in other ways, too. When the narrator describes him 'repeating some trivial movement or sound, until the repetition has bred a want, which is incipient habit' (*SM* 14), she echoes Darwin's accounts on habit and instinct and adapts his recurrent phrase 'incipient species' (*OS* 52 ff.).

Silas's spinning wheel is the physical embodiment of his developmental trajectory, which has lost both beginning and end: 'He hated the thought of the past; . . . and the future was all dark . . . Thought was arrested by utter bewilderment, now its old narrow pathway was closed' (*SM* 12). He exists out of time, off the progressive developmental path. Because 'his life had reduced itself to the functions of weaving and hoarding, without any contemplation of an end towards which the functions tended' (*SM* 15), Silas is no longer the means to his own ends, as *Bildung* requires. Not that he is changeless: like Aldous Huxley's senescent anti-heroes, Silas ages without developing: 'though he was not yet forty, the children always called him "Old Master Marner"' (*SM* 15). This is a kind of growth but only 'the slow growth of sameness in the brownish web' (*SM* 16).

Assuming Silas is an avatar of Darwin's caterpillar, Eliot obviously saw its repetitions as pathology. One of *Silas Marner*'s primary plots concerns Silas's gradual recovery from his addiction to 'gold [which] had kept his thoughts in an ever-repeated circle, leading to nothing beyond itself' (*SM* 106). Eppie's arrival triggers this recovery, partly because her needs provide a purpose for his gold, partly because her own progressive development begins to guide his:

> Eppie was an object compacted of changes and hopes that forced his thoughts onward, and carried them far away from their old eager pacing towards the same blank limit – carried them away to the new things that would come with the coming years. (*SM* 106)

Without end or beginning, Silas's obsessive weaving had no temporality, but Eppie's 'growing into knowledge' reinstates time – which is to say direction – in his life. It is worth noting that this temporality is not unidirectional: Silas finds hope for the future by rekindling links to the past: 'his mind was growing into memory' (*SM* 106). The linear mechanisms Darwin attributes to habit parallel the plotting of Silas's *Bildung* plot: only by recovering his social aptitudes, the knowledge of plants he learned from his mother, and the name of his lost little sister, can he see 'his soul, long stupefied in a cold narrow prison, . . . unfolding too, and trembling gradually into full consciousness' (*SM* 106). This retrospective temporality, however, ultimately serves Silas's 'growing purpose' to move 'continually onward' (*SM* 111). Like Darwin's singer 'interrupted in a song, or in repeating anything by rote', Silas must 'go back to recover the habitual train of thought' (*OS* 208).

Silas's compulsion and eventual recovery accord perfectly with the recapitulatory structure of the classical *Bildung* plot. This is certainly how Samuel Butler interprets Darwin's caterpillar in his Neo-Lamarckian manifesto *Life and Habit*. Having quoted Darwin's account of Huber's experiment, Butler charmingly admits that his entire theory of evolution, an alternative to Darwinism, must have been 'unconsciously taken . . . from this passage' in *The Origin of Species* (1890: 225). The thesis of *Life and Habit* is simple: true knowledge is acquired through repetition, which becomes habitual then completely unconscious, so that 'consciousness of knowledge vanishes on the knowledge becoming perfect' (1890: 17). Butler's notion of 'knowledge' is broad indeed, comprehending the ability to perform involuntary actions like breathing, metabolising or even growing from a fertilised egg. This view is necessarily recapitulatory: Butler's comments on Darwin's caterpillar in *Life and Habit* (1890: 224–5) make it clear that habit, or 'unconscious knowledge' (1890: 17), is the desirable outcome of ancestral learning repeated time and again over the generations. The more automatic an action, the more we owe to the ancestors who practised it on our behalf. 'We may observe', writes Butler, 'in this ascending scale, imperfect as it is, that the older the habit the longer the practice, the longer the practice the more knowledge – or, the less uncertainty' (1890: 13). A pianist must practise for years, struggling and stumbling, in order to play a sonata effortlessly; a caterpillar can metamorphose into a butterfly effortlessly, that skill having been perfected ages ago by its distant ancestors. For Butler, the confusions of Darwin's young apple leaf miner prove that habit keeps development on track. What survives of the past is good and worth repeating in the present; tinkering with the sequence of habitual actions throws development off its progressive line. In his scientific theorising, then, Butler like Eliot sees the embarrassment of Darwin's caterpillar as a pathology.

In his fiction, however, Butler approaches the caterpillar's confusions differently, anticipating modernist experiments by presenting it not as a developmental failure but as a completely different kind of life history. In *The Way of All Flesh*, a fictive elaboration of Lamarckian theories promoted in *Life and Habit*, Ernest Pontifex breaks the cycle of abuse and paternal domination which ruined childhood for generations of Pontifexes. In Ernest's case the past is *not* worth repeating, which is why he puts up his own children for adoption, sheltering them from familial influence. It is in this context that we must interpret the appearance of Darwin's caterpillar in the novel. Mr Overton, the narrator, reports that Ernest

> read Mr Darwin's books as fast as they came out and adopted evolution as an article of faith. 'It seems to me', he said once, 'that I am like one of those caterpillars which, if they have been interrupted in making their hammock, must begin again from the beginning . . .'. I do not know whether the analogy holds good or not, but I am sure Ernest's instinct was right in telling him that after a heavy fall he had better begin life again at a very low stage. (Butler 1977: 342; ellipsis in original)

Ernest's repeated reversions to 'a very low stage' occur at the cusp of maturity, when, according to Butler, inherited knowledge is weakest, when the habits accrued over aeons give way to the uncertainties of new knowledge. The younger we are, the more we already know from our ancestral past (this is effectively a paraphrase of recapitulation theory); as we age, though, we must grope about uncertainly in order to keep growing. As Butler memorably asserts in *Life and Habit*, 'it is the young and fair, then, who are the truly old and the truly experienced; it is they who alone have a trustworthy memory to guide them' (1890: 299). He continues:

> The whole charm of youth lies in its advantage over age in respect of experience, and where this has for some reason failed, or been misapplied, the charm is broken. When we say that we are getting old, we should say rather that we are getting new or young, and are suffering from inexperience, which drives us into doing things which we do not understand, and lands us, eventually, in the utter impotence of death. (Butler 1890: 299)

Whereas the juvenile have lots of accumulated ancestry to guide their habits and automatic actions, adults at the end of ontogeny are untrained for what comes next. This is a sorry state, according to the conservative Butler, for whom inherited habit could only be good. From another perspective, which Overton seems to endorse, the lack of precedent which comes with older age is an open-ended opportunity for self-invention, even repeated self-reinventions. The no longer young are on their own, which is also to say they are truly their own. This is how Ernest strives to remain, through his caterpillar-like reversions, on the cusp of the new. Unsure of his place in the world, Ernest abandons many projects before turning to authorship. Even then, his choice of vocation allows him to perpetuate rather than resolve the cycles of interrupted development: in his book, he repeatedly defers closure by adopting, with every new chapter, a new persona and opinion, by making a new beginning.

Beginning again is stranger still in *Alice's Adventures in Wonderland*. Instead of growing up, Alice simply grows; sometimes she shrinks. Her developmental confusions are brought home when she meets a caterpillar who asks a deceptively simple question: 'Who are *you*?' (Carroll 1992: 40). Alice does not know. 'I know who I *was* when I got up this morning', she explains, 'but I think I must have changed several times since then' (Carroll 1992: 40–1). As if to compensate for her ignorance, Alice tries educating the caterpillar about its own imminent transformations: 'you have to turn into a chrysalis – you will someday, you know – and then after that into a butterfly' (Carroll 1992: 41). But her confidence evaporates when the caterpillar dismisses the developmental forecast before returning to his initial question: '"Who are *you*?" (Carroll 1992: 41). This, of course, 'brought them back again to the beginning of the conversation' (Carroll 1992: 41). The question disturbs Alice not only because she lacks an answer but also because its repetition marks the failure of productive exchange; a conversation should lead somewhere, not go in circles. Anticipating modernist fictions of recurrence and deferred maturity, the 'advice from a caterpillar' (Carroll 1992: 40) breaks with conventional modes of communication and development. For it is Alice, not the caterpillar, who is 'much embarrassed': it is her maturation which has become anarchic, a movement whose goal, if it has one, is unpredictable. If Alice is worried about her situation, however, there is something liberatingly childlike about 'chang[ing] several times' a day (Carroll 1992: 41). Thus *Alice's Adventures in Wonderland* is, according to Daniel Bivona, 'a tale of a little girl's arrested development, an anti-*Bildungsroman* . . . [U]nable to extract herself from the games which play her except by disrupting them, Alice is condemned to a cyclical plot of failed development' (1990: 71–2). This sounds a lot like Darwin's caterpillar. It could also serve as the dust cover blurb for one of Beckett's novels. In her mutability, indeed, Alice prefigures the manic transmutations of 'all these Murphys, Merciers and Malones' (*UN* 345).

Beckett's Caterpillar Logic

After reading *The Origin of Species* in 1932, Beckett complained to Thomas MacGreevy that he had 'never read such badly written catlap', adding, 'I only remember one thing: *blue-eyed cats are always deaf*' (2009: 111). His fiction and notes show he remembered more than that, and he even seems to have re-read *The Origin* (Van Hulle and Nixon 2013: 202–5). Darwin's clearest contribution to Beckett's art is the caterpillar whose mode of locomotion, immaturity, fleshiness and developmental embarrassment perfectly suit his style, his plot-jamming, his character's psychology and the flow of his dialogues. As a larva, the stage of moth life history devoted to feeding, the caterpillar makes an excellent mascot for Beckett's inexorably embodied narratives (Connor 2014: 17), and the larva of the apple leaf miner is a peculiarly Beckettian creature: as its name suggests, it feeds by tunnelling within leaves, marking them with a distinctive vermiform pattern. Darwin's caterpillar therefore joins the Beckett's bestiary of blind or half-blind burrowers,[4] including the human crawlers of *Molloy* and *How It Is*. 'I am constantly working in the dark', Beckett famously told Alec Reid, adding that 'for me to talk about my writing' would be 'impossible', 'like an insect leaving his cocoon' (qtd in Abbott 1996: xi). The caterpillar's most congenial feature, though, is its inability to complete its metamorphosis on the way to maturity. A perpetual juvenile, Darwin's caterpillar mirrors Beckett's notoriously deferred endings. Its cyclical interruptions, like those of Beckett's novels, make its life history a case of what Judith Roof calls 'perverse narrative', 'a narrative about narrative dissolution, a narrative that continually short-circuits, that both frustrates and winks at the looming demagogue of reproduction' (1996: xxiv).

Darwin's caterpillar makes three explicit appearances in Beckett's early fiction, the first in 'Echo's Bones' (1934). In this difficult story Belacqua complains, sometimes quoting Darwin verbatim:

> my memory has gone to hell altogether . . . If you can't give me a better cue than that I'll have to be like the embarrassed caterpillar and go back to my origins . . . He was working away at his hammock . . . and not doing a damn bit of harm to man or beast, when up comes old Monkey-brand bursting with labour-saving devices. The caterpillar was far from feeling any benefit. (Beckett 2014: 42)

The caterpillar returns in *Murphy*, when Miss Counihan interrupts her own speech midway, inspiring Wylie to comment that 'she will have to go right back to the beginning, like Darwin's caterpillar' (*MU* 122). It reappears finally, and most humorously, in *Watt*:

> The point I was raising, said Mr O'Meldon, when I was interrupted, is this, that of the two columns of figures here before me this afternoon, the one, or – He has said this twice already, said Mr MacStern. If not three times, said Mr de Baker. Go on from where you left off, said Mr Magershon, not from where you began. Or are you like Darwin's caterpillar? Darwin's what? said Mr de Baker. Darwin's caterpillar? said Mr Magershon. What was the matter with him? said Mr MacStern. The matter with him was this, said Mr Magershon, that when he was distracted in the building of his hammock – . Are we here to discuss caterpillars? said Mr O'Meldon. Raise your point for the love of God. (*W* 193–4)

The point is, of course, that he will never get to the point. As the fitful conversation demonstrates, the caterpillar is no longer a mere allusion: its iterative developmental short-circuiting has infected *Watt*'s style and plotting (such as it is).

Often mentioned by scholars, and granted its own entry in *The Grove Companion to Samuel Beckett* (Ackerley and Gontarski 2004: 125–6), the caterpillar's significance has yet remained underexamined. Kathryn Chiong suggestively calls 'caterpillar logic . . . the model for Samuel Beckett's production, where series upon series go on from where they begin, where "going on" finally takes priority over all ends' (1998: 63), but her discussion of caterpillars is metaphorical and unrelated to biology. More intriguingly, Kirsten Shepherd-Barr links Beckett's use of Darwin's caterpillar with 'Haeckel's recapitulation theory' (2015: 249). They are indeed connected but, as we shall see, Shepherd-Barr overlooks a crucial structural and ideological mismatch between the caterpillar's repeated beginnings and the ontogenetic recapitulation of phylogeny. In fact, the reversionary dynamics of Darwin's caterpillar supply one of modernism's most insistently anti-recapitulatory manoeuvres.

Watt contains Beckett's last explicit reference to Darwin's caterpillar, after which it seems to disappear. In fact it merely goes to ground, weaving itself more and more into the fabric of the texts, as a structural and stylistic principle which effectively embodies Beckett's aesthetic and philosophy of becoming. Caterpillar logic is evident in 'First Love', when the woman sings songs 'so disjointedly, skipping from one to another and finishing none' (Beckett 1995: 30); it is manifest in Krapp's playing, interrupting, rewinding and re-playing his tapes, continually 'embarking on a new . . . retrospect' (Beckett 2006: 218; ellipsis in original); it recurs as late as *Worstward Ho* (1983), in the iterations of 'ever tried. Ever failed. No matter. Try again. Fail again. Fail better' (Beckett 1996: 89). Long after Beckett stopped mentioning the caterpillar, then, its movement continues, in increasingly distilled form, until nothing remains of the insect but a 'non-narrative' yet fully dynamic 'aesthetic of recommencement' (Abbott 1994: 103, 109). Recommencement is a process of beginning again fundamentally distinct from the forms of rebirth or resurrection implied by Haeckel's term for perfect recapitulation, 'palingenesis'. Beckett's recommencements occur perversely before the end of anything, and lead only to further premature new beginnings. Beckett's characters elude the trappings of a well-wrought life by repeatedly 'beginning all over again' (*MO* 8), advancing in 'fits and starts' (*MD* 208) and 'not coming to the point' (*MD* 315). Rather than move forwards, they find 'it was the only way to progress, to stop' (*MO* 86). In many cases, the spectre of the caterpillar is obvious. In *The Unnamable*, the narrator compares himself unmistakably to the caterpillar in Huber's experiment, forced by tormentors to repeat his incomplete development:

> It is only when they see me stranded that they take up again the thread of my misfortunes, judging me insufficiently vitalized to bring them to a successful conclusion alone. But instead of making the junction, I have often noticed this, I mean *instead of resuming me at the point where I was left off, they pick me up at a much later stage*, perhaps thereby hoping to induce in me the illusion that I had got through the interval all on my own (*UN* 376; emphasis added)

Agency plays no part in this vision of development, and there is no sign of *Bildung*'s gradual progress towards enlightenment, self-knowledge, or vocation. In its stead is 'a succession of irregular loops, . . . invariably unpredictable in direction, that is to say determined by the panic of the moment' (*UN* 372).

Explicit or not, Beckett's uses of Darwin's caterpillar paint a picture of development completely unlike that of *Silas Marner*, where habitual repetition was a problem to be solved in order for the plot to continue to its end. But Beckett's caterpillar logic does suggest a kind of development nonetheless; it does not simply indicate total disintegration. His narrators may be obsessed with nothingness, death, silence and immobility, but they describe and, by describing, create selves and worlds which are curiously lively. If their dynamism is hard to recognise, it may be because deviations from the forward momentum of plot can look a lot like stasis. Those who read *Molloy* as a simple 'story of decomposition', suggests Michael D'Arcy, misrepresent Beckett's narrative by 'arrest[ing] the movement of reversal that it enacts' (2014: 68) and overlooking the 'intensification of the reversibility between . . . enlightenment and mythic regression' (2014: 71). In a similar vein, Amanda Dennis protests that to read *The Unnamable* as an 'impasse is to miss the proliferation of alternatives and spatial possibilities that grow out of periods of radical indecision' (2015: 181). What replaces the singular Enlightenment plot, Dennis continues, is a variety of 'ways of moving *within* one's material surroundings' – 'tunneling, sprouting, germinating' (2015: 183) – like a caterpillar mining through a leaf.

Revisionary readings such as these exploit contradictions inherent in metamorphic narratives. Though easily appropriated into allegories of individual and historical rebirth, metamorphosis also troubles the narrative simplicity of Brunel's 'palingenetic myth' (1974: 166):

> sometimes everything topples over; progress becomes retrogression. This reversal, a paradoxical motionless movement, is probably less explicable by the Hegelian schema of degradation to the lower animal images of past ages, than as the play of contradictory forces and the feeling for what is forbidden. (Brunel 1974: 124)

The reversionary impulse in metamorphosis, then, is not atavistic, in the sense that it does not simply demote the body to some lower or more primitive state. In terms remarkably similar to Edward Carpenter's thoughts on the creative potential of 'the reversionary process' (1898: 246), Brunel suggests that the 'reversal' of progress is not degradation but a kind of exploration. Against the determinism and teleology of the palingenetic myth (and its biological manifestation, the biogenetic law), incomplete metamorphosis generates the productive forces of play, contradiction, transgression. As Ann Banfield notes in another context, for Beckett

> it is only via a conception of history, both personal and literary, that runs counter to the myth of progress . . . that all can 'change utterly', that an individual might escape the round of generation, . . . that art can find a language to say something new. (Banfield 2003: 7)

For Alain Robbe-Grillet, a kindred contemporary of Beckett, the potential newness of modern narrative comes from its anti-narrative strategies. In the modern novel, he writes, 'the instant denies continuity' (1963: 133) and time loses its fluidity:

> If temporality satisfies the waiting, instantaneity disappoints it; likewise spatial discontinuity emancipates us from the traps of the anecdote. These descriptions whose movements remove all belief in the things described, these artificial protagonists without identity; this present that invents itself ceaselessly, as though one with the act of writing, repeating itself, doubling itself, modifying itself, contradicting itself, without ever accumulating enough to constitute a past – which is to say, a 'story' in the traditional sense. (Robbe-Grillet 1963: 133–4)

Describing his own method of burying narration in description, Robbe-Grillet also sheds light on Beckettian narrators, who exist only in their utterances, in a perpetual present 'without ever accumulating enough to constitute a past' (1963: 134). And yet, as the end of 'The End' attests, the narrator is not completely severed from 'the traps of the anecdote', revealing Beckett's simultaneous debt to and defiance of biographical narrative: 'The memory came faint and cold of the story I might have told, a story in the likeness of my life, I mean without the courage to end or the strength to go on' (1995: 99).

What kind of life do Beckett's narratives resemble? None, claims Martha Nussbaum, who, wary of Beckett's fiction, points out that real 'stories contain and teach forms of feeling, forms of life' (1988: 226). Her implication is that Beckett's fiction, by abandoning story, cannot perform these salutary tasks. But could there be a feeling and lesson in the form of a caterpillar's looping? Is it that 'unconscious memory' is a better guide to action than reflection, as Samuel Butler claims in *Life and Habit*? Is it an allegory of the individual's ramified potentialities, the many stories a protagonist might choose to live, as Butler seems to propose in *The Way of All Flesh*? Is it a glitch in the developmental system which reveals through failure what a good life might otherwise be, as George Eliot suggests in *Silas Marner*? For Beckett, the looping caterpillar inverts the logic of the biogenetic law, in which the multiple losers in the struggle for existence – those who were deleted from the phylogenetic record and therefore from the recapitulation of phylogeny in all subsequent ontogenies – enjoy (or suffer) a transient life between interruption and beginning again.

Beckett's Caterpillar Logic: Development through the Loop

So what is development, for Beckett? 'In what did the change *consist*?' wonders Arsene in *Watt* (*W* 44), prompting this answer: 'What was changed was existence off the ladder . . . This I am happy to inform you is the reversed metamorphosis' (*W* 44). Recapitulation posits an ascending ladder to the acme of evolution; Beckett's 'reversed metamorphosis' decouples development from any necessary direction or goal: 'so descend, so mount, rung by rung', adds Arsene (*W* 45). In stark contrast with recapitulation, the changes chronicled in *Watt* and in Beckett's later works refute recapitulation's 'long chain of consistence, a chain stretching from the long dead to the far unborn' (*W* 134), 'the ordaining of a being to come by a being past' (*W* 136). Glossing the latter quotation, Beausang aptly notes that 'the principle of reverse metamorphosis gives rise to an equality between before and after, so that genetic priority loses all validity' (1996: 504). Chronological progression provides the means of subsuming the biographical plot to the framework of recapitulation, thus upholding principles of 'genetic priority' which equate actualisation with the fulfilment, which is to say the exhaustion, of potentialities. Recursive departures from linearity preserve *Bildung*'s ideal content (the endless unfolding of potentiality) by giving it a radically new form.

As a governing figure in Beckett's fiction from *Watt* to *How It Is*, Darwin's caterpillar fails repeatedly to reach the chrysalis stage that precedes winged maturity. For Beckett, however, this failure to repeat the successful metamorphoses of its ancestors is not a failure of development but, rather, a way to explore creative alternatives to past life histories. In this capacity, it evokes the spectre of recapitulatory progress, but only to repudiate it. Both Molloy and Macmann abandon the erect bodily carriage traditionally associated with human divinity, preferring the postures of so-called lower animals. 'Abandon[ing] erect motion, that of man' (*MO* 98), Molloy resorts to 'crawling on his belly, like a reptile' (*MO* 99), as will Moran in his wake. Similarly, Macmann

> was by temperament more reptile than bird and could suffer extensive mutilation and survive, happier sitting than standing and lying down than sitting, so that he sat and lay down at the least pretext and only rose again when the élan vital or struggle for life began to prod him in the arse again. (*MD* 276)

Macmann's atavistic posture mirrors his refusal to procreate, despite the messianic connotations of his name (Son of Man). An anti-Noah, he puts another kind of stop to evolutionary progress: faced with a rainstorm worthy of the Deluge, he is unable to grasp

> that he must not stop and lie down, but on the contrary press forward . . . for he was no more than human, than the son and grandson and greatgrandson of humans. But between him and those grave and sober men . . . there was this difference, that his semen had never done any harm to anyone. So his link with his species was through his ascendants

> only, who were all dead, in the fond hope they had perpetuated themselves. But the better late than never thanks to which true men, true links, can acknowledge the error of their ways and hasten on to the next, was beyond the power of Macmann . . . (*MD* 273–4)

Nowhere does Beckett's 'antagonism to linking' (Connor 2014: 199) so clearly implicate biological processes. Macmann's refusal to procreate makes him the severance between past and future. Analogous to the caterpillar's failure to link egg to adult stages of moth development, Macmann's response to the genealogical imperative is profoundly anti-recapitulation. To sever the genealogical connection is to make one's ontogeny the end of the phylogenetic line. Refusing to perpetuate his family line, Macmann frees himself from the dubious glory of being a link in the progressive development of future forms.

Whatever awaits Beckett's characters, it is not survival through procreation – a 'very pretty' (*MD* 220) and therefore probably 'false' story (*MD* 221), according to Malone, who favours instead an ontogenetic version of reproduction as self-reinvention. 'On the threshold of being no more I succeed in being another' (*MD* 220). He then elaborates, in language reminiscent once again of Huber's experiment:

> I began again, to try and live, cause to live, be another, in myself, in another. How false all this is. No time now to explain. I began again. But little by little with a different aim, no longer in order to succeed, but in order to fail. Nuance. (*MD* 221)

Malone's self-portrait as an ever-renewing self violates the characterological premises of the modern biographic plot; this enables him, like Macmann, to break the isomorphism between recapitulation and the *Bildung* plot. Rather perversely, then, Malone's and Macmann's failure to have 'perpetuated themselves' (*MD* 274) is heroic and flattering to the self in a manner hard to square with the typical image of Beckett: the accent shifts away from the individual as a means to future generations towards the individual as an end in itself, no matter how unsatisfying that end may be.

Here and everywhere, Beckett delivers an unrelenting attack on the biogenetic law and its various manifestations, mocking or travestying its progressivism and analogical 'neatness of identifications' (Beckett 1961: 3). Yet it is easy to be misled by structural parallels between recapitulation and the looping of Darwin's caterpillar. In *Theatre and Evolution from Ibsen to Beckett*, Kirsten Shepherd-Barr treats the looping of Darwin's caterpillar as a microcosmic version of 'Haeckel's recapitulation theory' (2015: 249). There are indeed some similarities, but they are superficial. Shepherd-Barr equates habit and recapitulation, claiming that 'habit is embodied recapitulation' (2015: 250). Though not exactly incorrect (as I discuss above in relation to Samuel Butler), this claim conceals the fact that in Huber's experiment the caterpillar's habit does not enable but, rather, prevents the completion of ontogeny, a necessary step in turning the recapitulation of past phylogeny into evolutionary progress. Unable to finish its hammock, the caterpillar cannot metamorphose into a chrysalis, let alone a reproductive adult moth. Despite Haeckel's iconoclastic style, recapitulation theory was at heart an Enlightenment narrative of the 'exploits of the human race, in its slow ascension towards the light' (*MO* 147), whereas Darwin's caterpillar is 'much embarrassed' (*OS* 208) because it has lost that plot.

This contrast is perhaps most evident in *Murphy*'s Celia, who epitomises the larval reversions and reconstitutions Beckett opposes to recapitulatory development. Developing backwards, Celia 'was in her mind . . . a girl, a child, an infant . . . Penelope's curriculum was reversed, the next day and the next it was all to do over again, the coils of her life to be hackled into tow all over again' (*MU* 86). This evocative passage, with its conceit of fibres and textiles, shows Celia 'teasing the oakum of her history' until 'she had no history' (*MU* 86). Thus she reverses the weaving process, in which tangled plant fibres ('tow', *OED* n^1) are 'hackled', that is 'split, straightened, and combed out' ('hackle', *OED* v^3). A delightful pun on Haeckel, 'hackled into tow' suggests a reversionary breach of the biogenetic law. Recapitulatory development should move *out of* and not '*into* tow'; the tangle of fibres should be straightened 'so as to be in a condition for spinning' ('hackle', *OED* v^3). Despite superficial resemblances between recapitulation and the repetitions of Darwin's caterpillar, then, Celia confounds the Haeckelian plot by retreating into the 'dark' of 'larval existence' (*MU* 42).

Beckett's caterpillar logic is an entomological manifestation of the 'developmental view' recently proposed by Marco Bernini, who writes that 'the interruption' of two co-implicated phenomena, bodily motion and narrative continuity, 'returns Beckett's creatures to the underdeveloped crawling stages of infants' (2015: 45). In this reversionary light, Michael Beausang is right to claim that 'the recapitulation motif almost always functions in Beckett as an expression that disguises tautology. Thus, we are tempted to suppose the existence of a very close connection between Huber's caterpillar, reverse metamorphosis, and narcissistic or autoparodic construction in the novel' (1996: 504). Not progressive or end-directed, what looks like recapitulation turns out to be 'reversed metamorphosis' (*W* 44), a change not for the better, not really a regression, but a way of dynamically staying put. One thinks here of the Red Queen in *Through the Looking-Glass*, who explains that in her country 'it takes all the running *you* can do, to keep in the same place' (Carroll 1992: 145). When Hamm in *Endgame* insists on killing a flea, otherwise 'humanity might start from there all over again!' (Beckett 2006: 108), he does transpose the failed development of Darwin's caterpillar onto evolutionary history, but this historical vision is closer to Nietzsche's eternal recurrence than to Haeckel's palingenesis. Recapitulation is not really a repetition, or else it is repetition with an improvement – it is a handing down of torches, each individual stepping back into past generations only to gather the momentum for its leap forward.

In *How It Is*, Beckett's most Darwinian work, the narrator is well aware that his tendency to begin again, to repeat with variation but without direction, runs counter to recapitulatory progressivism. It is not rebirth or redemption he embodies when 'I recapitulate' but 'other certainties the mud the dark' and their hidden possibilities (*HII* 2). He spurns 'the eternal straight line' (*HII* 33) of the *Bildung* plot, favouring a zigzag course of 'sudden swerve[s]' and dodges at 'forty-five degrees' and 'right angle[s]' (*HII* 34). Only for very short bursts, 'two yards', does he chart a 'straight line' (*HII* 34), and then only because linearity is so engrained: 'such is the force of habit' (*HII* 34). The zigzag turns propulsion into reversion, the destination being not a goal but a beginning. Rather than moving ever forwards and upwards, the narrator's repetitions satisfy his certainty that there is 'only one thing to do go back' (*HII* 33). He revels in 'the losses of the species' (*HII* 33), whereas recapitulation would involve successive species acquisitions, the progression up the evolutionary ladder to the human apex. In a significant inversion of the recapitulatory plot, then, the narrator's caterpillar-looping sees his humanity not as a goal but as a past, youthful condition: 'I was young I clung to the species we're talking of the species the human' (*HII* 33). But now the thought of ascending the evolutionary tree appears to be a travesty, a symptom of becoming 'mad or worse transformed à la Haeckel' (*HII* 29). The alarming prospect of moving up the evolutionary tree 'à la Haeckel' is, for Beckett's narrator, a fate worse than circling aimlessly in universal muck. Now, after his lifelong repetitions, he identifies instead with so-called lower animals, 'the different orders of the animal kingdom beginning with the sponges' (*HII* 27). The figure of the end is therefore not the half-angelic young man poised before the 'luminous Future' (A. Huxley 2004: 14) but a 'Worm' who will 'go on squirming at the end of the line' (*UN* 386).

The broken developmentalism of caterpillar logic is embodied in several Beckettian devices, from contradiction and false endings to clauses linked with comma splices or, in *How It Is* and later texts, with no punctuation at all. Compounding clauses suggests simultaneous open-endedness and self-containment, a situation Steven Connor aptly likens to a 'leaking parenthesis, closed on one side and open on the other, as though the comma were an abbreviated form of an opening bracket that never finds its corresponding closing form' (2014: 58). If a grammatical sentence is a mini-narrative analogous to complete metamorphosis, then a series of clauses connected by comma splices mimics an interrupted developmental sequence which resumes itself repeatedly instead of reaching a full stop. Such syntax does not lend itself to communicative clarity or narrative coherence,[5] but clarity and coherence are not highly valued in modernist theories of selfhood and consciousness. A complementary but more radical effect is produced by Beckett's systematic use of denarration, which dissolves clear relations between story and discourse and, by extension, dissolves the sense of a singular, recoverable chronology (Richardson 2008: 52–3). The device fatally compromises the linear irreversible temporality on which, as we have seen, recapitulatory development plots are founded. When a narrator retracts his narration, the speaking 'I' performs a narratological reversion, recovering the potentialities of the beginning without yet fully erasing what was narrated. Malone identifies this dynamic with Darwin's caterpillar when he reflects on the rightness of 'stop[ping] in the middle of a tedious and perhaps futile task' (*MD* 243):

> a great number of tasks are of this kind, without a doubt, and the only way to end them is to abandon them . . . The moment comes when one desists, because it is the wisest thing to do, discouraged, but not to the extent of undoing all that has been done. (*MD* 243)

Dirk Van Hulle has coined for this form of development a felicitous phrase: 'creative undoing' (2014a: 183–212). In *The Unnamable* in particular, the task of self-writing links selfhood to the act of narration, making it vulnerable to cancellations, erasures, rewritings and contradictions but also to creative redoing. This dynamic is embodied in *The Unnamable*'s figure Worm, one of Beckett's most literal avatars of Darwin's caterpillar. Steven Connor identifies the 'crepuscular non-figure of Worm' as a fly maggot (2014: 159), but the taxonomically vague 'worm' is just as likely to mean caterpillar. Debating the point is futile, of course, not least because maggots living in putrefaction and perpetual caterpillars are equally Beckettian creatures. Each is the vermiform larval stage preceding a chrysalis and then a dramatically different, winged adult; each is an 'incipient, almost-creature . . . whose role seems to be to bore out a pure space of hypothetical existence, which is meant never to be real enough to be falsified' (Connor 2014: 59–60).

Whatever Worm is, he exemplifies Beckett's developmental logic as not a repudiation but, rather, as an absurd extreme of Goethe's notion of narrating *Bildung* through deferral: 'the novel must move slowly and the sentiments of the main personage must, in some way or another, hold up [*aufhalten*] the progression of the whole towards its resolution' (Goethe 1989: 185). Using the caterpillar principle to hold up – to defer – progression forever, Beckett's characters refuse death-by-ending: 'The last step!' scoffs the Unnamable, 'I who could never manage but the first' (*UN* 380). Never past beginning, Beckett's characters never stop. They refuse to follow plot beyond the beginning, 'that moment at which story, or "life" is stimulated from quiescence into a state of narratability, into a tension, a kind of irritation, which demands narration' (P. Brooks 1985: 103). Always 'somewhere on a road, moving, between a beginning and an end, gaining ground, losing ground' (*UN* 357), Beckett's characters inhabit a perpetual state of formation which eschews the finality of form.

Instead of exploding the *Bildungsroman*'s attempt to narrate the shape of a life, then, Beckett's style, attenuated plots and deferred endings may come closer than classical forms to the ideal of *Bildung*. To be sure, the cycles of Darwin's caterpillar clash with some defining features of the *Bildung* plot, notably its progressive temporality and its holistic organicism. More profoundly, however, they recover a feature of organicism which Beckett would not relinquish: the dynamism and open-endedness Goethe celebrates in both life and art. As a form of development, beginning again and again ensures an indefinite state of incipience and potentiality. We saw in Huxley's treatment of neoteny that extended larval existence can confer developmental and evolutionary advantages. In Huxley, metamorphosis is deferred until the time is right; in Beckett, it is deferred forever. 'Irresolution is the secret for not ageing', says Édouard in *Les Faux-monnayeurs* (Gide 1975: 324), and indeed Beckett's recurrent use of the embarrassed caterpillar produces a kind of formal and characterological neoteny, a retention of potentiality which grants his decrepit characters an apparently inexhaustible vitality. Adulthood, in the sense of being in one's prime physically, mentally and socially, is an age unknown to Beckett's characters. When he is not mortally senescent, the Unnamable is 'acting the infant' (*UN* 369), watching as 'the ceiling rises and falls, rises and falls, rhythmically, as when I was a foetus' (*UN* 323). Lemuel retreats to a chrysalis-like 'cell' and 'swathe[s] himself in his two blankets as in swaddlings and over and above this rough and ready cocoon he [wears] his cloak' (*UN* 322). Like Anthony Beavis, these neotenous characters embody 'a principle of change pregnant with possibilities' (*UN* 390). Unable to convert potentiality into achievement, they fulfil a precondition of true *Bildung* or – more accurately – defer the completion of development in which *Bildung* itself is inevitably a casualty.

Through their iterative movements, Beckett's versions of Darwin's caterpillar give narrative form to a condition of inexhaustible potentiality and multifariousness, a condition idealised by theorists of *Bildung*, yet compromised by attempts to narrate *Bildung* in linear time. In lieu of the butterfly allegory's set programme, they enact the formative dynamism of the 'process of differentiation, variation, and transformation that Goethe seeks to articulate under the headings of "metamorphosis"' (Pfau 2010: 9) and '"perpetual transfiguration"' (Pfau 2010: 16). How fitting, then, that the narrator of *How It Is* refers to his life-giving, ever-changing speech in the same breath as he apostrophises two immature lifeforms: 'this voice its promises and solaces all imagination dear bud dear worm' (*HII* 57). The worm, an incomplete moth or butterfly, is linked to the 'bud', the undifferentiated plant organ which can generate a flower, leaf or branch, and perhaps the archetypal '*leaf*', in which, according to Goethe, 'lies the true Proteus who can hide or reveal himself in all vegetal forms' (1982: 363). Also pertinent to Beckett is the 'bud' as an organ of asexual reproduction. Goethe believed 'reproduction by bud is just as interesting as reproduction by seed' (1982: 364), but his theory of metamorphosis clearly favours the latter: 'propagation through two genders', he claims, is 'the pinnacle of nature', the top of the 'spiritual ladder' (1988: 76). Beckett, as we have seen in the figure of Macmann, prefers somatic regeneration over sexual reproduction. Darwin's caterpillar suggests, through its repeated deferrals, a refusal to reach literal sexual maturity, symbolic of spiritual elevation and narrative closure.

Postponing the end, Beckett's characters do not change in the old recognisable way, but they do change. They do little else, in fact: their existence is an infinite series of 'great inward metamorphoses' (*MO* 185). As early as *Murphy*, the unified figure of the hero on a singular trajectory gives way to

> a perpetual coming together and falling asunder of forms . . . Neither elements nor states, nothing but forms becoming and crumbling into the fragments of a new becoming, without love or hate or any intelligible principle of change. Here there was nothing but commotion and the pure forms of commotion. Here he was not free, but a mote in the dark of absolute freedom. He did not move, he was a point in the ceaseless unconditional generation and passing away of line. (*MU* 65–6)

In this echo of Pater's 'continual vanishing away, that strange, perpetual weaving and unweaving of ourselves' (1919: 236), Beckett situates his characters at the productive edge of chaos, poised between generative activity and disintegration. More anarchic than inert, the dynamic of Beckett's prose is not entropic, though it has been read this way by Sara Crangle (2010: 182–3), Laura Salisbury (2012: 131–4) and others. It is in fact neg-entropic, a quality also noted by Gordon Armstrong (1993) and by Michael Worton (1994). Exhaustion is always close at hand, but Beckett's prose like his characters appears to be energised by the imminence of entropic dissolution. Even the pauses and silences are no more endings than that precarious stillness when the boulder of Sisyphus teeters on the peak. Movement inevitably begins again.

This perpetual motion narrative is most evident in *How It Is*. Having described itself as a neat closed structure – 'before Pim with Pim after Pim how it is three parts' (*HII* 1) – the novel eventually acknowledges an indefinite future lying somewhere beyond part three, the possibility of 'part six ten fourteen so on' (*HII* 91). This possibility entails another: an infinite number of parts, and as many selves to inhabit. Thus the determinism of 'how it will be' (*HII* 97) and the actuality of 'how it is' (*HII* 97) give way to the conditional, to the 'possible formulation' (*HII* 98), to 'how it would be' (*HII* 80). The end of the novel is not final. It is just the end of the 'present formulation', which is the beginning of 'this new formulation namely this new life' (*HII* 107). As the narrative proceeds, the neat tripartite division of the narrator's life-course is undone by a dangerous – and liberating – supplemental logic:

> in trying to present in three parts or episodes an affair which all things considered involves four one is in danger of being incomplete that to this third part now ending at last a fourth should normally be appended in which would be seen among a thousand and one other things scarcely or not at all to be seen in the present formulation (*HII* 97)

Exposing the artificially of endings, the narrator's reference to the involuted *One Thousand and One Nights* also suggests a biographical narrative in which 'various times [are] mixed up' (*HII* 79).[6] Like Scheherazade's life, which is sustained by tales left unfinished, the fragmented *Bildung* plots of *How It Is* promise 'a new development' (*HII* 59) in the loopy logic of Darwin's caterpillar: 'then of a sudden like all that starts starts again no knowing set forth forth again' (*HII* 44). Though the narrator's life is 'this old life old words same old scraps millions of times each time the first' (*HII* 100), repetition inevitably entails productive variation. The narrative is 'ill-heard ill-murmured ill-heard ill-recorded' (*HII* 100), admits the narrator, whose 'whole life [is] a gibberish garbled' (*HII* 100). If his repetitions seek, through trial and error, to match the narrative of his life to its empirical reality, just as Haeckel demanded that ontogeny faithfully repeat phylogeny, he necessarily fails and maybe fails better. Beckett's statements on the need not to succeed are legendary, but his compatriot Elizabeth Bowen says it as well, and more clearly: 'If revolutions do not fail, they fail you' (1998: 166).

If the *Bildungsroman* is an allegory of return to the Garden of Eden, as Helena Feder (2014) contends, then Beckett fundamentally rewrites the allegory. The origin is no longer the Word, for his novels permit at most 'the first syllable' (*MO* 126). It's not much, but it's not nothing. The first syllable only partially determines the rest of the word, the rest of the sentence – hence the concurrent impulse to finish and the drive to go on, for 'the search for the means to put an end to things, an end to speech, is what enables the discourse to continue' (*UN* 341). There is a wonderful irony in using endurance for endurance's sake as a creative principle, displacing former notions such as entelechy, vitalism or *Bildungstrieb*. Thus the Unnamable resigns himself 'to begin again, to start again from nowhere, from no one and from nothing and win to me again, to me here again, by fresh ways to be sure, or by the ancient ways, unrecognizable at each fresh faring' (*UN* 343). This manic changeability is beholden to no generic structure, archetype or finality, which is not to say it is pure formlessness or, as Frank Kermode defines formlessness, 'change without potentiality' (1967: 138).

The narrative unfolds, Kermode continues, in a truly 'human time' (1967: 139), undetermined by the form-giving power of the end; thus

> the future is a fluid medium in which I try to actualize my potency, though the end is unattainable . . . The faring forward is all right, and fits the old desire to know what happens next; but the denial of all causal relation between disparate *kairoi* [supreme moments] . . . makes form impossible. (Kermode 1967: 139)

Yet as Kermode also points out, Beckett never fully eliminates linkages between the epiphanic *kairoi* (1967: 116), leaving vestiges of the *Bildung* plot in the iterations of the caterpillar's looping. Beckett replaces the plot of development with directionless deve*loop*ment (if I may), and though we cannot direct our lives along its 'devious winding ways' (*MO* 64), we may to our surprise recognise ourselves in it.

In *Molloy*, Moran calls himself 'a grown man thinking he is done with surprises' (*MO* 125), but if he, like 'Murphy, Watt, Yerk, Mercier and all the others' (*MO* 154), takes his lead from Darwin's caterpillar, he is not really 'grown' and thus not 'done with surprises'. Most surprising about Beckett's narratives is that they lead downward so predictably and yet remain, through their perpetual movement, 'fertile in surprises' (*UN* 360). This movement, specifies the Unnamable, is 'not in a straight line I need hardly say, but in a sharp curve which, if I continued to follow it, seemed likely to restore me to my point of departure, or to one adjacent' (*UN* 360). In the manner of Darwin's caterpillar the Unnamable goes on:

> I must have got embroiled in a kind of inverted spiral, I mean one the coils of which, instead of widening more and more, grew narrower and narrower and finally, given the kind of space in which I was supposed to evolve, would come to an end for lack of room. Faced then with the material impossibility of going any further I should no doubt have had to stop, unless of course I elected to set off again at once in the opposite direction, to unscrew myself as it were, after having screwed myself to a standstill, which would have been an experience rich in interest and fertile in surprises . . . (*UN* 360)

In this gleeful parody of the Hegelian spiral, the Unnamable is 'screwed' indeed, having reached an impasse. Still, a screw can be 'unscrew[ed]' and put to new uses. Life's journey is not a predetermined path, for Beckettian *Bildung* is 'well furnished with loopholes' (*UN* 362), suggesting not only a faulty argument but also the potential freedom through hidden escape routes. It also hints at a leaf riddled by the mining of a caterpillar. And so, the Unnamable predicts, 'at my next appearance, if I ever appear again, all will be new,

new and strange' (*UN* 381). Nothing could be more Darwinian than that. As Darwin writes of the mindless, directionless iterations of natural section, 'by the repetition of this process, a new variety might be formed' (*OS* 91).

More clearly perhaps than any other author featured in this book, Beckett's caterpillar logic illustrates how biology can inspire or bolster reversionary experiments with the *Bildung* plot. Even after a second great war and the Holocaust, or perhaps especially then, his novels persist in experimenting with the problem of life history. The lives endured by Beckett's characters never cease to reflect their historical moment, though not in a way Herder, Hegel, or Haeckel would have embraced or even recognised: they 'keep dying in a dying age' (*HII* 9), and so they 'grow mortal again' (*HII* 7). For Catherine Coquio, the indeterminacy of beginning retains its 'poeticizing force' even in the aftermath of Auschwitz because 'the utopia of the undetermined is by definition counter-ideological' even as it owes its status to the fate of the 'exterminated' (1998: 385–6).

Reversion, for Beckett as for the authors featured in earlier chapters, is therefore a critical but not cynical response to the ideal and promise of development. For the Unnamable, the answer is not to abandon development but to reimagine its possible shapes by means of trial and error:

> let us go back as planned, afterwards we'll fall forward as projected. The reverse would be more like it. But not by much. Upstream, downstream, what matter, I begin by the ear, that's the way to talk. Before that it was the night of time. Whereas ever since, what radiance! (*UN* 402)

Though it may well be 'an ironical radiance' (*MU* 70), it betrays a hope that characterises the reversionary strategies we have explored in various modernist *Bildungsromane*. That this hope might draw on the strange, disturbing and exhilarating models of post-Darwinian biology is clear in one of the Unnamable's great unfinished sentences: 'My good-will at certain moments is such, and my longing to have floundered however briefly, however feebly, in the great life torrent streaming from the earliest protozoa to the very latest humans, that I, no parenthesis unfinished. I'll begin again' (*UN* 366).

Notes

1. In *The Water-Babies*, Charles Kingsley uses metamorphosis to merge ontogeny and phylogeny with a Christian narrative of life and afterlife:

   > Does not each of us . . . go through a transformation just as wonderful as that of a sea-egg, or a butterfly? and do not reason and analogy, as well as Scripture, tell us that that transformation is not the last? and that, though we shall be, we know not, yet we are here but as the crawling caterpillar, and shall be hereafter as the perfect fly? (Kingsley 2008: 82–3)

   For a cultural history of butterfly metamorphosis, see Gallagher (2009: 158–61).

2. On 'the infinity of the process of *Bildung*' (2006: 72), Christiane Thompson writes that '*Bildung* would then be the always different and unsuccessful revealing of the history of self-withdrawal and thus would form a critical and aporetic category in our relation to ourselves and to the world' (2016: 85).
3. *Silas Marner*'s emphasis on chance has motivated Darwinian readings by Levine (1988a: 138) and by K. M. Newton (2011: 128–30), but its plot is more providential than contingent.
4. Beside worms, Beckett favours other burrowing animals. He compared himself to 'a mole in a molehill' (qtd in Abbott 1996: xi). 'What a Misfortune' in *More Pricks than Kicks* features the 'occasionally blind' 'tucu-tucu' (Beckett 1994: 113), an unmistakable allusion to the 'frequently blind' rodent 'tuco-tuco' mentioned by Darwin (*OS* 137). Watt's mode of locomotion makes him 'a headlong tardigrade' (a microscopic animal whose name means 'slow-stepper') (*W* 30). The narrator of 'The End' has 'lived too long among rats' (Beckett 1995: 95).
5. Molloy discovers the communicative limitations of the caterpillar principle when he tries speaking to his mother by knocking on her skull. Knocking four times to ask for 'money', Molloy realises she cannot understand because she cannot count 'beyond two' – and two knocks means 'no':

   > the distance was too great for her, from one to four. By the time she came to the fourth knock she imagined she was only at the second, the first two having been erased from her memory as completely as if they had never been felt. (*MO* 16)

6. Beckett's allusion to the *Thousand and One Nights* recalls how the other great modernist poet of reiteration, Gertrude Stein, depicts development – in endlessly repeating characters who 'have arabian nights inside them' (1995: 121).

CONCLUSION

The foregoing chapters add to the already substantial refutation of C. P. Snow's comment on 'how very little of twentieth-century science has been assimilated into twentieth-century art' (1998: 16). More specifically, they redress the relative lack of attention paid to biology in studies of literature and science in the early twentieth century. By highlighting ways in which biology helped quicken the modernist imagination, the preceding chapters also counter the tendency among literary critics to focus on biology's negative aspects and applications, especially genetic determinism and biopolitical control over human bodies. The go-to modernist text in this context is of course *Brave New World*. Important as they are, these perspectives can overshadow other manifestations of biological theory in modernism. Often overlooked are texts which, like Huxley's *Eyeless in Gaza* and *After Many a Summer*, subtly work biology into narrative structure and character construction. These incorporations are not incompatible with the more visible, thematic biological engagements that interest most critics; as most of the chapters in this book attest, explicit references often serve to signal and confirm covert formal experiments with biology (thus my biological reading of *Eyeless in Gaza*'s structure was both triggered and endorsed by Huxley's seemingly trivial allusion to axolotl metamorphosis). But structural engagements with biology are liable to be overlooked or overshadowed by more explicit biological content.

Biology's role in life narratives is a significant point of continuity linking the earliest *Bildungsromane* to those still being published today. It also represents a unique lens into the ways in which the genre has changed over the course of its history. I have already discussed these continuities and differences in the context of Victorian and modernist *Bildungsromane*. In the remaining pages I briefly survey how paradigm shifts in biology since the 1950s have registered in contemporary novels of formation, differentiating them from their early to mid-century counterparts. A literary history of biology and the contemporary novel would thus have to consider modernist antecedents but also account for ways in which biology has changed in focus and scope since the Second World War.

In 1953, when Beckett published *The Unnamable*, *Nature* published Watson and Crick's ground-breaking article on the structure of DNA. The subsequent molecular revolution has had several consequences which would impact how authors treat relations between biology and *Bildung*. The most important is the eclipse of embryology by the rise of molecular genetics. Though embryology has since made something of a comeback, most notably in evolutionary-developmental biology (Evo-Devo), it has not reclaimed the importance it had in the days of Haeckel or even Julian Huxley. As the gene and the DNA molecule became the figureheads for biology in the popular imagination, the metaphorical ground in the life sciences shifted, displacing organicist with computational metaphors – from formation to information (Keller 1995: 18–21). Even Ian McEwan's *Nutshell* (2016), narrated by a foetus, is more concerned with genetics than with embryology.

In contemporary novels of formation, biology manifests itself most visibly in the generic clash between the *Bildung* plot and the genealogical plot, a dynamic already present in *Howards End*. Elsewhere I have coined the term *genic novel* to describe *Bildungsromane* in which a genetic plot underlies the primary developmental plot (Newman 2016b). In such novels, development is interrupted by genealogical analepses and, more rarely, prolepses: history and individual life are not parallel but co-implicated and seemingly co-determining. Already present in Zola and exacerbated in post-Mendelian novels such as Forster's *The Longest Journey*, this pattern has become so common in contemporary fiction that it may easily elude detection. When genes play an overt role in the narrative, however, relations between present development and genetic past (or future) can be rather more unsettling, as in such novels as Anthony Burgess's *M/F* (1971), Salman Rushdie's *Midnight's Children* (1981), Ann-Marie MacDonald's *Fall on Your Knees* (1996), Simon Mawer's *Mendel's Dwarf* (1997) and Margaret Drabble's *The Peppered Moth* (2000). The most striking exemplars of the genic novel, both of them evincing sophisticated knowledge of genetics and incorporating it into their narrative structure, are Jeffrey Eugenides's *Middlesex* (2002) and Zadie Smith's *White Teeth* (2000). In Smith's novel, the progressive *Bildung* plot of mixed-race and immigrant children is insistently if often farcically muddled by 'an imperative secreted in the genes' (2007: 525). They find themselves caught between the lures of Western culture, including the tantalising promise of classical *Bildung*, and racialised bodies 'genetically designed with another country in mind, another climate' (Smith 2007: 266). This biological inheritance is coupled with an equally complicated cultural legacy: in Smith's proleptic vision at the end of the novel, England will be inherited by Irie Jones and the twins Millat and Magid Iqbal, which is not to say they have not also been burdened by family histories going back to the 1857 Indian Rebellion, the 1907 Kingston earthquake or the post-War hunt for Nazi eugenicists.

Such admixtures of developmental and generational plotting take several distinctive forms in contemporary fiction. Most unsettling is the fusion of biographical and genealogical chronotopes in the clone *Bildungsroman*, an increasingly common variant of the genic novel. Such novels supplement the genic novel's formal anachronies with the doubled (tripled, quadrupled . . .) developmental lines of the protagonist's clones. Examples include Fay Weldon's *The Cloning of Joanna May* (1989), Eva Hoffman's *The Secret* (2001), the 'Sonmi-451' episodes of David Mitchell's *Cloud Atlas* (2004) and Kazuo Ishiguro's *Never Let Me Go* (2005). Another variation is the procreative *Bildungsroman*, such as Doris Lessing's *The Fifth Child* (1988) and Tim Parks's *Goodness* (1991), in which parents assume responsibility for the development of children profoundly afflicted by hereditary disorders. Here the child's developmental plot is separated from the issue of *Bildung*, which is divested onto the parents. The biology of ageing has also helped reshape the form and content of contemporary *Bildungsromane*, most notably in Saul Bellow's complex engagement with Lamarckism in *Henderson the Rain King* (1955) and Margaret Drabble's Huxleyan exploration of neoteny, thyroid hormone and *Bildung* in the autumnal romance *The Sea Lady* (2006). Less easily recognisable as a *Bildungsroman*, yet clearly sharing the genre's concern with identity, growing up and artistic realisation, is Ali Smith's inventive *How to Be Both* (2014), a latter-day *Orlando* whose allusions to the DNA molecule find formal expression in the narrative's doubled, helical structure. Most recently, yet perhaps closest to the modernist concerns with reversionary development and evolution, is Louise Erdrich's reproductive dystopia *Future Home of the Living God* (2017), which finds humanity 'climbing back down the swimming-pool ladder into the primordial soup' (2017: 68).

My list above is partial, not least because it neglects a lot of pertinent science fiction. It is beyond the scope of this book even to outline the many ways in which biology continues to inform the plotting of *Bildung*. These ways include an expansion of the *Bildungsroman*'s content, most importantly in relation to the identity of the protagonist. New ways of conceiving the biology of gender, sexuality, race, age and ability all contribute to making *Bildung* possible for individuals in groups formerly excluded from its promises. Of course modernist (and more recent) biology has not prevented developmental narratives from being normative and exclusionary. Racism, homophobia and patriarchy have all too evidently survived the demise of the scientific theories in which they once opportunistically found support. Prejudice can thrive with, without and against scientific evidence. But for what it's worth (and I think it is worth a lot), biology, when 'freed from the mental strait-jacket of recapitulation' (de Beer 1940: 141), broke some persistent habits of mind. In doing so it has, I hope, helped foment the critical activity which comes, as H. Porter Abbott has argued, from having 'to adjust to, to understand' the unwieldy models science foists upon us, enlisting our minds into an 'active resistance to the narrative frames of common experience' (2003: 148).

So I return to the idea of the *Bildungsroman* as a thought experiment, a notion akin to Jed Esty's proposal 'that the bildungsroman . . . always serves as a laboratory for reflection about the place of the individual self in larger histories' (2012: 213). Esty's symptomatic approach, his notion of literary experiment as a 'reflection' of larger cultural forces, highlights the importance of the historical forces underlying modernist innovation. I have approached experiment differently, more in line with my past practice as a biologist: as a set of artificial constraints placed on natural conditions in order to learn something new about the world. In 'Science in Literature' Simon Mawer reminds readers of *Nature* that '"What if?" is the question posed in both literature and science . . . And just as scientists employ thought experiments to focus their ideas, so a work of literature is a thought experiment about this uncertain human condition' (2005: 299).

Innovative literature is particularly important in this respect. Modernist fiction and its successors would thus illustrate Robbe-Grillet's claim that the novel uses experiment not to reject reality but, rather, to approach ever closer to it:

> The discovery of reality cannot continue along its forward course unless we abandon the used-up forms. Unless we believe the world is now fully known (in which case the wise thing to do is stop writing), there is nothing to do but to try going on – not to 'do better', but to advance into still-unknown paths, where a new writing becomes necessary. (Robbe-Grillet 1963: 136)

If literature is worth writing, reading and studying, it cannot merely confirm expectations and beliefs; it must continue to surprise. For Michel Butor, this is the very point and function of the novel, whose power lies in its triple ability to 'denounce' outmoded beliefs, to 'explore' new ones and to 'adapt' our mind to the implications of these new perspectives (1992: 10). As Richard Dawkins argues in an intriguingly similar vein, 'thought experiments are not supposed to be realistic' (2008: 4), and they must indeed often be *un*realistic. Percy Shelley says as much in his preface to Mary Shelley's *Frankenstein*. The novel, he insists, does not 'merely weav[e] a series of supernatural terrors' (2012: 49), for though the construction of the monster may be 'impossible as a physical fact' (2012: 49), it nevertheless 'affords a point of view to the imagination for the delineating of human passions more comprehensive and commanding than any which the ordinary relations of existing events can yield' (2012: 49). *Frankenstein* is a thought experiment, using an unnatural premise in order to depict human nature. It is a gothic tale of horror but also an allegory of moral education, a study into the psychology of rebellion, exclusion and sociality, a *Bildungsroman* thoroughly informed by the radical new ideas of the emergent field of biology.

Frankenstein thus anticipates the novels examined in *Modernist Life Histories*, novels which likewise explore, with help from new biology, how characters who 'cannot develop as they are supposed to develop' might yet 'develop what [they] have' (*HE* 335). As long as novelists recognise how much biology inheres in developmental narratives, the *Bildungsroman* will have occasion to adapt itself to new scientific models of how our bodies grow and change in time. The early twentieth century, like the early nineteenth, was such a period of rapid and dramatic change in the life sciences. What is especially important about the nexus of biology and *Bildung* in the early decades of the twentieth century is that no single alternative emerged to replace the biogenetic law. Ontogeny conceived as a recapitulation of phylogeny gave way to dynamic mosaic formations and relativistic differentials in developmental timing. The diversity of developmental plots enabled by such a conception is modelled by the frenzied repetitions, reversions and renewals of *How It Is* and summarised in that novel's variations on the phrase 'this new formulation namely this new life' (*HII* 107). This is not to deny the basic reality of time's arrow and ageing. 'Of course we grow old', writes Forster, but then, he adds, 'a great book must rest on something more than an "of course"' (*AN* 26). This 'something more' may not end up amounting to very much. It may do little more than make some room for the 'ever changing aspects of the never changing life' (*HII* 52). But perhaps this is not so little after all. It is perhaps in order to highlight these 'ever changing aspects' that fiction continues to renew itself, even when its subject matter – development in the *Bildungsroman* – remains apparently constant. 'Fiction', argues Woolf, 'far from having reached its full height, . . . is in a state of growth and development; we scarcely know on opening a new novel what to expect' (*EVW* ii.238). In this way at least, modernist fiction really is the mirror of our own life histories.

BIBLIOGRAPHY

Abbott, H. Porter (1994), 'Beginning Again: The Post-Narrative Art of *Texts for Nothing* and *How It Is*', in John Pilling (ed.), *The Cambridge Companion to Beckett*, Cambridge: Cambridge University Press, pp. 106–23.

Abbott, H. Porter (1996), *Beckett Writing Beckett: The Author in the Autograph*, Ithaca: Cornell University Press.

Abbott, H. Porter (2003), 'Unnarratable Knowledge: The Difficulty of Understanding Evolution by Natural Selection', in David Herman (ed.), *Narrative Theory and the Cognitive Sciences*, Stanford: Center for the Study of Language and Information, pp. 143–62.

Abbott, H. Porter (2010a), 'The Legacy of Samuel Beckett', in S. E. Gontarski (ed.), *A Companion to Samuel Beckett*, Malden, MA: Wiley-Blackwell, pp. 73–83.

Abbott, H. Porter (2010b), 'Narrating Conversion in an Age of Darwinian Gradualism', *StoryWorlds: A Journal of Narrative Studies* 2, 1–18.

Abel, Elizabeth (1983), 'Narrative Structure(s) and Female Development: The Case of *Mrs Dalloway*', in Elizabeth Abel, Marianne Hirsh and Elizabeth Langland (eds), *The Voyage In: Fictions of Female Development*, Hanover: University Press of New England, pp. 161–85.

Ackerley, Chris J. and Stanley E. Gontarski (2004), *The Grove Companion to Samuel Beckett: A Reader's Guide to His Works, Life, and Thought*, New York: Grove Press.

Adler, Jeremy D. (2005), 'Natural Science and the Making of Modern German Literature', in Rüdiger Görner (ed.), *Tales from the Laboratory, Or, Homunculus Revisited*, Munich: Iudicium, pp. 39–54.
A. E. R. (1921), 'Views and Reviews: The New Humanism – I', *The New Age* 30: 4, 34–5.
Aithal, S. Krishnamoorthy (1984), 'Huxley's *Eyeless in Gaza*', *Explicator* 42: 3, 46–9.
Alaimo, Stacy (2010), *Bodily Natures: Science, Environment, and the Material Self*, Indianapolis: Indiana University Press.
Allan, J. McGrigor (1869), 'On the Real Differences in the Minds of Men and Women', *Journal of the Anthropological Society of London* 7, 195–219.
Alt, Christina (2010), *Virginia Woolf and the Study of Nature*, Cambridge: Cambridge University Press.
Anderton, Joseph (2016), *Beckett's Creatures: Art of Failure after the Holocaust*, New York: Bloomsbury.
Argyle, Gisela (2002), *Germany as Model and Monster: Allusions in English Fiction, 1830s–1930s*, Montreal: McGill-Queen's University Press.
Armstrong, Gordon S. (1993), 'Cultural Politics and the Irish Theatre: Samuel Beckett and the New Biology', *Theatre Research International* 18: 3, 215–21.
Armstrong, Tim (2012), 'The Human Animal: Biological Tropes in Interwar Poetry', in John Robert Holmes (ed.), *Science and Modern Poetry*, Liverpool: Liverpool University Press, pp. 101–15.
Attridge, Derek (2000), *Joyce Effects: On Language, Theory, and History*, Cambridge: Cambridge University Press.
Auden, W. H. (1977), *The English Auden: Poems, Essays and Dramatic Writings 1927–1939*, ed. Edward Mendelson, London: Faber & Faber.
Bakhtin, Mikhail (1981), *The Dialogic Imagination: Four Essays*, ed. Michael Holquist, trans. Caryl Emerson and Michael Holquist, Austin: University of Texas Press.
Bakhtin, Mikhail (1984), *Speech Genres and Other Late Essays*, ed. Caryl Emerson and Michael Holquist, trans. Vern W. McGee, Austin: University of Texas Press.
Banfield, Ann (2003), 'Beckett's Tattered Syntax', *Representations* 84: 1, 6–29.
Baron, Scarlett (2013), 'Joyce, Darwin and Literary Evolution', in John Nash (ed.), *James Joyce in the Nineteenth Century*, Cambridge: Cambridge University Press, pp. 183–99.
Barthes, Roland (1970), *S/Z*, Paris: Seuil.
Bates, David William (2002), *Enlightenment Aberrations: Error and Revolution in France*, Ithaca: Cornell University Press.
Bateson, William (1913), *Mendel's Principles of Heredity*, New York: Putnam.
Bateson, William (1921), 'The Determination of Sex', *Nature* 106: 2675, 719–21.

Bateson, William (2009), *William Bateson, Naturalist: His Essays and Addresses*, ed. Beatrice Bateson, Cambridge: Cambridge University Press.

Beausang, Michael (1996), '*Watt*: Logic, Insanity, Aphasia', trans. Valérie Galiussi, *Style* 30: 3, 495–513.

Beckett, Samuel [1953] (1959), *Watt*, New York: Grove Press.

Beckett, Samuel [1929] (1961), 'Dante. . . Bruno. Vico.. Joyce', in *Our Exagmination Round his Factification for Incamination of Work in Progress*, London: Faber & Faber, pp. 1–22.

Beckett, Samuel [1938] (1973), *Murphy*, London: Picador.

Beckett, Samuel (1993), *Dream of Fair to Middling Women*, ed. Eoin O'Brien and Edith Fournier, New York: Arcade.

Beckett, Samuel [1934] (1994), *More Pricks than Kicks*, New York: Grove Press.

Beckett, Samuel (1995), *The Complete Short Prose, 1929–1989*, ed. S. E. Gontarski, New York: Grove Press.

Beckett, Samuel (1996), *Nohow On: Company, Ill Seen Ill Said, Worstward Ho*, New York: Grove Press.

Beckett, Samuel [1955] (1997a), *Molloy*, trans. Samuel Beckett with Patrick Bowles, in *Molloy, Malone Dies, The Unnamable*, New York: Everyman, pp. 1–199.

Beckett, Samuel [1956] (1997b), *Malone Dies*, trans. Samuel Beckett, in *Molloy, Malone Dies, The Unnamable*, New York: Everyman, pp. 201–328.

Beckett, Samuel [1958] (1997c), *The Unnamable*, trans. Samuel Beckett, in *Molloy, Malone Dies, The Unnamable*, New York: Everyman, pp. 329–476.

Beckett, Samuel (2006), *The Complete Dramatic Works*, London: Faber & Faber.

Beckett, Samuel [1961] (2007), *How It Is*, trans. Samuel Beckett, New York: Grove Press.

Beckett, Samuel (2009), *The Letters of Samuel Beckett, Volume I: 1929–1940*, ed. George Craig, Martha Dow Fehsenfeld, Dan Gunn and Lois More Overbeck, Cambridge: Cambridge University Press.

Beckett, Samuel (2014), *Echo's Bones*, ed. Mark Nixon, London: Faber & Faber.

Beer, Gillian (1996), *Virginia Woolf: The Common Ground*, Edinburgh: Edinburgh University Press.

Beer, Gillian (2000), *Darwin's Plots: Evolutionary Narrative in Darwin, George Eliot and Nineteenth-Century Fiction*, 2nd edn, Cambridge: Cambridge University Press.

Beiser, Frederick (2011), *The German Historicist Tradition*, Oxford: Oxford University Press.

Bender, Bert (2011), 'Nature in Naturalism', in Keith Newlin (ed.), *The Oxford Handbook of American Literature Naturalism*, Oxford: Oxford University Press, pp. 52–68.

Benstock, Bernard (1976), 'A Light from Some Other World: Symbolic Structure in *A Portrait of the Artist*', in Thomas Staley and Bernard Benstock (eds), *Approaches to Joyce's Portrait: Ten Essays*, Pittsburgh: University of Pittsburgh Press, pp. 185–211.

Benzel, Kathryn (1994), 'Reading Readers in Virginia Woolf's *Orlando: A Biography*', *Style* 28: 2, 169–82.

Benzenhöfer, Udo (1989), 'Joyce and Embryology: Giulio Valenti's *Lezioni Elementari di Embriologia* as Source for "Oxen of the Sun"', *James Joyce Quarterly* 26: 5, 608–11.

Beplate, Justin (2005), 'Joyce, Bergson, and the Memory of Words', *Modern Language Review* 100: 2, 298–312.

Bergson, Henri [1907] (2007), *L'Évolution créatrice*, ed. Frédéric Worms, Paris: Presses universitaires de France.

Berman, Antoine (1992), *The Experience of the 'Foreign': Culture and Translation in Romantic Germany*, trans. S. Heyvaert, Albany: State University of New York Press.

Berman, Jessica (2011), *Modernist Commitments: Ethics, Politics, and Transnational Modernism*, New York: Columbia University Press.

Bernini, Marco (2015), 'Crawling Creating Creatures: On Beckett's Liminal Minds', *European Journal of English Studies* 19: 1, 39–54.

Bersani, Leo (2004), 'Against *Ulysses*', in Derek Attridge (ed.), *James Joyce's* Ulysses: *A Casebook*, Oxford: Oxford University Press, pp. 201–29.

Birgy, Philippe (1997), '*Point Counterpoint*: Le journal de Philip Quarles et la théorie du modernisme en littérature', *Études Britanniques Contemporaines* 11, 37–45.

Birke, Lynda (1999), 'Bodies and Biology', in Janet Price and Margrit Shildrick (eds), *Feminist Theory and the Body: A Reader*, New York: Routledge, pp. 42–9.

Bivona, Daniel (1990), *Desire and Contradiction: Imperial Visions and Domestic Debates in Victorian Literature*, New York: Manchester University Press.

Bixby, Patrick (2009), *Samuel Beckett and the Postcolonial Novel*, Cambridge: Cambridge University Press.

Black, Joel (2000), 'Scientific Models', in Marshall Brown (ed.), *The Cambridge History of Literary Criticism, Volume 5: Romanticism*, Cambridge: Cambridge University Press, pp. 115–37.

Boehm, Beth (1992), 'Fact, Fiction, and Metafiction: Blurred Gen(d)res in *Orlando* and *A Room of One's Own*', *The Journal of Narrative Technique* 22: 3, 191–204.

Boes, Tobias (2006), 'Modernist Studies and the *Bildungsroman*: A Historical Survey of Critical Trends', *Literature Compass* 3: 2, 230–43.

Boes, Tobias (2012), *Formative Fictions: Nationalism, Cosmopolitanism, and the Bildungsroman*, Ithaca: Cornell University Press.

Bolaki, Stella (2011), *Unsettling the Bildungsroman: Reading Contemporary Ethnic American Women's Fiction*, New York: Rodopi.

Bolin, John (2013), *Beckett and the Modern Novel*, Cambridge: Cambridge University Press.

Bolton, Jonathan (2010), *'Blighted Beginnings': Coming of Age in Independent Ireland*, Lewisburg, PA: Bucknell University Press.

Booth, Wayne (1983), *The Rhetoric of Fiction*, 2nd edn, Chicago: University of Chicago Press.

Bowen, Elizabeth [1935] (1998), *The House in Paris*, New York: Anchor.

Bowen, Elizabeth [1929] (2000), *The Last September*, New York: Anchor.

Bowers, Paul Alan (1999), '"Variability in Every Tongue": Joyce and the Darwinian Narrative', *James Joyce Quarterly* 36: 4, 869–88.

Bowers, Paul Alan (2009), '"Charley, You're My Darwing!" Sexual Selection in the Joycean Nursery', *Journal of Modern Literature* 32: 4, 34–42.

Bowler, Peter (1984), *Evolution: The History of an Idea*, Berkeley: University of California Press.

Bowler, Peter (1988), *The Non-Darwinian Revolution: Reinterpreting a Historical Myth*, Baltimore: Johns Hopkins University Press.

Boyd, Brian (1990), *Vladimir Nabokov: The Russian Years*, Princeton: Princeton University Press.

Bredeck, Gregory (1997), '"Queer Superstitions": Forster, Carpenter, and the Illusion of (Sexual) Identity', in Robert K. Martin and George Piggford (eds), *Queer Forster*, Chicago: University of Chicago Press, pp. 29–58.

Briggs, Julia (2005), *Virginia Woolf: An Inner Life*, New York: Harvest.

Brivic, Sheldon (2006), 'The Disjunctive Structure of Joyce's *Portrait*', in R. B. Kershner (ed.), *A Portrait of the Artist as a Young Man*, 2nd edn, New York: Bedford/St. Martin's, pp. 279–98.

Brontë, Charlotte [1847] (2008), *Jane Eyre*, New York: Signet.

Brooks, Daniel and E. O. Wiley (1988), *Evolution as Entropy: Toward a Unified Theory of Biology*, 2nd edn, Chicago: University of Chicago Press.

Brooks, Peter (1985), *Reading for the Plot: Design and Intention in Narrative*, New York: Vintage.

Brooks, Peter (1993), *Body Work: Objects of Desire in Modern Narrative*, Cambridge, MA: Harvard University Press.

Brooks, William Keith (1883), *The Law of Heredity: A Study of the Cause of Variation, and the Origin of Living Organisms*, 2nd edn, New York: John Murphy.

Brown, Penny (1992), *The Poison at the Source: The Female Novel of Self-Development in the Early Twentieth Century*, London: Palgrave Macmillan.

Brown, Richard (1985), *James Joyce and Sexuality*, Cambridge: Cambridge University Press.

Bruce, A. B. (1910), 'The Mendelian Theory of Heredity and the Augmentation of Vigour', *Science* 32: 827, 627–28.

Bruford, W. H. (1975), *The German Tradition of Self-Cultivation: Bildung from Humboldt to Thomas Mann*, Cambridge: Cambridge University Press.

Brunel, Pierre (1974), *Le Mythe de la métamorphose*, Paris: Armand Colin.

Bryden, Mary (ed.) (2013), *Beckett and Animals*, Cambridge: Cambridge University Press.

Bryher [1920/1923] (2000), *Two Novels: Development and Two Selves*, ed. Joanne Winning, Madison: University of Wisconsin Press.

Budgen, Frank (1960), *James Joyce and the Making of Ulysses*, Bloomington: Indiana University Press.

Burgess, Anthony (1988), 'Martyr and Myth-Maker', in Harold Bloom (ed.), *James Joyce's Portrait of the Artist as a Young Man: Modern Critical Interpretations*, New York: Chelsea House, pp. 43–54.

Butler, Samuel [1872] (1890), *Life and Habit*, London: Longmans, Green.

Butler, Samuel [1903] (1977), *The Way of All Flesh*, New York: Hart.

Butor, Michel (1992), *Essais sur le roman*, Paris: Gallimard.

Bynum, Caroline Walker (2005), *Metamorphosis and Identity*, New York: Zone Books.

Campbell, Joseph and Henry Morton Robinson (1968), *A Skeleton Key to Finnegans Wake*, New York: Viking.

Caputi Daileader, Celia (2013), 'Othello's Sister: Racial Hermaphroditism and Appropriation in Virginia Woolf's *Orlando*', *Studies in the Novel* 45: 1, 56–79.

Carney, James (2012), 'The Buzzing of B: The Subject as Insect in Beckett's *Molloy*', in James Carney, Michael O'Sullivan and Karl White (eds), *Beckett Re-Membered: After the Centenary*, Newcastle-upon-Tyne: Cambridge Scholars, pp. 224–37.

Carpenter, Edward (1898), *Angels' Wings: Essays on Art and its Relation to Life*, London: Swan Sonnenschein.

Carpenter, Edward [1908] (1918), *The Intermediate Sex: A Study of Some Transitional Types of Men and Women*, London: Allen & Unwin.

Carroll, Lewis [1865/1871] (1992), *Alice's Adventures in Wonderland* and *Through the Looking-Glass and What Alice Found There*, ed. Roger Lancelyn Green, Oxford: Oxford University Press.

Caserio, Robert L. (1999), *The Novel in England, 1900–1950: History and Theory*, New York: Twayne.

Castle, Gregory (2006), *Reading the Modernist Bildungsroman*, Orlando: University of Florida Press.

Castle, Gregory (2013), 'My Self, My Other: Modernism and Postcolonial Bildung in Assia Djebar's *Algerian Quartet*', *Modern Fiction Studies* 59: 3, 628–48.

Castle, Gregory (2015), 'Destinies of *Bildung*: Belatedness and the Modernist Novel', in Gregory Castle (ed.), *A History of the Modernist Novel*, Cambridge: Cambridge University Press, pp. 483–507.

Caughie, Pamela (2013), 'The Temporality of Modernist Life Writing in the Era of Transsexualism: Virginia Woolf's *Orlando* and Einar Wegener's *Man Into Woman*', *Modern Fiction Studies* 59: 3, 501–25.

Cerrato, Laura (1993), 'Postmodernism and Beckett's Aesthetics of Failure', *Samuel Beckett Today/Aujourd'hui* 2, 21–30.

Cervetti, Nancy (1996), 'In the Breeches, Petticoats, and Pleasures of *Orlando*', *Journal of Modern Literature* 20: 2, 165–75.

Channing, Jill (2005), 'Magical Realism and Gender Variability in *Orlando*', *Virginia Woolf Miscellany* 67, 11–13.

Cheah, Pheng (2003), *Spectral Nationality: Passages of Freedom from Kant to Postcolonial Literatures of Liberation*, New York: Columbia University Press.

Cheng, Vincent (1995), *Joyce, Race, and Empire*, Cambridge: Cambridge University Press.

Cheng, Vincent (2004), *Inauthentic: The Anxiety Over Culture and Identity*, New Brunswick: Rutgers University Press.

Childs, Donald (2001), *Modernism and Eugenics: Woolf, Eliot, Yeats, and the Culture of Degeneration*, Cambridge: Cambridge University Press.

Chiong, Kathryn (1998), 'Naumann's Beckett Walk', *October* 86, 61–81.

Churchill, Frederick B. (2007), 'Living with the Biogenetic Law: A Reappraisal', in Manfred D. Laubichler and Jane Maienschein (eds), *From Embryology to Evo-Devo: A History of Developmental Evolution*, Cambridge, MA: MIT Press, pp. 37–81.

Clayton, Jay (2016), 'The Modern Synthesis: Genetics and Dystopia in the Huxley Circle', *Modernism/Modernity* 23: 4, 875–96.

Clissold, Bradley (2007), 'Heredity and Disinheritance in Joyce's *Portrait*', in Allan Hepburn (ed.), *Troubled Legacies: Narrative and Inheritance*, Toronto: University of Toronto Press, pp. 191–218.

Conklin, Edwin Grant (1928), 'Evolution as Shown by the Advancement of the Individual Organism', in Frances Mason (ed.), *Creation by Evolution*, New York: Macmillan, pp. 49–80.

Connor, Steven (2014), *Beckett, Modernism and the Material Imagination*, Cambridge: Cambridge University Press.

Conrad, Joseph [1899] (1976), *Lord Jim*, Harmondsworth: Penguin.

Cope, Edward Drinker (1887), *The Origins of the Fittest: Essays on Evolution*, New York: Appleton.

Cope, Jackson (1962), 'The Rhythmic Gesture: Image and Aesthetic in Joyce's *Ulysses*', *ELH* 29: 1, 67–89.

Coquio, Catherine (1998), 'L'Homme-sans: Poésie de l'indéterminé, histoire des exterminés', in Valérie-Angélique Deshoulières (ed.), *Poétiques de l'indéterminé: Le caméléon au propre et au figuré*, Clermont-Ferrand: Association des Publications de la Faculté des Lettres et Sciences Humaines de Clermont-Ferrand, pp. 381–403.

Cormack, Alistair (2008), *Yeats and Joyce: Cyclical History and the Reprobate Tradition*, London: Ashgate.

Cosmoi, M. M. (1920), 'World Affairs', *The New Age* 28: 7, 75–77.

Crangle, Sara (2010), *Prosaic Desires: Modernist Knowledge, Boredom, Laughter, and Anticipation*, Edinburgh: Edinburgh University Press.

Crawford, Hugh (2011), 'Modernism', in Bruce Clarke and Manuela Rossini (eds), *The Routledge Companion to Literature and Science*, London: Routledge, pp. 508–17.

Crowley, Tony (2010), 'James Joyce and Lexicography: "I Must Look that Word up. Upon my Word I Must" (*Logodaedalus*, "One Who Is Cunning in Words", 1611)', *Dictionaries* 31, 87–90.

Cullingford, Elizabeth Butler (2000), 'Phoenician Genealogies and Oriental Geographies: Joyce, Language and Race', in Derek Attridge and Marjorie Howes (eds), *Semicolonial Joyce*, Cambridge: Cambridge University Press, pp. 219–39.

Daiches, David (1939), *The Novel and the Modern World*, Chicago: University of Chicago Press.

Daleski, H. M. (1985), *Unities: Studies in the English Novel*, Athens, GA: University of Georgia Press.

D'Arcy, Michael (2014), 'Beckett's Trilogy and the Deaths of (Auto)biographical Form', *Samuel Beckett Today/Aujourd'hui* 26, 63–77.

Darwin, Charles [1859] (1964), *On the Origin of Species: A Facsimile of the First Edition*, Cambridge, MA: Harvard University Press.

Darwin, Charles [1871] (1981), *The Descent of Man, and Selection in Relation to Sex*, Princeton: Princeton University Press.

da Silva, Stephen (1988), 'Transvaluing Immaturity: Reverse Discourses of Male Homosexuality in E. M. Forster's Posthumously Published Fiction', *Criticism* 40: 2, 237–72.

Davidson, Percy (1914), *The Recapitulation Theory and Human Infancy*, New York: Teachers College, Columbia University.

Davies, Paul (1994), 'Three Novels and Four *Nouvelles*: Giving Up the Ghost Be Born at Least', in John Pilling (ed.), *The Cambridge Companion to Beckett*, Cambridge: Cambridge University Press, pp. 43–66.

Dawkins, Richard (2004), *The Ancestor's Tale: A Pilgrimage to the Dawn of Life*, Boston: Houghton-Mifflin.

Dawkins, Richard (2006), *The Selfish Gene*, 3rd edn, Oxford: Oxford University Press.

Dawkins, Richard (2008), *The Extended Phenotype: The Long Reach of the Gene*, Oxford: Oxford University Press.

Dawkins, Richard (2009), *The Greatest Show on Earth: The Evidence for Evolution*, New York: Free Press.

Deane, Seamus (1990), 'Joyce the Irishman', in Derek Attridge (ed.), *The Cambridge Companion to James Joyce*, Cambridge: Cambridge University Press, pp. 32–54.

Deane, Seamus (2000), 'Dead Ends: Joyce's Finest Moments', in Derek Attridge and Marjorie Howes (eds), *Semicolonial Joyce*, Cambridge: Cambridge University Press, pp. 21–36.

de Beer, Gavin (1930), *Embryology and Evolution*, Oxford: Clarendon.

de Beer, Gavin (1938), 'Embryology and Evolution', in Gavin de Beer (ed.), *Evolution: Essays on Aspects of Evolutionary Biology*, Oxford: Clarendon, pp. 57–78.

de Beer, Gavin (1940), *Embryos and Ancestors*, Oxford: Clarendon.

de Beer, Gavin (1951), *Vertebrate Zoology: An Introduction to the Comparative Anatomy, Embryology and Evolution of Chordate Animals*, 2nd edn, London: Sidgwick & Jackson.

de Beer, Gavin (1962), *Reflections of a Darwinian: Essays and Addresses*, London: Thomas Nelson & Sons.

Deese, R. S. (2014), *We Are Amphibians: Julian and Aldous Huxley on the Future of the Species*, Berkeley: University of California Press.

de Gay, Jane (2006), *Virginia Woolf's Novels and the Literary Past*, Edinburgh: Edinburgh University Press.

de la Durantaye, Leland (2016), *Beckett's Art of Mismaking*, Cambridge, MA: Harvard University Press.

Delbaere-Garant, Jeanne (1977), 'From the Moocow to Navelless Eve: The Spiral Growth of Stephen Dedalus', *Revue des langues vivantes* 43, 131–41.

Deming, Robert (ed.) (1970), *James Joyce: The Critical Heritage*, London: Routledge and Paul.

Dennis, Amanda (2015), 'Radical Indecision: Aporia as Metamorphosis in Beckett's *The Unnamable*', *Journal of Beckett Studies* 24: 2, 180–97.

Dettmar, Kevin (2010), 'The Materiality and Historicity of Language in *A Portrait of the Artist as a Young Man*', in Sean Latham (ed.), *James Joyce*, Portland: Irish Academic, pp. 67–82.

Deutsch, David (2010), 'Reconnecting Music to *Howards End*: Forster's Aesthetics of Inclusion', *Literature Interpretation Theory* 21, 163–86.

DiBattista, Maria (2009), *Imagining Virginia Woolf: An Experiment in Critical Biography*, Princeton: Princeton University Press.

DiBattista, Maria and Emily Wittman (2014), 'Introduction', in Maria DiBattista and Emily Wittman, *Modernism and Autobiography*, Cambridge: Cambridge University Press, pp. xi–xx.

Dickens, Charles [1861] (1996), *Great Expectations*, London: Penguin.

Dilthey, Wilhelm [1910] (1985), 'Friedrich Hölderlin', trans. Joseph Ross, in Rudolf A. Makkreel and Frithjof Rodi (eds), *Selected Works, Vol. V: Poetry and Experience*, Princeton: Princeton University Press, pp. 303–84.

Doherty, Gerald (2008), *Pathologies of Desire: The Vicissitudes of the Self in James Joyce's A Portrait of the Artist as a Young Man*, New York: Lang.

Dorland, Tamera (1997), '"Contrary to the Prevailing Current"? Homoeroticism and the Voice of Maternal Law in "The Other Boat"', in Robert K. Martin and George Piggford (eds), *Queer Forster*, Chicago: University of Chicago Press, pp. 193–219.

Douglas, Erin (2009), '"That was a terrible thing to do to a flower": Floral Pleasures and Changeable Bodies in Virginia Woolf's *Orlando* and Jeanette Winterson's *The PowerBook*', *Virginia Woolf Miscellany* 75, 13–15.

Douglas, James Archibald (1909), 'The Carboniferous Limestone of County Clare (Ireland)', *Quarterly Journal of the Geological Society* 65, 538–86.

Dowden, Edward (1877), 'The Scientific Movement and Literature', *The Contemporary Review* 30, 558–78.

Drabble, Margaret (2008), *The Sea Lady*, Toronto: Emblem.

'drivel, *n*[2]' (2016), *OED Online*, Oxford University Press, <http://www.oed.com.myaccess.library.utoronto.ca/view/Entry/57794?rskey=QYmuCT&result=2&isAdvanced=false> (last accessed 17 October 2016).

Ebbatson, Roger (1982), *The Evolutionary Self: Hardy, Forster, Lawrence*, Totowa, NJ: Barnes & Noble.

Eddington, Arthur (1928), *The Nature of the Physical World*, Cambridge: Cambridge University Press.

Edelman, Lee (2004), *No Future: Queer Theory and the Death Drive*, Durham, NC: Duke University Press.

Eder, M. D. (1909), 'The New Biology', *The New Age* 5: 10, 192–3.

Eide, Marian (1998), 'The Woman of the Ballyhoora Hills: James Joyce and the Politics of Creativity', *Twentieth-Century Literature* 44: 4, 377–93.

Eimer, G. H. Theodor (1890), *Organic Evolution as the Result of the Inheritance of Acquired Characteristics, According to the Laws of Organic Growth*, trans. J. T. Cunningham, London: Macmillan.

Eliot, George [1861] (1996), *Silas Marner*, Mineola, NY: Dover.

Eliot, T. S. [1943] (2001), *Four Quartets*, London: Faber & Faber.

Elkins, Amy (2010), 'Old Pages and New Readings in Virginia Woolf's *Orlando*', *Tulsa Studies in Women's Literature* 29: 1, 131–6.

Ellis, Havelock (1905), *Studies in the Psychology of Sex: Sexual Selection in Man*, Philadelphia: Davis.

Ellis, Havelock (1906), *Studies in the Psychology of Sex: Sexual Inversion*, Philadelphia: Davis.

Ellis, Lorna (1999), *Appearing to Diminish: Female Development and the British Bildungsroman, 1750–1850*, Lewisburg, PA: Bucknell University Press.

Ellmann, Maud (1982), 'Polytropic Man: Paternity, Identity and Naming in *The Odyssey* and *A Portrait of the Artist as a Young Man*', in Colin MacCabe (ed.), *James Joyce: New Perspectives*, Bloomington: Indiana University Press, pp. 73–104.

Ellmann, Maud (2010), *The Nets of Modernism: Henry James, Virginia Woolf, James Joyce and Sigmund Freud*, Cambridge: Cambridge University Press.

Ellmann, Richard (1965), *James Joyce*, Oxford: Oxford University Press.

Erdrich, Louise (2017), *Future Home of the Living God*, New York: HarperCollins.

Ermarth, Elizabeth Deeds (1998), *Realism and Consensus in the English Novel*, Edinburgh: Edinburgh University Press.

Esty, Jed (2012), *Unseasonable Youth: Modernism, Colonialism, and the Fiction of Development*, Oxford: Oxford University Press.

Ewart, J. C. (1894), 'The Development of the Skeleton of the Limbs of the Horse, with Observations on Polydactyly, Part II', *Journal of Anatomy and Physiology* 28, 342–69.

Fassler, Barbara (1979), 'Theories of Homosexuality as Sources of Bloomsbury's Androgyny', *Signs* 5: 2, 237–51.

Faulkner, William [1951] (2011), *Requiem for a Nun*, New York: Vintage.

Feder, Helena (2014), Ecocriticism and the Idea of Culture: Biology and the Bildungsroman, New York and London: Routledge.

Felski, Rita (1989), *Beyond Feminist Aesthetics: Feminist Literature and Social Change*, Cambridge, MA: Harvard University Press.

Felski, Rita (1995), *The Gender of Modernity*, Cambridge, MA: Harvard University Press.

Felski, Rita (2009), 'After Suspicion', *Profession* 2009, 28–35.

Feshbach, Sidney (1967), 'A Slow and Dark Birth: A Study of the Organization of *A Portrait of the Artist as a Young Man*', *James Joyce Quarterly* 4: 4, 289–300.

Firchow, Peter (1981), 'Germany and Germanic Mythology in *Howards End*', *Comparative Literature* 33: 1, 50–68.

Fitch, Tecumseh (2010), *The Evolution of Language*, Cambridge: Cambridge University Press.

Fitzpatrick, William (1974), 'The Myth of Creation: Joyce, Jung, and *Ulysses*', *James Joyce Quarterly* 11: 2, 123–44.

Ford, Ford Madox (1908), *Mr Apollo: A Just Possible Story*, London: Methuen.

Forster, E. M. (1972a), *The Life to Come and Other Stories*, ed. Oliver Stallybrass, London: Arnold.

Forster, E. M. (1972b), *Two Cheers for Democracy*, ed. Oliver Stallybrass, London: Arnold.

Forster, E. M. [1910] (1973), *Howards End*, ed. Oliver Stallybrass, London: Arnold.

Forster, E. M. [1927] (1974), *Aspects of the Novel and Related Writings*, ed. Oliver Stallybrass, London: Arnold.

Forster, E. M. (1975), *Where Angels Fear to Tread*, ed. Oliver Stallybrass, London: Arnold.

Forster, E. M. (1978), *A Passage to India*, ed. Oliver Stallybrass, London: Arnold.

Forster, E. M. (1980), *Arctic Summer and Other Fiction*, ed. Elizabeth Heine and Oliver Stallybrass, London: Arnold.

Forster, E. M. (1983), *Selected Letters*, vol. 1, ed. Mary Lago and P. N. Furbank, Cambridge, MA: Belknap Press.

Forster, E. M. (1984), *The Longest Journey*, ed. Elizabeth Heine, London: Arnold.

Forster, E. M. (1985), *Commonplace Book*, ed. Philip Gardner, London: Scholar.

Forster, E. M. (1999), *Maurice*, ed. Philip Gardner, London: Deutsch.

Forster, E. M. (2008), *The Critic as Creator and Other Writings*, ed. Jeffrey Heath, Toronto: Dundurn.

Fraiman, Susan (1994), *Unbecoming Women: British Women Writers and the Novel of Development*, New York: Columbia University Press.

Frazer, James [1909] (2007), *Psyche's Task: A Discourse Concerning the Influence of Superstition on the Growth of Institutions*, New York: Cosimo.

Freedgood, Elaine and Cannon Schmitt (2014), 'Denotatively, Technically, Literally', *Representations* 125: 1, 1–14.

Freud, Sigmund [1939] (1961), *Civilization and Its Discontents*, ed. and trans. James Strachey, New York: Norton.

Friedman, Susan Stanford (2015), 'Religion, Intersectionality, and Queer/Feminist Narrative Theory: The *Bildungsromane* of Ahdaf Soueif, Leila Aboulela, and Randa Jarrar', in Robyn Warhol and Susan Lanser (eds), *Narrative Theory Unbound: Queer and Feminist Interventions*, Columbus: Ohio State University Press, pp. 101–22.

Friedman, Susan Stanford (2017), 'Both/And: Critique and Discovery in the Humanities', *PMLA* 132: 2, 344–51.

Froula, Christine (1996), *Modernism's Body: Sex, Culture, and Joyce*, New York: Columbia University Press.

Gaipa, Mark (1995), 'Culture, Anarchy, and the Politics of Modernist Style in "Oxen of the Sun"', *Modern Fiction Studies* 41: 2, 195–217.

Gallagher, David (2009), *Metamorphosis: Transformations of the Body and the Influence of Ovid's Metamorphoses on Germanic Literature of the Nineteenth and Twentieth Centuries*, New York: Rodopi.

Garstang, Sylvia and Walter Garstang (1928), 'On the Development of Botrylloides', *Quarterly Journal of Microscopical Science* 72, 1–45.

Garstang, Walter (1922), 'The Theory of Recapitulation: A Critical Re-statement of the Biogenetic Law', *Journal of the Linnean Society of London, Zoology* 35: 232, 81–101.

Garstang, Walter (1928), 'The Morphology of the Tunicata, and Its Bearing on the Phylogeny of Chordates', *Quarterly Journal of Microscopical Science* 72, 51–187.

Gates, R. Ruggles (1921), 'The Genetics of Sex', *Nature* 107: 2696, 571–2.

Gaultier, Jules de (1903), *La Fiction universelle: Deuxième essai sur le pouvoir d'imaginer*, Paris: Société du Mercure de France.

Geddes, Patrick and J. Arthur Thomson (1889), *The Evolution of Sex*, London: Scribner's.

Genette, Gérard (1982), *Palimpsestes: La littérature au second degré*, Paris: Seuil.

Gide, André [1925] (1975), *Les Faux-monnayeurs*, Paris: Gallimard.

Gifford, Don with Robert J. Seidman (1989), *Annotations to Ulysses*, 2nd edn, Berkeley: University of California Press.

Gigante, Denise (2009), *Life: Organic Form and Romanticism*, New Haven: Yale University Press.

Goethe, Johann Wolfgang von [1816–17] (1982), *Italian Journey, 1786–1788*, trans. W. H. Auden and Elizabeth Mayer, San Francisco: North Point Press.

Goethe, Johann Wolfgang von (1988), *Scientific Studies*, ed. and trans. Douglas Miller, New York: Suhrkamp.

Goethe, Johann Wolfgang von [1895–6] (1989), *Wilhelm Meister's Apprenticeship*, ed. and trans. Eric Blackall with Victor Lange, Princeton: Princeton University Press.

Gohlman, Susan (1990), *Starting Over: The Task of the Protagonist in the Contemporary Bildungsroman*, New York: Garland.

Goldschmidt, Richard (1917), 'Intersexuality and the Endocrine Aspect of Sex', *Endocrinology* 1: 4, 433–56.

Goldschmidt, Richard (1918), 'A Preliminary Report on Some Genetic Experiments Concerning Evolution', *American Naturalist* 52: 613, 28–50.

Goldschmidt, Richard (1921), 'The Determination of Sex', *Nature* 107: 2703, 780–4.

Gontarski, S. E. (2008), 'An End to Endings: Samuel Beckett's Endgame(s)', in Minako Okamuro, *Borderless Beckett/Beckett sans frontières*, ed. Minako Okamuro, Naoya Mori, Bruno Clément, Sjef Houppermans, Angela Moorjani and Anthony Uhlmann, New York: Rodopi, pp. 419–29.

Goodlad, Lauren M. E. (2005), 'Toward a Victorianist's Theory of Androgynous Experiment', *Victorian Studies* 47: 2, 215–29.

Gordon, John (2003), *Physiology and the Literary Imagination: Romantic to Modern*, Orlando: University of Florida Press.

Gordon, John (2004), *Joyce and Reality: The Empirical Strikes Back*, Syracuse: University of Syracuse Press.

Gose, Elliott B., Jr (1985), 'Destruction and Creation in *A Portrait of the Artist as a Young Man*', *James Joyce Quarterly* 22: 3, 259–70.

Goudge, T. A. (1961), *The Ascent of Man: A Philosophical Study of the Theory of Evolution*, Toronto: University of Toronto Press.

Gould, Stephen Jay (1977), *Ontogeny and Phylogeny*, Cambridge, MA: Harvard University Press.

Gould, Stephen Jay (1979), *Ever Since Darwin*, New York: Norton.

Gould, Stephen Jay (1982), *The Panda's Thumb: More Reflections in Natural History*, New York: Norton.

Gould, Stephen Jay (1984), *Hen's Teeth and Horse's Toes*, New York: Norton.

Gould, Stephen Jay (1996), *The Mismeasure of Man*, New York: Norton.

Green, Henry [1926] (2008), *Blindness*, in *Nothing, Doting, Blindness*, London: Vintage.

Greene, Graham [1951] (2000), *The End of the Affair*, London: Penguin.

Greenslade, William (1994), *Degeneration, Culture and the Novel 1880–1940*, Cambridge: Cambridge University Press.

Griffin, Roger (1991), *The Nature of Fascism*, New York: St. Martin's Press.

'hackle, *v*[3]' (2016), *OED Online*, Oxford University Press, <http://www.oed.com.myaccess.library.utoronto.ca/view/Entry/83056?rskey=JJKdDK&result=5&isAdvanced=false> (last accessed 25 November 2016).

Haeckel, Ernst (1876), *The History of Creation: Or the Development of the Earth and Its Inhabitants by the Action of Natural Causes*, trans. Ray Lankester, London: Henry S. King.

Haeckel, Ernst (1883), *The Evolution of Man: A Popular Exposition of the Principal Points of Human Ontogeny and Phylogeny*, London: Kegan Paul.

Haeckel, Ernst (1900), *Riddle of the Universe*, trans. Joseph McCabe, London: Harper & Brothers.

Haeckel, Ernst (1903), *The Pedigree of Man, and Other Essays*, trans. Edward Aveling, London: Bonner.

Haeckel, Ernst (1904), *The Wonders of Life: A Popular Study of Biological Philosophy*, trans. Joseph McCabe, London: Watts.

Haldane, J. B. S. (1913), *Mechanism, Life and Personality: An Examination of the Mechanistic Theory of Life and Mind*, London: John Murray.

Haldane, J. B. S. (1932), 'The Time of Action of Genes, and Its Bearing on Some Evolutionary Problems', *American Naturalist* 66: 702, 5–24.

Haldane, J. B. S. [1923] (1995), 'Daedalus, or The Science of the Future', in Krishna Dronamraju (ed.), *Haldane's Daedalus Revisited*, Oxford: Oxford University Press, pp. 23–50.

Hall, G. Stanley (1904), *Adolescence: Its Psychology and Its Relations to Physiology, Anthropology, Sociology, Sex, Crime, Religion and Education*, 2 vols, New York: Appleton.

Hardin, James (1991), 'Introduction', in James Hardin (ed.), *Reflection and Action: Essays on the Bildungsroman*, Columbia: University of South Carolina Press, pp. iv–xxvii.

Hardy, A. C. (1958), 'Escape from Specialization', in Julian Huxley, A. C. Hardy and E. B. Ford (eds), *Evolution as a Process*, 2nd edn, London: Allen & Unwin, pp. 122–42.

Hardy, Thomas (1998), *Selected Poems*, London: Penguin.

Harley, Alexis (2015), *Autobiologies: Charles Darwin and the Natural History of the Self*, Lewisburg, PA: Bucknell University Press.

Hart, Clive (1993), 'Gaps and Cracks in *Ulysses*', *James Joyce Quarterly* 30: 3, 427–37.

Hartung, Heike (2016), *Ageing, Gender, and Illness in Anglophone Literature: Narrating Age in the Bildungsroman*, New York: Routledge.

Heard, Gerald (1941), *Man the Master*, New York: Harper.

Hegel, G. W. F. [1807] (1979), *Phenomenology of Spirit*, trans. A. V. Miller, Oxford: Oxford University Press.

Helt, Brenda (2010), 'Passionate Debates on "Odious Subjects": Bisexuality and Woolf's Opposition to Theories of Androgyny and Sexual Identity', *Twentieth-Century Literature* 56: 2, 131–67.

Henderson, Linda Dalrymple (2007), 'Modernism and Science', in Astradur Eysteinsson and Vivian Liska (eds), *Modernism*, vol. 1, Philadelphia: John Benjamins, pp. 383–403.

Hepburn, Allan (2007), 'Introduction: Inheritance and Disinheritance in the Novel', in Allan Hepburn (ed.), *Troubled Legacies: Inheritance and the Novel*, Toronto: University of Toronto Press, pp. 3–25.

Herz, Judith Scherer (1978), 'The Double Nature of Forster's Fiction: *A Room with a View* and *The Longest Journey*', *ELH* 21: 4, 254–65.

Herz, Judith Scherer (2008), 'Miss Avery in the Garden with the Sword', *GLQ: A Journal of Lesbian and Gay Studies* 14: 4, 603–8.

Ho, Janice (2015), *Nation and Citizenship in the Twentieth-Century British Novel*, Cambridge: Cambridge University Press.

Hovanec, Caroline (2013), 'Zoological Modernism: Literature, Science, and Animals in Early Twentieth-Century Britain', PhD thesis, Vanderbilt University, Nashville.

Howes, Marjorie (2000), '"Goodbye Ireland I'm Going to Gort": Geography, Scale, and Narrating the Nation', in Derek Attridge and Marjorie

Howes (eds), *Semicolonial Joyce*, Cambridge: Cambridge University Press, pp. 58–77.

Hulme, T. E. (1994), *Collected Writings*, ed. Karen Csengeri, Oxford: Clarendon.

Humboldt, Wilhelm von [1851] (1969), *The Limits of State Action*, ed. and trans. J. W. Burrow, Cambridge: Cambridge University Press.

Hurst, C. Herbert (1893), 'The Recapitulation Theory', *Natural Science* 2, 195–241.

Hussakof, L. (1910), 'Vertebrate Paleontology and the Evidences for Recapitulation', *Popular Science Monthly* 77: 15, 305–7.

Hutchings, William (1978), 'Ontogenesis/Phylogenesis: The Pattern of Historical Development in Chapter IV of *A Portrait*', *James Joyce Quarterly* 15: 4, 339–46.

Huxley, Aldous (1923), *Antic Hay*, London: Chatto & Windus.

Huxley, Aldous (1925), *Those Barren Leaves*, London: Chatto & Windus.

Huxley, Aldous (1926a), *Essays New and Old*, London: Chatto & Windus.

Huxley, Aldous (1926b), *Jesting Pilate: An Intellectual Holiday*, New York: Doran.

Huxley, Aldous (1927), *Proper Studies*, London: Chatto & Windus.

Huxley, Aldous (1928), *Point Counter Point*, London: Chatto & Windus.

Huxley, Aldous (1931), *Music at Night*, London: Chatto & Windus.

Huxley, Aldous (1936a), *Eyeless in Gaza*, London: Chatto & Windus.

Huxley, Aldous (1936b), *The Olive Tree and Other Essays*, London: Chatto & Windus.

Huxley, Aldous (1937), *Ends and Means: An Enquiry into the Nature of Ideals and into the Methods Employed for Their Realization*, London: Chatto & Windus.

Huxley, Aldous (1939), *After Many a Summer Dies the Swan*, London: Chatto & Windus.

Huxley, Aldous (1944), *Time Must Have a Stop*, New York: Harper & Brothers.

Huxley, Aldous (1956), *Adonis and the Alphabet*, London: Chatto & Windus.

Huxley, Aldous (1963), *Literature and Science*, London: Chatto & Windus.

Huxley, Aldous (2002), *Complete Essays, Volume IV: 1956–1963*, ed. Robert S. Baker and James Sexton, Chicago: Dee.

Huxley, Aldous [1921] (2004), *Crome Yellow*, Mineola, NY: Dover.

Huxley, Aldous [1932] (2007a), *Brave New World*, Toronto: Vintage.

Huxley, Aldous (2007b), *Selected Letters*, ed. James Sexton, Chicago: Dee.

Huxley, Julian (1920a), 'Metamorphosis of Axolotl Caused by Thyroid-Feeding', *Nature* 104: 2618, 435.

Huxley, Julian (1920b), 'Recent Work on Heredity – I', *Discover* 1: 7, 199–203.

Huxley, Julian (1922a), 'Ductless Glands and Development: Amphibian Metamorphosis Considered as Consecutive Dimorphism, Controlled by Glands of Internal Secretion', *The Journal of Heredity* 13: 8, 349–58.

Huxley, Julian (1922b), 'Experiments on Amphibian Metamorphosis and Pigment Responses in Relation to Internal Secretions', *Proceedings of the Royal Society of London, Series B* 93: 649, 36–53.

Huxley, Julian (1922c), 'Sex and Its Determination – II', *Discover* 3: 33, 237–41.

Huxley, Julian (1922d), 'Some Recent Advances in the Biological Theory of Sex', *Journal of the Royal Society of Arts* 70: 3610, 188–202.

Huxley, Julian (1923a), 'Ductless Glands and Development – II: Amphibian Metamorphosis Considered as Consecutive Dimorphism, Controlled by Glands of Internal Secretion', *The Journal of Heredity* 14: 1, 3–11.

Huxley, Julian (1923b), 'The Physiology of Sex-Determination', *Nature* 112: 2826, 927–30.

Huxley, Julian (1923c), *Essays of a Biologist*, New York: Knopf.

Huxley, Julian (1925a), 'Experimentally-Induced Metamorphosis in Echinus', *American Naturalist* 62: 681, 363–76.

Huxley, Julian (1925b), 'Studies on Amphibian Metamorphosis – II', *Proceedings of the Royal Society of London, Series B* 98: 688, 113–46.

Huxley, Julian (1932), *Problems of Relative Growth*, New York: Dial.

Huxley, Julian (1947), *Evolution and Ethics: 1893–1943*, ed. Julian Huxley, London: Pilot.

Huxley, Julian [1931] (1968), *Africa View*, New York: Greenwood.

Huxley, Julian and Gavin de Beer (1934), *Elements of Experimental Embryology*, Cambridge: Cambridge University Press.

Huxley, Julian and E. B. Ford (1925), 'Mendelian Genes and Rates of Development', *Nature* 116: 2928, 861–3.

Huxley, Julian and A. C. Haddon (1936), *We Europeans: A Survey of 'Racial' Problems*, London: Jonathan Cape.

Huxley, Julian and Lancelot T. Hogben (1922), 'Experiments on Amphibian Metamorphosis and Pigment Responses in Relation to Internal Secretions', *Proceedings of the Royal Society of London, Series B* 93: 649, 36–53.

Jaffe, Aaron (2016), 'Introduction: Who's Afraid of the Inhuman Woolf?', *Modernism/Modernity* 23: 3, 491–513.

Jakobson, Roman (1968), *Child Language: Aphasia and Phonological Universals*, New York: Mouton.

James, William [1897/1898] (1960), *The Will to Believe and Other Essays in Popular Philosophy* and *Human Immortality*, New York: Dover.

James, William [1902] (1985), *The Varieties of Religious Experience: A Study in Human Nature*, London: Penguin.

James, William [1890] (2007), *The Principles of Psychology*, New York: Cosimo.

Jameson, Fredric (1982), *The Political Unconscious: Narrative as a Socially Symbolic Act*, Ithaca: Cornell University Press.

JanMohamed, Abdul and David Lloyd (1990), 'Introduction: Toward a Theory of Minority Discourse: What Is to Be Done?', in Abdul JanMohamed and David Lloyd (eds), *The Nature and Context of Minority Discourse*, Oxford: Oxford University Press, pp. 1–16.

Janusko, Robert (1983), *The Sources and Structures of James Joyce's 'Oxen'*, Ann Arbor: UMI Research.

Jejcic, Marie (2006), 'Corps errants chez Beckett: Un sujet héroïque', *Samuel Beckett Today/Aujourd'hui* 17, 176–90.

Jenkinson, John Wilfrid (1909), *Experimental Embryology*, Oxford: Clarendon.

Jennings, H. S. (1930), *The Biological Basis of Human Nature*, New York: Norton.

Joyce, James (1939), *Finnegans Wake*, London: Faber & Faber.

Joyce, James (1959), *The Critical Works of James Joyce*, ed. Ellsworth Mason and Richard Ellmann, New York: Viking.

Joyce, James [1904] (1968a), 'A Portrait of the Artist', in *A Portrait of the Artist as a Young Man: Text, Criticism, and Notes*, ed. Chester G. Anderson, Harmondsworth: Penguin, pp. 257–66.

Joyce, James [1916] (1968b), *A Portrait of the Artist as a Young Man: Text, Criticism, and Notes*, ed. Chester G. Anderson, Harmondsworth: Penguin.

Joyce, James (1969), *Stephen Hero*, ed. John Slocum and Herbert Cahoon, London: Jonathan Cape.

Joyce, James (1977), *Joyce in Padua*, ed. and trans. Louis Berrone, New York: Random House.

Joyce, James [1922] (1993), *Ulysses: The 1922 Text*, Oxford: Oxford University Press.

Joyce, Stanislaus [1958] (2003), *My Brother's Keeper*, ed. Richard Ellmann, Cambridge, MA: Da Capo.

Jung, Carl (1990), *The Collected Works. Volume Seven: Two Essays on Analytical Psychology*, 2nd edn, ed. Herbert Read, Michael Fordham and Gerhard Adler, trans. R. F. C. Hull, New York: Routledge.

Kadvany, John (2001), *Imre Lakatos and the Guises of Reason*, Durham, NC: Duke University Press.

Kaivola, Karen (1999), 'Revisiting Woolf's Representations of Androgyny: Gender, Race, Sexuality, and Nation', *Tulsa Studies in Women's Literature* 18: 2, 235–61.

Kane, Michael (1999), *Modern Men: Mapping Masculinity in English and German Literature, 1880–1930*, New York: Cassell.

Kant, Immanuel (2003), *Political Writings*, 2nd edn, ed. H. S. Reiss, trans. H. B. Nisbet, Cambridge: Cambridge University Press.

Keller, Evelyn Fox (1995), *Refiguring Life: Metaphors of Twentieth-Century Biology*, New York: Columbia University Press.

Kenner, Hugh (1948), 'The *Portrait* in Perspective', *The Kenyon Review* 10: 3, 361–81.

Kenner, Hugh (1971a), 'Joyce and the 19th Century Linguistics Explosion', *Atti del Third International James Joyce Symposium*, Trieste: Università degli studi, pp. 45–52.

Kenner, Hugh (1971b), *The Pound Era*, Berkeley: University of California Press.

Kermode, Frank (1967), *The Sense of an Ending: Studies in the Theory of Fiction*, Oxford: Oxford University Press.

Kermode, Frank (2009), 'E. M. Forster and the Art and Science of the Novel', *New England Review* 30: 3, 106–15.

Kiberd, Declan (1995), *Inventing Ireland: The Literature of the Modern Nation*, Cambridge, MA: Harvard University Press.

King, Mary C. (1998), 'Hermeneutics of Suspicion: Nativism, Nationalism, and the Language Question in "Oxen of the Sun"', *James Joyce Quarterly* 35: 2/3, 349–71.

Kingsley, Charles [1863] (2008), *The Water-Babies*, ed. Richard Kelly, Plymouth: Broadview.

Koestler, Arthur (1971), *The Case of the Midwife Toad*, London: Pan.

Kontje, Todd (1993), *The German Bildungsroman: History of a National Genre*, Columbia, SC: Camden House.

Lavrin, Janko (1920), 'Germany and Culture', *The New Age* 26: 24, 383–5.

Lawrence, D. H. [1920] (1981), *Women in Love*, London: Penguin.

Lawrence, Karen (1986), 'Gender and Narrative Voice in *Jacob's Room* and *A Portrait of the Artist as a Young Man*', in Morris Beja, Phillip Herring, Maurice Harmon and David Norris (eds), *James Joyce: The Centennial Symposium*, Urbana: University of Illinois Press, pp. 31–8.

Lawrence, Karen (1992), 'Orlando's Voyage Out', *Modern Fiction Studies* 38: 1, 253–77.

Leavis, F. R. (1952), *The Common Pursuit*, Harmondsworth: Penguin.

Lehleiter, Christine (2015), *Romanticism, Origins, and the History of Heredity*, Lewisburg, PA: Bucknell University Press.

Lehmann, Rosamond [1927] (2013), *Dusty Answer*, London: Virago.

Levenson, Michael (1985), 'Stephen's Diary in Joyce's *Portrait* – The Shape of Life', *ELH* 52: 4, 1017–35.

Levenson, Michael (1991), *Modernism and the Fate of Individuality: Character and Novelistic Form from Conrad to Woolf*, Cambridge: Cambridge University Press.

Levine, George (1988a), *Darwin and the Novelists: Patterns of Science in Victorian Fiction*, Cambridge, MA: Harvard University Press.

Levine, George (1988b), 'The Novel as Scientific Discourse: The Example of Conrad', *NOVEL: A Forum on Fiction* 21: 2/3, 220–7.

Lewis, Gilbert (1926), *The Anatomy of Science*, New Haven: Yale University Press.

Lewis, Pericles (2000), *Modernism, Nationalism, and the Novel*, Cambridge: Cambridge University Press.

Lewis, Wyndham (1927), *Time and Western Man*, London: Chatto & Windus.

'life history, *n*[1]' (2015), *OED Online*, Oxford University Press, <http://www.oed.com/view/Entry/272406> (last accessed 6 January 2016).

'life history, *n*[2]' (2015), *OED Online*, Oxford University Press, <http://www.oed.com/view/Entry/272406> (last accessed 6 January 2016).

Lima, Maria Helena (1993), 'Decolonizing Genre: Jamaica Kincaid and the *Bildungsroman*', *Genre* 26: 4, 431–60.

Lloyd, David (1987), *Nationalism and Minor Literature: James Clarence Mangan and the Emergence of Irish Cultural Nationalism*, Berkeley: University of California Press.

Lombroso, Cesare (1898), 'Regressive Phenomena in Evolution', trans. I. W. Howerth, *The Monist* 8: 3, 377–83.

Macaulay, Rose (1924), *Told by an Idiot*, New York: Boni & Liveright.

MacBride, E. W. (1914), *Text-book of Embryology, Volume 1: Invertebrata*, ed. Walter Heape, London: Macmillan.

MacBride, E. W. (1925), 'The Blindness of Cave-Animals', *Nature* 116: 2927, 818.

MacBride, E. W. (1930), 'Embryology and Recapitulation', *Nature* 125: 3163, 883–5.

MacBride, E. W. (1932), 'The Inheritance of Acquired Characters', *Nature* 129: 3268, 900–1.

McCallum, E. L. and Mikko Tuhkanen (2011), 'Becoming Unbecoming: Untimely Mediations', in E. L. McCallum and Mikko Tuhkanen (eds), *Queer Times, Queer Becomings*, Albany: State University of New York Press, pp. 1–21.

McCullers, Carson [1946] (2004), *The Member of the Wedding*, New York: Mariner.

MacDonald, Rónán (2014), 'The "Fascination of What I Loathed": Science and Self in Yeats's *Autobiographies*', in Maria DiBattista and Emily Wittman (eds), *Modernism and Autobiography*, Cambridge: Cambridge University Press, pp. 18–30.

McDuffie, Allen (2009), 'Joseph Conrad's Geographies of Energy', *ELH* 76: 1, 75–98.

McKinney, Michael and Kenneth McNamara (1991), *Heterochrony: The Evolution of Ontogeny*, New York: Plenum.

McNamara, Kenneth (1997), *Shapes of Time: The Evolution of Growth and Development*, Baltimore: Johns Hopkins University Press.

McNamara, Kenneth and Michael McKinney (2002), 'Heterochrony, Disparity, and Macroevolution', *Paleobiology* 31: 2S, 17–26.

Maienschein, Jane (ed.) (1986), *Defining Biology: Lectures from the 1890s*, Cambridge, MA: Harvard University Press.

Majumdar, Robin (ed.) (1997), *Virginia Woolf: The Critical Heritage*, London: Routledge.

Malik, Charu (1997), 'To Express the Subject of Friendship: Masculine Desire and Colonialism in *A Passage to India*', in Robert K. Martin and George Piggford (eds), *Queer Forster*, Chicago: University of Chicago Press, pp. 221–36.

Mao, Douglas (2008), *Fateful Beauty: Aesthetic Environments, Juvenile Development, and Literature 1860–1960*, Princeton: Princeton University Press.

Markley, A. A. (2001), 'E. M. Forster's Reconfigured Gaze and the Creation of a Homoerotic Subjectivity', *Twentieth-Century Literature* 47: 2, 268–92.

Marshall, Arthur Milnes (1891), 'Presidential Address', *Report of the Sixteenth Meeting of the British Association for the Advancement of Science*, London: John Murray, pp. 826–52.

Marshall, Arthur Milnes (1893), *Vertebrate Embryology: A Text-book for Students and Practitioners*, New York: Putnam.

Martin, Robert K. (1997), '"It Must Have Been the Umbrella": Forster's Queer Begetting', in Robert K. Martin and George Piggford (eds), *Queer Forster*, Chicago: University of Chicago Press, pp. 255–74.

Martini, Fritz (1991), 'Bildungsroman: Term and Theory', in James Hardin (ed.), *Reflection and Action: Essays on the Bildungsroman*, Columbia: University of South Carolina Press, pp. 1–25.

Martland, Arthur (1999), *E. M. Forster: Passion and Prose*, London: Gay Men's Press.

Matz, Jesse (2000), '*Maurice* in Time', *Style* 34: 2, 188–211.

Maugham, Somerset [1919] (1990), *The Moon and Sixpence*, London: Mandarin.

Mawer, Simon (2005), 'Science in Literature', *Nature* 434: 7031, 297–9.

Mayoux, J.-J. (1930), 'À Propos d'*Orlando* de Virginia Woolf', *Europe* 22: 85, 117–22.

Mayr, Ernst (1982), *The Growth of Biological Thought: Diversity, Evolution, and Inheritance*, Cambridge, MA: Harvard University Press.

Mayr, Ernst (1994), 'Recapitulation Reinterpreted: The Somatic Program', *Quarterly Review of Biology* 69: 2, 223–32.

Meacham, Jack (1997), 'Autobiography, Voice, and Developmental Theory', in Eric Amsel and K. Ann Renninger (eds), *Change and Development: Issues of Theory, Method, and Application*, Mahwah, NJ: Lawrence Erlbaum, pp. 43–60.

Meckier, Jerome (1969), *Aldous Huxley: Satire and Structure*, London: Chatto & Windus.

Medalie, David (2002), *E. M. Forster's Modernism*, New York: Palgrave.

Mensch, Jennifer (2013), *Kant's Organicism: Epigenesis and the Development of Critical Philosophy*, Chicago: University of Chicago Press.

Micir, Melanie (2012), 'The Queer Timing of *Orlando: A Biography*', *Virginia Woolf Miscellany* 82, 11–13.

Miller, Brook (2013), *Self-Consciousness in Modern British Fiction*, New York: Palgrave Macmillan.

Miller, Gavin (2008), 'Animals, Empathy, and Care in Naomi Mitchison's *Memoirs of a Spacewoman*', *Science Fiction Studies* 35: 2, 251–65.

Miller, Hugh (1857), *The Testimony of the Rocks; or, Geology in Its Bearings to the Two Theologies, Natural and Revealed*, Boston: Gould & Lincoln.

Miller, J. Hillis (1982), *Fiction and Repetition: Seven English Novels*, Cambridge, MA: Harvard University Press.

Minden, Michael (1997), *The German Bildungsroman: Incest and Inheritance*, Cambridge: Cambridge University Press.

Miracky, James (2003), *Engendering the Novel: Gender and Genre in Woolf, Forster, Sinclair, and Lawrence*, New York: Routledge.

Mitchell, Breon (1976), '*A Portrait* and the *Bildungsroman* Tradition', in Thomas Staley and Bernard Benstock (eds), *Approaches to Joyce's Portrait: Ten Essays*, Pittsburgh: University of Pittsburgh Press, pp. 61–76.

Mitchell, Peter Chalmers (1912), *The Childhood of Animals*, New York: Frederick Stokes.

Mitchell, Robert (2014), *Experimental Life: Vitalism in Romantic Science and Literature*, Baltimore: Johns Hopkins University Press.

Montagu, Ashley (1938), 'The Concept of Atavism', *Science* 87: 2264, 462–3.

Montagu, Ashley (1955), 'Time, Morphology, and Neoteny in the Evolution of Man', *American Anthropologist* 57, 13–27.

Montagu, Ashley (1989), *Growing Young*, 2nd edn, Granby, MA: Bergin & Garvey.

Moran, Patricia (2015), 'Shame, Subjectivity, and Self-Expression in Cora Sandel and Jean Rhys', *Modernism/Modernity* 22: 4, 713–34.

Moretti, Franco (2000), *The Way of the World: The Bildungsroman in European Culture*, 2nd edn, trans. Albert Sbragia, New York: Verso.

Morgan, C. Lloyd (1896), *Habit and Instinct*, London: Edward Arnold.

Morgan, Thomas Hunt (1919), *A Critique of the Theory of Evolution*, Princeton: Princeton University Press.

Morgenstern, Karl [1819] (2009), 'On the Nature of the *Bildungsroman*', trans. Tobias Boes, *PMLA* 124: 2, 650–9.

Morrison, Paul (2015), '*Maurice*, or Coming Out Straight', in Robyn Warhol and Susan S. Lanser (eds), *Narrative Theory Unbound: Queer and Feminist Interventions*, Columbus: Ohio State University Press, pp. 253–74.

Morrisson, Mark (2002), 'Why Modernist Studies and Science Studies Need Each Other', *Modernism/Modernity* 9: 4, 675–82.

Muir, Edwin [1927] (1987), *The Marionette*, London: Hogarth.

Müller-Sievers, Helmut (1997), *Self-Generation: Biology, Philosophy, and Literature around 1800*, Stanford: Stanford University Press.

Murdoch, Iris (1961), 'Against Dryness: A Polemical Sketch', *Encounter* 88, 16–20.

Murphy, Richard T. (2013), 'Monuments of Unageing Embarrassment: Brinsley MacNamara and the *Bildungsroman* in the Irish Free State', *New Hibernia Review* 17: 4, 74–92.

Murphy, Ruth (2016), 'Kipling's *Just So Stories*: The Recapitulative Child and Evolutionary Progress', in Elisabeth Wesseling (ed.), *The Child Savage, 1890–2010: From Comics to Games*, Farnham: Ashgate.

Musil, Robert [1906] (2013), *The Confusions of Young Master Törless*, trans. Christopher Moncrieff, Richmond: Alma Classics.

Nelson, Scott R. (1992), 'Narrative Inversion: The Textual Construction of Homosexuality in E. M. Forster's Novels', *Style* 26: 2, 310–26.

Newman, Daniel Aureliano (2016a), 'Kin Selection, Mendel's "Salutary Principle", and the Fate of Characters in Forster's *The Longest Journey*', in Christine Lehleiter (ed.), *Fact and Fiction: Literature and Science in the German and European Context*, Toronto: University of Toronto Press, pp. 247–71.

Newman, Daniel Aureliano (2016b), 'Plot Counter Plot: Genetics and Generic Strain in the Modernist Novel of Formation', *Intervalla* 4, 30–69.

Newton, K. M. (2011), *Modernizing George Eliot: The Writer as Artist, Intellectual, Proto-Modernist, Cultural Critic*, New York: Bloomsbury.

Norris, Margot (1985), *Beasts of the Modern Imagination: Darwin, Nietzsche, Kafka, Ernst, and Lawrence*, Baltimore: Johns Hopkins University Press.

Norris, Margot (1992), *Joyce's Web: The Social Unraveling of Modernism*, Austin: University of Texas Press.

Nussbaum, Martha (1988), 'Narrative Emotions: Beckett's Genealogy of Love', *Ethics* 98: 2, 225–54.

Nuttall, G. Clarke (1908), 'Mendel and His Theory of Heredity', *Contemporary Review* 83: 495, 528–38.

O'Brien, Flann [1939] (2001), *At Swim-Two-Birds*, London: Penguin.

Ohi, Kevin (2015), *Dead Letters Sent: Queer Literary Transmission*, Minneapolis: University of Minnesota Press.

Olby, Robert (1985), *Origins of Mendelism*, 2nd edn, Chicago: University of Chicago Press.

Oppenheimer, Jane (1967), *Essays in the History of Embryology and Biology*, Cambridge, MA: MIT Press.

O'Sullivan, James (2014), 'Time and Technology in *Orlando*', *ANQ: A Quarterly Journal of Short Articles, Notes, and Reviews* 27: 1, 40–5.

Parkes, Adam (1994), 'Lesbianism, History, and Censorship: *The Well of Loneliness* and the Suppressed Randiness of Virginia Woolf's *Orlando*', *Twentieth-Century Literature* 40: 4, 434–60.

Parkes, Adam (2013), 'Varieties of Modernist Im/personality', *Modern Fiction Studies* 59: 3, 668–76.

Parkin-Gounelas, Ruth (1991), *Fictions of the Female Self: Charlotte Brontë, Olive Schreiner, Katherine Mansfield*, London: Macmillan.

Parsons, Deborah (2007), *Theorists of the Modernist Novel: James Joyce, Dorothy Richardson, Virginia Woolf*, New York: Routledge.

Pater, Walter [1873] (1919), *The Renaissance: Studies in Art and Poetry*, London: Macmillan.

Pater, Walter [1895] (1920), *Greek Studies: A Series of Essays*, London: Macmillan.

Patke, Rajeev (2013), *Modernist Literature and Postcolonial Studies*, Edinburgh: Edinburgh University Press.

Paul, Jean-Marie (2011), 'Image de l'homme, image de la nature dans le roman de formation goethéen', in Mai Lequan (ed.), *Goethe et la Naturphilosophie*, Paris: Klincksieck, pp. 271–85.

Pearson, Nels (2015), *Irish Cosmopolitanism: Location and Dislocation in James Joyce, Elizabeth Bowen, and Samuel Beckett*, Miami: University Press of Florida.

Peppis, Paul (2014), *Sciences of Modernism: Ethnography, Sexology, and Psychology*, Cambridge: Cambridge University Press.

Peters, Gerald (1993), *The Mutilating God: Authorship and Authority in the Narrative of Conversion*, Boston: University of Massachusetts Press.

Pfau, Thomas (2010), '"All is Leaf": Difference, Metamorphosis, and Goethe's Phenomenology of Knowledge', *Studies in Romanticism* 49: 1, 3–41.

Plock, Vike Martina (2009), 'Medicine', in John McCourt (ed.), *James Joyce in Context*, Cambridge: Cambridge University Press, pp. 250–61.

Pratt, Annis (1981), *Archetypal Patterns in Female Fiction*, Bloomington: Indiana University Press.

Preston, Carrie (2009), 'Joyce's Reading Bodies and the Kinesthetics of the Modernist Novel', *Twentieth-Century Literature* 55: 2, 232–54.

Punday, Daniel (2003), *Narrative Bodies: Toward a Corporeal Narratology*, New York: Palgrave.

Punnett, R. C. (1907), *Mendelism*, 2nd edn, Cambridge: Bowes & Bowes.

Rabaté, Jean-Michel (2001), *James Joyce and the Politics of Egoism*, Cambridge: Cambridge University Press.

Rahman, Zia Haider (2014), *In the Light of What We Know*, New York: Picador.

Redfield, Marc (1996), *Phantom Formations: Aesthetic Ideology and the Bildungsroman*, Ithaca: Cornell University Press.

Reid, J. Archdall (1910), *The Laws of Heredity*, London: Methuen.

Reill, Peter Hanns (1986), 'Bildung, Urtyp and Polarity: Goethe and Eighteenth-Century Physiology', *Goethe Yearbook* 3, 139–48.

'reversion, *n*[1b]' (2017), *OED Online*, Oxford University Press, <http://www.oed.com/view/Entry/164800> (last accessed 28 October 2017).

Richards, Robert J. (1992), *The Meaning of Evolution: The Morphological Construction and Ideological Reconstruction of Darwin's Theory*, Chicago: University of Chicago Press.

Richards, Robert J. (2002), *The Romantic Conception of Life: Science and Philosophy in the Age of Goethe*, Chicago: University of Chicago Press.

Richards, Robert J. (2008), *The Tragic Sense of Life: Ernst Haeckel and the Struggle over Evolutionary Thought*, Chicago: University of Chicago Press.

Richardson, Brian (2000), 'Linearity and Its Discontents: Rethinking Narrative Form and Ideological Valence', *College English* 62: 6, 685–95.

Richardson, Brian (2008), 'Beyond Story and Discourse: Narrative Time in Postmodern and Nonmimetic Fiction', in Brian Richardson (ed.), *Narrative Beginnings: Theories and Practices*, Lincoln: University of Nebraska Press, pp. 47–63.

Ringueberg, Eugene (1884), 'Atavism Considered as a Conservative Agent in a State of Nature', *American Naturalist* 18: 5, 542–6.

Riquelme, John Paul (2013), 'Modernist Transformations of Life Narrative: From Wilde and Woolf to Bechdel and Rushdie', *Modern Fiction Studies* 59: 3, 461–79.

Robbe-Grillet, Alain (1963), *Pour un nouveau roman*, Paris: Éditions de Minuit.

Rogers, Janine (2015), *Unified Fields: Science and Literary Form*, Montreal: McGill-Queen's University Press.

Rohman, Carrie (2009), *Stalking the Subject: Modernism and the Animal*, New York: Columbia University Press.

Rohy, Valerie (2009), *Anachronism and Its Others: Sexuality, Race, Temporality*, Albany: State University of New York Press.

Roof, Judith (1996), *Come as You Are: Sexuality and Narrative*, New York: Columbia University Press.

Rosen, Jody R. (2006), 'Deviation and Acceleration: Time in the Story and Narrative of *Orlando*', *Virginia Woolf Miscellany* 70, 29–30.

Roux, Wilhelm [1894] (1986), 'The Problems, Methods, and Scope of Developmental Mechanics', trans. William Morton Wheeler, in Jane Maienschein (ed.), *Defining Biology: Lectures from the 1890s*, Cambridge, MA: Harvard University Press, pp. 106–48.

Ruse, Michael (2009), *Monad to Man: The Concept of Progress in Evolutionary Biology*, Cambridge, MA: Harvard University Press.

Russell, E. S. [1916] (1982), *Form and Function: A Contribution to the History of Animal Morphology*, Chicago: University of Chicago Press.

Russett, Cynthia Eagle (1991), *Sexual Science: The Victorian Construction of Womanhood*, Cambridge, MA: Harvard University Press.

Said, Edward (1975), *Beginnings: Intention and Method*, New York: Columbia University Press.

Salisbury, Laura (2012), *Samuel Beckett: Laughing Matters, Comic Timing*, Edinburgh: Edinburgh University Press.

Sanger, Charles Percy [1926] (1990), 'The Structure of *Wuthering Heights*', in William Sale, Jr. and Richard Dunn (eds), *Wuthering Heights: Authoritative Text, Backgrounds, Criticism*, 3rd edn, New York: Norton, pp. 331–6.

Saunders, Max (2010), *Self Impression: Life-Writing, Autobiografiction, and the Forms of Modern Literature*, Oxford: Oxford University Press.

Schiller, Friedrich [1794] (1967), *On the Aesthetic Education of Man in a Series of Letters*, ed. and trans. Elizabeth M. Wilkinson and L. A. Willoughby, Oxford: Clarendon.

Schlegel, Friedrich [1799] (1997), 'On Philosophy: To Dorothea', in Theory as Practice: A Critical Anthology of Early German Romantic Writings, ed. and trans. Jochen Schulte-Sasse, Haynes Horne, Andreas Michel, Elizabeth Mittman, Assenka Oksiloff, Lisa C. Roetzel and Mary R. Strand, Minneapolis: University of Minnesota Press, pp. 419–39.

Schmitt, Cannon (2009), *Darwin and the Memory of the Human: Evolution, Savages, and South America*, Cambridge: Cambridge University Press.

Schneider, B. Aubrey (1939), 'Effects of Feeding Thyroid Substance (Concluded)', *Quarterly Review of Biology* 14: 4, 431–50.

Scholes, Robert, James Phelan and Robert Kellogg (2006), *The Nature of Narrative: Fortieth Anniversary Edition*, Oxford: Oxford University Press.

Schreiner, Olive [1883] (1999), *Story of an African Farm*, Oxford: Oxford University Press.

Sedgwick, Eve Kosofsky (2003), *Touching Feeling: Affect, Pedagogy, Performativity*, Durham, NC: Duke University Press.

See, Sam (2010), 'The Comedy of Nature: Darwinian Feminism in Virginia Woolf's *Between the Acts*', *Modernism/Modernity* 17: 3, 639–67.

Seitler, Dana (2008), *Atavistic Tendencies: The Culture of Science in American Modernity*, Minneapolis: University of Minnesota Press.

Senn, Fritz (1978/1979), 'The Challenge: "Ignotas Animum" (An Old-Fashioned Close Guessing at a Borrowed Structure)', *James Joyce Quarterly* 16: 1/2, 123–34.

Senn, Fritz (1987), '*A Portrait*. Temporal Foreplay', *Études irlandaises* 12, 65–73.

Seshagiri, Urmila (2010), *Race and the Modernist Imagination*, Ithaca: Cornell University Press.

Sheehan, Paul (2004), *Modernism, Narrative and Humanism*, Cambridge: Cambridge University Press.

Shelley, Percy Bysshe [1818] (2012), 'Preface', *Frankenstein; or, the Modern Prometheus*, by Mary Wollstonecraft Shelley, London: Broadview, pp. 49–50.

Shepherd-Barr, Kirsten (2015), *Theatre and Evolution from Ibsen to Beckett*, New York: Columbia University Press.

Shumway, Waldo (1932), 'The Recapitulation Theory', *Quarterly Review of Biology* 7: 1, 93–9.

Shuttleworth, Sally (2010), *The Mind of the Child: Child Development in Literature, Science, and Medicine, 1940–1900*, Oxford: Oxford University Press.

Sinclair, May [1919] (2002), *Mary Olivier: A Life*, New York: New York Review Books.

Skeat, Walter (1884), *An Etymological Dictionary of the English Language*, 2nd edn, Oxford: Oxford University Press.

Slaughter, Joseph (2009), *Human Rights, Inc.: The World Novel, Narrative Form, and International Law*, New York: Fordham University Press.

Smith, Victoria L. (2006), '"Ransacking the Language": Finding the Missing Goods in Virginia Woolf's *Orlando*', *Journal of Modern Literature* 24: 9, 57–75.

Smith, Zadie (2007), *White Teeth*, London: Penguin.

Snow, C. P. [1959] (1998), *The Two Cultures*, Cambridge: Cambridge University Press.

Sorkin, David (1983), 'Wilhelm von Humboldt: The Theory and Practice of Self-Formation (*Bildung*), 1791–1810', *Journal of the History of Ideas* 44: 1, 55–73.

Spencer, Herbert (1861), *Education: Intellectual, Moral, and Physical*, London: Manwaring.

Spencer, Herbert (1878), *Illustrations of Universal Progress: A Series of Discussions*, New York: Appleton.

Spencer, Herbert (1882), *Principles of Sociology*, New York: Appleton.

Spencer, Theodore (1969), 'Introduction to the First Edition', in James Joyce, *Stephen Hero*, ed. John Slocum and Herbert Cahoon, London: Jonathan Cape, pp. 13–24.

Squier, Susan M. (1996), 'Embryologies of Modernism', *Modernism/Modernity* 3: 3, 145–53.

Steigerwald, Joan (2002), 'Goethe's Morphology: *Urphänomene* and Aesthetic Appraisal', *Journal of the History of Biology* 35, 291–328.

Stein, Gertrude [1925] (1995), *The Making of Americans*, Normal, IL: Dalkey Archive.

Sternberg, Meir (1990), 'Telling in Time (I): Chronology and Narrative Theory', *Poetics Today* 11: 4, 901–48.

Stockton, Kathryn Bond (2009), *The Queer Child, or Growing Sideways in the Twentieth Century*, Durham, NC: Duke University Press.

Straley, Jessica (2007), 'Of Beasts and Boys: Kingsley, Spencer, and the Theory of Recapitulation', *Victorian Studies* 49: 4, 583–609.

Sulloway, Frank J. (1992), *Freud, Biologist of the Mind: Beyond the Psychoanalytic Legend*, 2nd edn, Cambridge, MA: Harvard University Press.

Summers, Claude (1983), *E. M. Forster*, New York: Frederick Ungar.

Svevo, Italo [1923] (2001), *Zeno's Conscience*, trans. William Weaver, Toronto: Everyman.

Swales, Martin (1978), *The German Bildungsroman from Wieland to Hesse*, Princeton: Princeton University Press.

Swinnerton, H. H. (1938), 'Development and Evolution', in *Report of the Annual Meeting, 1938*, London: British Association for the Advancement of Science, pp. 57–84.

Swirski, Peter (2007), *Of Literature and Knowledge: Explorations in Narrative Thought Experiments, Evolution, and Game Theory*, New York: Routledge.

Taine, Hippolyte (1877), 'M. Taine on the Acquisition of Language by Children', *Mind* 2: 6, 252–9.

Tennyson, Alfred (1958), *Poems of Tennyson*, ed. Jerome H. Buckley, Boston: Houghton Mifflin.

Thompson, Christiane (2006), 'Adorno and the Borders of Experience: The Significance of the Nonidentical for a "Different" Theory of *Bildung*', *Educational Theory* 56: 1, 69–87.

Thompson, D'Arcy Wentworth (1917), *On Growth and Form*, Cambridge: Cambridge University Press.

Thomson, Douglass H. (1983), 'From Words to Things: Margaret's Progress in *Howards End*', *Studies in the Novel* 15: 2, 122–34.

Thomson, J. Arthur (1912), *Heredity*, 2nd edn, London: John Murray.

Thomson, J. Arthur (1917), 'Foundations of Bio-physics', *Nature* 100: 2498, 21–2.

Thornton, Weldon (1987), 'Voices and Values in *Ulysses*', in Robert D. Newman and Weldon Thornton (eds), *Ulysses: The Larger Perspective*, Newark: University of Delaware Press, pp. 244–70.

Thornton, Weldon (1994), *The Antimodernism of A Portrait of the Artist as a Young Man*, Syracuse, NY: Syracuse University Press.

'tow, *n*[1]' (2016), *OED Online*, Oxford University Press, <http://www.oed.com.myaccess.library.utoronto.ca/view/Entry/203990?rskey=wvpMQ8&result=2&isAdvanced=false> (last accessed 25 November 2016).

Trench, Richard Chenevix (1853), *On the Study of Words*, 6th edn, New York: Redfield.

Trilling, Lionel (1962), *E. M. Forster*, New York: New Directions.

Tropp, Sandra (2008), '"The Esthetic Instinct in Action": Charles Darwin and Mental Science in *A Portrait of the Artist as a Young Man*', *James Joyce Quarterly* 45: 2, 221–44.

Tuana, Nancy (1996), 'Fleshing Gender, Sexing the Body: Refiguring the Sex/Gender Distinction', *Southern Journal of Philosophy* 35S, 53–71.

Tyler, John Mason (1907), *Growth and Education*, New York: Houghton, Mifflin.

Valente, Joseph (1998), 'Thrilled by His Touch: The Aestheticizing of Homosexual Panic in *A Portrait of the Artist as a Young Man*', in Joseph Valente (ed.), *Quare Joyce*, Ann Arbor: University of Michigan Press, pp. 47–75.

Valente, Joseph (2000), '"Neither Fish Nor Flesh"; or How "Cyclops" Stages the Double-Bind of Irish Manhood', in Derek Attridge and Marjorie Howes (eds), *Semicolonial Joyce*, Cambridge: Cambridge University Press, pp. 96–127.

Van Hulle, Dirk (2014a), *Modern Manuscripts: The Extended Mind and Creative Undoing from Darwin to Beckett and Beyond*, London: Bloomsbury.

Van Hulle, Dirk (2014b), 'The Obidil and the Man of Glass: Denarration, Genesis and Cognition in Beckett's *Molloy, Malone meurt/Malone Dies* and *L'Innommable/The Unnamable*', in David Tucker, Mark Nixon and Dirk Van Hulle (eds), *Revisiting Molloy, Malone meurt/Malone Dies and L'Innommable/The Unnamable*, New York: Rodopi, pp. 25–39.

Van Hulle, Dirk and Mark Nixon (2013), *Samuel Beckett's Library*, Cambridge: Cambridge University Press.

Vitoux, Pierre (1972), 'Structure and Meaning in Aldous Huxley's *Eyeless in Gaza*', *Yearbook of English Studies* 2, 212–24.

Voituron, Yann, Michelle de Fraipont, Julien Issartel, Olivier Guillaume and Jean Clobert (2011), 'Extreme Lifespan of the Human Fish (*Proteus anguinus*): A Challenge for Aging Mechanisms', *Biological Letters* 7, 105–7.

Vuillet, Hélène (2012), 'Hermétiques métamorphoses: Un motif secret dans l'œuvre romanesque de Thomas Mann', in Florence Bancaud and Karine Winkelvoss (eds), *Poétiques de la Métamorphose dans l'espace germanique et européen*, Mont Saint Aignan: Presses universitaires de Rouen et du Havre, pp. 99–112.

Wasserman, Jerry (1980), 'Huxley's Either/Or: The Case for *Eyeless in Gaza*', *NOVEL: A Forum on Fiction* 13: 2, 188–203.

Watt, Donald (ed.) (1975), *Aldous Huxley: The Critical Heritage*, Boston: Routledge & Paul.

Weeks, Jeffrey (1977), *Coming Out: Homosexual Politics in Britain from the Nineteenth Century to the Present*, London: Quartet Books.

Wells, H. G. (1904), *Mankind in the Making*, 4th edn, London: Chapman & Hall.

Wells, H. G. [1896] (1996), *The Island of Doctor Moreau*, Mineola, NY: Dover.

Wells, H. G. [1909] (2005), *Tono-Bungay*, London: Penguin.

Wells, H. G., Julian S. Huxley and G. P. Wells [1929] (1937), *The Science of Life*, Garden City, NJ: Doubleday, Doran.

Welsh, Alexander (1973), 'Theories of Science and Romance, 1870–1920', *Victorian Studies* 17: 2, 135–54.

White, Leslie (2005), 'Vital Disconnection in *Howards End*', *Twentieth-Century Literature* 51: 1, 43–63.

White, Paula K. (1998), 'The Post-colonial Condition in the *Bildungsroman*: *Bildung* Gone Wrong in Tsitsi Dangarembga's *Nervous Conditions* and Jamaica Kincaid's *Annie John*', PhD thesis, Wichita State University.

Whittaker, Stephen (1987), 'Joyce and Skeat', *James Joyce Quarterly* 24: 2, 177–92.

Whitworth, Michael (2001), *Einstein's Wake: Relativity, Metaphor, and Modernist Literature*, Oxford: Oxford University Press.

Whitworth, Michael (2010), 'Science in the Age of Modernism', in Peter Brooker, Andrezej Gąsiorek, Deborah Longworth and Andrew Thacker (eds), *The Oxford Handbook of Modernisms*, Oxford: Oxford University Press, pp. 445–60.

Wilde, Alan (1991), *Horizons of Assent: Modernism, Postmodernism, and the Ironic Imagination*, Baltimore: Johns Hopkins University Press.

Wilde, Oscar (1996), *Plays, Prose Writings and Poems*, ed. Anthony Fothergill, London: Everyman.

Wilson, Aimee Armande (2016), *Conceived in Modernism: The Aesthetics and Politics of Birth Control*, New York: Bloomsbury.

Wilson, Edmund Beecher (1895), 'The Embryological Criterion of Homology', *Biological Lectures Delivered at the Marine Biological Laboratory at Wood's Holl*, Boston: Ginn, pp. 101–24.

Wilson, Edmund Beecher [1893] (1986), 'The Mosaic Theory of Development', in Jane Maienschein (ed.), *Defining Biology: Lectures from the 1890s*, Cambridge, MA: Harvard University Press, pp. 66–80.

Winkelvoss, Karine (2012), 'Introduction', in Florence Bancaud and Karine Winkelvoss (eds), *Poétiques de la Métamorphose dans l'espace germanique et européen*, Mont Saint Aignan: Presses universitaires de Rouen et du Havre, pp. 13–20.

Wolpert, Lewis (1992), *The Unnatural Nature of Science*, London: Faber & Faber.

Woolf, Virginia (1977), *The Letters of Virginia Woolf, Volume III: 1923–1928*, ed. Nigel Nicolson and Joanne Trautmann, New York: Harcourt Brace Jovanovich.

Woolf, Virginia [1922] (1992a), *Jacob's Room*, London: Penguin.

Woolf, Virginia (1992b), *Three Great Novels: Mrs Dalloway; To the Lighthouse; The Waves*, London: Penguin.

Woolf, Virginia [1928] (1993), *Orlando: A Biography*, New York: Harvest.

Woolf, Virginia [1929/1938] (1998), *A Room of One's Own/Three Guineas*, ed. Morag Shiach, Oxford: Oxford University Press.

Woolf, Virginia (1986–2011), *The Essays of Virginia Woolf*, ed. Andrew McNeillie, 6 vols, London: Hogarth.

Wordsworth, William (1958), *Selected Poems*, ed. Roger Sharrock, Chicago: Heinemann.

Worton, Michael (1994), '*Waiting for Godot* and *Endgame*: Theatre as Text', in John Pilling (ed.), *The Cambridge Companion to Beckett*, Cambridge: Cambridge University Press, pp. 67–87.

Yoshida, Hiromi (2007), *Joyce and Jung: The 'Four Stages of Eroticism' in A Portrait of the Artist as a Young Man*, New York: Lang.

Zimmerman, Bonnie (1983), 'Exiting from Patriarchy: The Lesbian Novel of Development', in Elizabeth Abel, Marianne Hirsh and Elizabeth Langland (eds), *The Voyage In: Fictions of Female Development*, Hanover: University Press of New England, pp. 244–57.

Zwierlein, Anne-Julia (2012), 'The Biology of Social Class: Habit Formation and Social Stratification in Nineteenth-Century *Bildungsromane* and Scientific Discourse', *Partial Answers* 10: 2, 335–60.

INDEX

CPSIA information can be obtained
at www.ICGtesting.com
Printed in the USA
JSHW050739090920
7725JS00001B/38

9 781474 439626